Depressed & Anxious

The

Dialectical Behavior Therapy

Workbook for Overcoming

Depression & Anxiety

THOMAS MARRA, PH.D.

New Harbinger Publications, Inc.

Distributed in Canada by Raincoast Books.

Copyright © 2004 by Thomas Marra
        New Harbinger Publications, Inc.
        5674 Shattuck Avenue
        Oakland, CA 94609

Cover design by Amy Shoup

ISBN 1-57224-363-5 Paperback

New Harbinger Publications' Web site address: www.newharbinger.com

08   07   06

10   9   8   7   6   5

Contents

Acknowledgments   v

Chapter 1
Mixed Anxiety and Depression: How DBT Can Work for You   1

Chapter 2
Dialectics of Anxiety and Depression   15

Chapter 3
Denying Your Right to Feel   52

Chapter 4
There Must Be Something Wrong with Me   65

Chapter 5
Meaning Making   73

Chapter 6
Mindfulness Skills   98

Chapter 7
Emotion Regulation   119

Chapter 8
Distress Tolerance Skills   169

Chapter 9

Strategic Behavior Skills   193

Symptoms and How to Treat Them   225

DBT Forms   230

References   252

Acknowledgments

Dialectical behavior therapy (DBT) is one of the most exciting developments in psychology. I wish I could say I created it, but I didn't. I owe Dr. Marsha Linehan, a brilliant psychologist at the University of Washington, for putting behavior therapy and other analytical techniques into the dialectical framework. The integration of behavior therapy and psychoanalytic approaches was first well developed by Paul Wachtel, while research exploration of emotions and adaptive capacity was published by Richard Lazarus. Psychiatrist Susan Bradley specifically brings together research and theory on affect regulation as a critical component of psychopathology. Each of these academics is due credit for their significant contributions to this book's clinical application to comorbid depression and anxiety. What I hope to do with this book is make DBT more understandable and expand it beyond its current focus such that the vast majority of individuals with anxiety and depression have access to its benefits.

I also need to thank the staff of Monterey Psychiatric Health Facility, who were tolerant of my attempt to apply these principles to every patient who was admitted to the facility. Thanks to Linda Weesner, RN, C, whose enthusiasm and devotion made application of these principles fun and workable and who presented a centered and work-oriented model for the rest of us to follow. To James Moran, Ph.D., whose leap of faith to obtain funding for our project made it a reality. To Wayne Welcher, MD, and Romeo Mariano, MD, our medical directors who were committed to more than just medication in the relief of human suffering. To Ann Thompson, Ph.D., and Stephanie Bouc, Ph.D., who as new psychologists demonstrated a willingness to apply these principles with precision and warmth. To Kathy Robertson, RN, C, whose deployment of mindfulness skills inspired patients and convinced all that reducing emotional suffering was achievable. And in fact, to the entire staff, too numerous to mention, who evidenced the humanism and compassion to make such an intensive approach truly work with all our patients. To Gary Andrews, who probably doesn't remember me, but provided early validation that there was nothing wrong with me. To Vicki Burney and Bonnie Hutcheon, who employed me in spite of my anxiety. To Drs. Ken Beauchamp, Martin Gipson, and Clifford Hand, who were my earliest teachers about dialectics even before Dr. Linehan published in this field and who were masters at validation. To Julian Meltzoff, Ph.D., who validated even while demanding scientific evidence.

Great thanks to Matthew McKay, Ph.D., editor-in-chief at New Harbinger Publications, who persuaded me to write this book after attending one of my workshops. Catharine Sutker, acquisitions manager, was patient and tolerant of my stubbornness, while Heather Mitchener, editorial manager, provided critical focus for the book. Carole Honeychurch, senior editor at New Harbinger, showed attention to detail, perseverance, and writing skill that transformed the book into a more readable and coherent document. And to my family (wife Judy and boys Daniel and Steven), who tolerated my obsessiveness while writing this.

Chapter 1

Mixed Anxiety and Depression: How DBT Can Work for You

Depression is when it takes energy to just move. You've lost your initiative, your ability and willingness to engage in activities. You want to do these things to fulfill your responsibilities, but it takes such tremendous effort. It's as if you're moving through thick mud just to be mobile, just to get things done that previously took little energy or effort. And the effort it takes now just to *live*, just to do the basic chores and tasks of life, requires so much more energy than ever before. But that's not all. In addition to feeling depressed, you also feel anxious. You question your every move: Maybe something bad will happen. Maybe you'll miss something important. Your muscles tighten up like some catastrophe is about to happen. You have no energy to *do* things, but seemingly boundless energy to feel panic, dread, negative anticipation about the future, and the sense that your world as you previously knew it has changed.

Mixing It Up

If you're feeling this way, you likely have *mixed anxiety and depression*—not just depression and not just anxiety. You have both, simultaneously. In the old days we called it "agitated depression," meaning the loss of energy and initiative but with substantial stress and anxiety. It is what professionals call *comorbid depression and anxiety* when you have both disorders at the same time.

Both depression and anxiety disorders can be easily misunderstood precisely because they share many of the same symptoms: you experience dread of the future, your anticipations and expectations are negative, it results in behavioral paralysis (you can't make decisions easily, everything is effortful, and you want to do nothing), and there is an essential loss of confidence in yourself. "There is something wrong with me," you think, and although you're not exactly certain what's wrong, you know that the problem is *within you* (there are also significant problems in the environment that are troublesome to you,

Mixed anxiety and depression is especially painful because it influences your emotions on a constant basis, causing you to be less influenced by the environment and the moment-by-moment experiences going on around you. It alienates you from others, takes away pleasure and joy from everyday living, and is confusing because it seems to change the rules of living to which you previously subscribed.

Fortunately, there is an answer to your emotional pain. It is called *dialectical behavior therapy* (DBT), and this book will teach you how to make it work for you. Is this book appropriate for you if you have only anxiety and not depression or only depression and not anxiety? DBT can be helpful for both conditions alone, but is an especially powerful set of strategies to use when people have mixed symptoms, because the exercises and procedures can kill two birds with one stone. DBT is designed for people who have lost hope and the sense of meaningfulness in life, who question their own ability to be influential in their world, who find their emotions intolerable, and who find that they try to escape and avoid important aspects of living. In short, DBT is extremely useful for people who experience both an anxiety disorder and depression.

How can you have two such different disorders at the same time? Mental-health professionals consider anxiety and depression disorders two different classifications, two distinct and rather unrelated sets of problems. In fact, there are even different medications designed to treat each disorder. There are several classes of antidepressant medications designed to treat depression or mood disorders, and different classes of medications to treat anxiety disorders. This is the way we're used to traditional medicine treating our problems, and it would be nice if your emotional problems could be placed into one neat little box, with only one strategy designed to deal with the one set of problems you have. But consider medicine and physical problems. Is it possible to have both a lower back problem *and* a headache? Of course it is, and it is no different for emotional or psychological problems. In fact, we know that long-term anxiety increases the probability of developing depression, and long-term depression causes people to feel anxious (Meichenbaum 1996). The recent statement of the International Consensus Group on Depression and Anxiety directly speaks to the high *comorbidity* (mixed) nature of both disorders, especially the most common anxiety disorder (generalized anxiety disorder) and depression (Ballenger et al. 2001). Mixed anxiety and depression may be more common among younger patients and less common in older patients (Colenda et al. 2002).

Why the Mix?

Why does anxiety tend to lead to depression and depression lead to anxiety? Well, living with anxiety for a long time *is* depressing. Anxiety can cause your muscles to ache, your concentration and attention to be impaired, your decision making to be slow and impaired, and your ability to experience joy muted. Who would not, over time, experience depression because they feel such symptoms? The same goes for depression. Over time, people lose the ability to find interest and amusement in simple pleasures; interest in food, sex, and interpersonal contact decreases; and sleep can be horribly disturbed. Alternatively, depression can cause people to try to fill up their internal void with food, drink, and sex. You may want to do nothing but sleep. Then the "environment" begins to protest: family members resent that you're not pulling your weight and have stopped being sensitive to and responsive toward them. Coworkers and supervisors become angry that your productivity on the job has decreased. People stop wanting to talk to you because much of what you have to say is negative and pessimistic (Coyne and Gotlib 1983). Your world as you knew it seems to be falling apart. Who would not, over time, become anxious about how others are demanding things from them that they no longer feel capable of performing?

Anxiety and depression are both negative spirals. One breeds the other, especially if the existence of either one is prolonged or severe.

Anxiety Disorders

To complicate matters, neither anxiety nor depression is a simple process. Instead, they are complex both in terms of their manifestations (how they are seen by others in your daily behavior) and their experience (how you see them in your private awareness). There are many anxiety disorders listed in the *Diagnostic and Statistical Manual of Mental Disorders* (American Psychiatric Association 1994), the bible of mental health.

Panic and Social Anxiety

With *panic attacks* you feel terror, fearfulness, shortness of breath, heart palpitations, and the anticipation of doom or losing control of yourself. These attacks often last only minutes, but they are so intense that afterward people obsess over the possibility that they will have another such attack, thus the "fear of the fear" syndrome that makes panic attacks an anticipatory disease. It has been estimated that as many as 70 percent of panic patients experience major depression at some point in their lives (McNally 1994), often at the same time they're having panic attacks. With *social anxiety disorder*, the anxiety is attached to social situations. When you anticipate having to meet unfamiliar people, or when you expect that you might be subject to public scrutiny (even if that "public" is only one person), you feel similar symptoms to panic attacks. With social anxiety disorder, the person learns that they can "control" their anxiety by simply avoiding social situations. They end up severely limiting their ability to socialize and lead normal lives in order to not feel the underlying anxiety.

Agoraphobia

Agoraphobia is a separate disorder related to panic attacks and social anxiety disorder. With agoraphobia you feel safe only when you are in certain environments. Your anxiety increases every time your "safe place" is unavailable, blocked, or becomes more distant. You feel okay only when at home, or in your car, when you are behind the wheel, and perhaps never when the doors are locked in your vehicle. The thought of being in a dark movie theatre, away from the exit doors, becomes intolerable. You do everything possible to stay in your safe places, and every new environment presents the challenge to identify escape routes in case you begin to panic. Any travel you might do is restricted, and anxiety increases the further away from your safe place you go. If agoraphobia remains untreated, the geography of your safe place can shrink until you are confined, like a prisoner, to your home or bedroom. The underlying fear is of the *anxiety itself*—you're afraid that you will have to endure nausea, an adrenalin rush the likes of which you would wish on no one, a pounding heart, and the feeling of doom that predicts utter annihilation.

Obsessive-Compulsive Disorder

An even more complex and potentially disabling anxiety disorder is *obsessive-compulsive disorder*. An *obsession* is an unwanted, negative thought that gets "stuck" in your mind. The thought can be totally illogical, and the person recognizes the irrationality and improbability of the negative thought. For example, you might think that your child will be killed if you don't keep your house clean and free of germs. This belief creates anxiety (pounding heart, short and shallow breathing, tightening of the neck and back muscles so severe that it causes physical pain, and perhaps dry mouth and the feeling that you will vomit). *Compulsions* are usually behaviors and are designed to avert the anticipated bad event. For example, you keep your house immaculate so that your child will not be killed. As you clean your house, more thoroughly than any surgeon would scrub their hands and arms before surgery, you find your anxiety associated with the obsession decreasing. The compulsive behavior (housecleaning) thus decreases the anxiety associated with the obsession (the thought that your child will die), and each time this occurs (you engage in the compulsion to reduce the obsession) the link between the two becomes stronger. You feel more compulsive urges even though your intent is to decrease the obsession. Both increase.

Post-traumatic Stress Disorder

In *post-traumatic stress disorder*, you have experienced a real and potentially life-threatening event. It might be a car accident, a robbery, war, rape, or having a loved one's life threatened (watching them be robbed, raped, or have a "near miss" fatal accident). After the event, you reexperience the trauma over and over again, like a bad horror movie to which you are subjected repeatedly against your will. Anything that reminds you of the previous event can bring back the full force of all the feelings you had during the original incident. It could be sights, smells, sounds, or even clothing associated with the original trauma. The post-traumatic stress patient is haunted by fear and will do almost anything to avoid reexperiencing the bad feelings. Like the panic disorder patient, you will avoid and escape every event that triggers your anxiety response. Your world begins to shrink, and it is totally understandable that depression will begin to "sit" on top of the anxiety.

Generalized Anxiety Disorder

Generalized anxiety disorder involves the experience of anxiety (restlessness, fatigue, muscle tension, irritability, heart palpitations, shortness of breath, and especially worry) that isn't connected to a specific event (as in post-traumatic stress disorder), or necessarily to simple social events (as in social anxiety disorder), isn't as intense or short as panic attacks, and is relatively unrelated to your geographic location (as in agoraphobia). With generalized anxiety disorder you have longer-term anxiety that is more likely to be prompted or caused by general worry and negative anticipations of the future. With this disorder you think that something is going to go wrong, and you worry about it as if it's happening or certain to happen in the future.

I mention only the main anxiety disorders, but even from these brief descriptions you can see that anxiety disorders are complex. They can have different causes, different *triggers* (things that cause them to happen), and different effects on you. With anxiety disorders, you're dealing with more than the stresses and strains of everyday life. You are dealing with intense bodily discomfort in the form of muscle tension, uncomfortable body temperature, intestinal and gastric distress, rapid or labored breathing, dryness of mouth, and hyperreactivity of your body. And all of these difficult symptoms may or may not relate to anything "real" going on in the here and now of your life. But the anxiety is very real and very painful, and it can last a long time. This is bound to be depressing.

Depression Disorders

Depression can be just as debilitating as an anxiety disorder, and sometimes even worse. Depressive disorders, what mental-health professionals call "mood disorders," can be divided into three large categories: major depressive disorder, bipolar disorders, and dysthymic disorder.

Major Depressive Disorder

Major depressive disorder is what most people think of when they think of depression: tearfulness, loss of interest, weight loss or gain, inability to get to sleep or desire to sleep all the time, loss of energy and initiative, feelings of worthlessness or guilt, inability to concentrate or sustain attention, feeling slowed down or keyed up, thoughts of death or suicide, irritability, feelings of emptiness, and feelings of hopelessness.

Professionals refer to *clinical* depression because many times a person will not report feelings of worthlessness or sadness, but will exhibit all of the other signs and symptoms of depression (sleep disturbance, loss of interest in sex, loss of appetite, and loss of energy) without the conscious awareness of the feeling components (agony, helplessness, hopelessness, thoughts of suicide, and extreme pessimism). The person is depressed, but they are not consciously aware of it.

Bipolar Disorders

Bipolar disorder has all or many of the characteristics of major depressive disorder, but for periods of time the person feels elated, grandiose, energetic, angry, or irritable in between periods of great sadness and loss of energy. The two "poles" of energy and lethargy, sadness and anger, loss of initiative and hyperactivity, inability to function and inability to stop, shame and "superpower" (either with aggression and irritability or with unwarranted elation and ebullience) come and go in cycles over time.

In *cyclothymic disorder* (the "little brother" of bipolar disorder), you don't lose contact with your typical self, but go through cycles of no energy and inappropriately high energy. With cyclothymic disorder your symptoms don't quite make the mark for a bipolar disorder, but do exhibit variability in mood that is marked and interferes with your ability to function well in the world.

Bipolar disorders are definitely considered neurochemical imbalances, and most evidence suggests that bipolar disorders are inherited genetically. The fact that bipolar disorders have a neurochemical basis makes them even more confusing. You feel strongly, but can't easily discriminate if the feeling is based on an objective environmental event that prompts the feeling, or is a direct reflection of the chemical imbalance. More than other disorders, bipolar disorders make you distrust your emotions (and for good reason, since sometimes you feel very strongly with no event from the environment making you feel this way).

Dysthymic Disorder

With *dysthymic disorder* you don't feel the full force of a major depressive episode, where it's almost impossible to take action or get anything done. But dysthymic disorder does make life feel like a constant struggle—a struggle that has gone on for very long periods of time. Pessimism, lack of energy, and loss of hope have become normal, and you have become so accustomed to this state of affairs that anything else would seem alien.

Mixed Anxiety and Depression

Anxiety and depression disorders are complex, and, unfortunately, they are prevalent. The Anxiety Disorders Association of America (2003) estimates that nineteen million U.S. residents have a diagnosable anxiety disorder of sufficient severity to need treatment (not just the stressed out busy person who has too much on their plate), and the National Institute of Mental Health (2003) estimates that a similar number of Americans have a mood disorder so severe that they need treatment. Twenty-six percent of the adult female population and 12 percent of adult males will experience a depression episode sometime during their life (National Institutes of Health 1991). We have known for a long time that depression and anxiety disorders can be mixed, or comorbidly experienced (Brown, Antony, and Barlow 1995; Maser and Cloninger 1990). In fact, so many people experience mixed anxiety and depression that Zinberg and his colleagues (1994) proposed that an entirely new diagnosis be created to describe it (a mixed anxiety-depressive disorder). The new *Diagnostic and Statistical Manual of Mental Disorders* will not come out for several years, so it will be interesting to see if the proposal to create an entirely new diagnostic category for mixed anxiety and depression receives the attention it deserves.

The Role of Medications

The focus of this book is on psychological procedures that cure. There is now abundant evidence, both scientific and anecdotal, that psychological interventions designed to treat depression, anxiety, and most emotional disorders work (Seligman 1995a, b). They work by providing a safe environment within which you can deal with your complex feelings rather than avoid or escape them, by teaching you how to reduce tension and avoid panic, and by changing thoughts and directly influencing feelings. However, I would be remiss if I did not mention the exceptions. There is equally abundant evidence that certain emotional disorders require medication. Those who have bipolar disorder (Rothbaum and Astin 2000) or severe cases of obsessive-compulsive disorder *need* medication. Psychological procedures (such as the ones presented in this book) can help immensely to improve your reaction to these disorders, but they do not and cannot cure the underlying process that causes these classes of disorder. Medication, unfortunately, can't cure them either. But medication offers the best hope of reducing the symptoms so that life becomes tolerable again.

Bipolar Disorder

With bipolar disorder, there is an alternation between down feelings and up feelings. The diagnosis used to be called "manic-depressive disorder," but this was confusing to people because "manic" implies euphoria (excessively and inappropriately high feelings), and in fact the up phase of bipolar disorder can manifest in anger, irritability, and agitation (certainly not euphoric feelings, as most of us would consider them). There is a biologically based lack of regulation of emotions in bipolar disorder. Some researchers believe that there may be some connection between bipolar disorders and seizure disorders, since many of the same medications can effectively treat both. We don't fully understand what the biological processes for bipolar disorders are at this point, but we know that few people are able to effectively manage their lives the way they would like to without the assistance of medication.

Of course, the research literature offers differing perspectives. Some researchers argue that psychotherapeutic approaches should be added to medication treatment for bipolar patients (Huxley, Parikh, and Baldessarini 2000; Rivas-Vazquez et al. 2002), while others argue that psychological approaches alone are just as effective (Basco 2000) or that only medication treatment is effective (Rothbaum and Astin 2000).

Obsessive-Compulsive Disorder

With obsessive-compulsive disorder (OCD), you feel tremendous anxiety unless you engage in certain behaviors in very specific ways. Very superstitious behaviors result (irrational behaviors, either in your mind or actual behavior you engage in externally), and you feel compelled to engage in them. These behaviors can interfere with life because they become chained together until you have to do so many things in order to feel normal that your life becomes unmanageable. Some people have symptoms that interfere with life and cause emotional pain, but they are still able to function. These individuals can use behavioral techniques alone to solve their issues (Kolar and Bojanin 2001). However, if your symptoms of OCD are so severe that attempts to use behavioral strategies alone would be cruel, the addition of medication to your treatment program is the only wise course of action.

Mild to moderate OCD can be treated without medication (Kolar and Svetomir 2001). The intensity of the symptoms and how disabling they are to everyday functioning should determine if and when you're willing to attempt psychological and behavioral technologies without medication. While this book recommends psychological treatment strategies for depression and anxiety, if you have symptoms that don't respond to environmental and psychological strategies pursued with gusto over time, I would highly recommend you consult with a psychiatrist as well as a psychologist in order to have every tool available to you to help reduce your emotional suffering.

General Anxiety

On the other hand, many anxiety disorders are best treated *without* medications. Why? Benzodiazepines or antianxiety agents are really only Band-Aids. They relieve symptoms without treating the underlying disorder. Moreover, they are habit-forming. Used over a lengthy period of time, you will be treating your addiction rather than your anxiety disorder. Some anxiety disorders, such as panic disorder, can respond well to very short-term medication treatment to reduce the intensity of symptoms, followed by psychological intervention (Heldt et al. 2003). Both medication and psychological approaches alone have been shown effective for generalized anxiety disorder (Gorman 2003). Some data suggest that medications may have an edge over psychological therapies in the treatment of social phobias (Fedoroff and Taylor 2001).

Depression

What about depression? Do you need to take an antidepressant medication in order to overcome the helplessness, hopelessness, and sense of powerlessness that comes with this disorder? The answer has to do with the severity of the depression. If you're feeling suicidal, definitely seek psychiatric consultation for medication. If you feel like giving up but don't have thoughts of killing yourself, a DBT approach alone may be effective. Generally, antidepressants are more effective when your depression is experienced in your body more than in your mind: If you have difficulty getting your body out of bed, feeding yourself, getting to sleep, or generating interest in sexual activity, then antidepressants are more likely to be helpful to you. If, instead, your depression is more expressed in your head (you doubt yourself, you show little initiative, you are pessimistic, you find reasons to be critical rather than supportive of others) rather than your body, then a DBT approach alone may work for you.

Antidepressants are effectively used by about half of those who try them. This is not surprising. Depression can be primarily controlled by biological factors (genetics) or by environmental factors (what is going on in the immediate world around you). If the cause is primarily biological, a biological solution (medication) is the quickest and most effective solution. If the cause is environmental (your thought process, or your social, occupational, academic, or family constellation), a more psychological approach is called for, such as the DBT principles outlined in this book. So, it depends on the severity of the depression whether medication will help treat your depression. While some researchers argue that there is no difference in the magnitude of effect between psychological and psychiatric interventions (Casacalenda, Perry, and Looper 2002), most research indicates that a combination of medication and psychotherapy is most effective (de Jonghe et al. 2001; Strunk and DeRubeis 2001). Some just argue that any conclusions are premature because studies are flawed and we don't have enough information (Klein 2000). Others go further and state that all information on medication treatment of depression is propaganda (Fava 2002). There is some evidence that antidepressants are more effective than psychological approaches for elderly patients

(Scazufca and Matsuda 2002), but combined or even solo psychological approaches have also been shown effective for older people with depression (Arean and Cook 2002).

DBT endorses a *biopsychosocial* model of recovery, incorporating biological, psychological, and environmental factors, and medications can play an important (and sometimes critical) role in emotional health. Consult with your physician if you have questions about the appropriateness of medications for your particular disorder.

The separation of "mental" from "physical" ailments is an artificial one that few educated professionals now accept (see, for example, Baily 2002; McLaren 2002). Your body has a head, and your head has processed a history of experiences that lead you to behave in certain ways. You interpret what your body experiences. To image that your body operates without psychology, or that psychology operates without your body, is to oversimplify the complex and rich interaction that actually occurs.

What Is DBT?

In dialectical behavior therapy the "dialectics" address conflicting demands and wants, and "behavior" refers to having strategic goals you constantly compare with your actions. DBT is thus a process to use your feelings to obtain your goals in spite of severe obstacles. DBT will assist you to better regulate your emotions to serve your goals, help you to face your feelings without terror, increase your sense of personal identity, improve your judgment, sharpen your observational skills, and reduce the sense of crisis in your life.

The following list outlines some of the basic aspects of DBT:

◊ a method of identifying conflicts that control your life

◊ a way of analyzing competing needs and forming better compromises

◊ an approach that places great focus on your feelings as valid pieces of information

◊ a set of techniques that help you to deal with your feelings better

◊ a set of strategies that places greatest emphasis on your own objectives

◊ a series of exercises that help you understand the function of your emotions, increasing your knowledge of yourself

◊ behavioral techniques that increase your ability to regulate and control your emotions

◊ a set of procedures that assists you to reduce avoidance and escape as core strategies in handling emotional difficulties

◊ processes that increase your comfort with your identity, reducing self-blame

◊ strategies to reduce urgency and impulsivity, thus improving your judgment

◊ mindfulness training to improve your observational skills

◊ strategies to reduce self-absorption and self-consciousness, thus increasing your ability to accurately perceive events

◇ skills to increase your ability to tolerate emotional pain

◇ self-soothing skills to reduce tension and crisis in your life

How DBT Can Help

If you have mixed, or comorbid, anxiety and depression (symptoms of both sets of disorders), as many people do, then your quality of life has probably shrunk substantially. That is where DBT comes in. DBT is ideally suited to help those with mixed anxiety and depression because DBT offers interventions designed to treat the emotions themselves (see Linehan 1993a; Brodsky and Stanley 2002). If you look at high anxiety and high depression as existing along a continuum of arousal (being overaroused or underaroused), then interventions or techniques designed to make arousal more stable and under conscious control will work for both sets of disorders. With both anxiety and depression, your world shrinks. You react more to your thoughts and less to the world itself, because you become self-absorbed. Mindfulness (chapter 6) is a strategy that helps you to be less self-absorbed and more influenced by the world around you. The world is ever-changing, offering multiple ways for you to be influenced and to have new feelings emerge. Mindfulness skills offer an important and critical method of "getting out" of your depressing thoughts and your anxious body.

Both depression and anxiety involve processes that make you overreact to threat cues and underreact to safety cues. The threat cues can come from inside (the "there is something wrong with me" syndrome) or from outside (being controlled by the environment rather than controlling the environment). With mixed anxiety and depression, safety cues (those things that predict you are not endangered, but in fact will survive comfortably) tend to be ignored. DBT helps you to pay more attention to safety cues, and to deal more effectively with threat cues. DBT thus offers interventions to help you challenge negative self-evaluations (chapters 3, 4, 7, and 8) and to be more behaviorally strategic in controlling your environment (chapter 9).

Both anxiety and depression involve a sense of hopelessness and lack of control over your life. Meaning shrinks. With depression, less and less seems important enough to expend the little energy you have (if you have major depressive disorder). With bipolar disorder, you become less focused on what is important *and* what's trivial. With anxiety disorders, you focus on unimportant details and become fixated on a few issues, missing the forest for the trees. DBT offers a new map for meaning making (chapter 5) that helps keep you focused on what is actually important.

Both depression and anxiety intensify your feelings. You feel helpless to control feelings, and to tolerate feelings that are out of your control. Both sets of disorders, over time, make you distrust and seek to avoid your feelings in general. DBT offers a new perspective on your emotions (chapter 7) that can assist you in overcoming your tendency to engage in such fear-based responses.

DBT is thus about decreasing your anxiety and depression symptoms, becoming more responsive and affected by potentially uplifting aspects of your environment, being more strategic in living your life in order to promote a sense of calm and tranquillity, regulating or tolerating emotions effectively, and not letting your current emotional state define who you are or what you're capable of. By teaching you DBT, this book will help you work on all of these aspects.

The Role of Escape and Avoidance

DBT is a different approach than others because it encourages you to identify conflicts and then resolve them in different ways. In both anxiety and depression, many people adopt two common strategies: emotional escape and emotional avoidance. You don't like feeling anxious, so you avoid situations that make you anxious. You don't like feeling depressed, so you escape situations that place demands on you. Emotional avoidance and escape are powerful psychological processes, but they make your anxiety and depression worse. Why? Because each time you avoid or escape, both the anxiety and depression are strengthened. You become even more fearful of the thing or process you're avoiding. It becomes an even bigger bogeyman chasing you. Each time you escape a situation that taxes your sense of competence, you feel more depressed because you feel even less competent and hopeful. And each time you successfully avoid a situation that makes you anxious, you make similar situations seem more daunting in the future.

In addition to offering specific ways to change your behavior and boost your coping skills, DBT helps you get out of the avoidance trap by focusing on the underlying conflicts and compromises you've made that push you toward anxiety and depression.

If you're still in doubt, the following self-test will help you decide if this book is the right approach for you.

DBT: Is It for You?

High Emotional Arousal	Yes	No
I feel tense, stressed, or on edge even when there is nothing immediately confronting me in the moment.		
I can't seem to relax as much as I would like to, even when I try.		
My hands shake or I'm anticipating failure a good deal of the time.		
I jump when a loud noise comes, even though I later find it wasn't anything dangerous.		
It takes me a lot longer than other people to relax.		
I'm always prepared or expecting something bad to happen to me.		
I feel vulnerable, like many things can hurt me, even though no one in particular is trying to hurt me.		
My emotions always seem to be "on" or prepared to be "on," even though I try to be calm and relaxed.		
I feel depressed.		
My feelings are intense, but I just can't get moving.		
Sometimes I just wish I would die.		

High Emotional Sensitivity	Yes	No
It doesn't take much to get me going (I react emotionally to even minor events).		
Many times "emotional" commercials make me cry.		
I wear my feelings on my sleeve in that, when I feel something, I typically express it openly.		
Other people tell me I'm an emotional person.		
I believe I feel my emotions more intensely than others do.		
When someone else hurts, I frequently hurt with them.		
I seem to be keyed in to what others are thinking and feeling.		

Slow Reduction in Emotional Tension	Yes	No
Once I feel an emotion, it's hard for me to stop feeling it.		
My strong emotions seem to last forever.		
I can't stop feeling anxious or depressed without great effort.		

Distrust of Emotions	Yes	No
My feelings frequently don't tell me how I should best behave or what to do next.		
I can't trust my gut reactions like others seem to be able to do.		
I wish I could eliminate my feelings, since they seem to get in my way rather than help me most of the time.		

Emotional Escape	Yes	No
When I feel tense, I do everything possible in order to feel differently as fast as possible.		
When someone hurts me, I immediately leave the room, usually no matter what the consequences or how it will look.		
When I begin to feel down or depressed, I can't stand it.		
I can't stand strong emotions, even if they are normal.		

Emotional Avoidance	Yes	No
I stay away from people who make me uncomfortable, even if they are not mean to me.		
I avoid situations and people who have hurt me in the past, even when this is difficult to do.		
I do whatever I can to avoid being hurt, even though I may miss opportunities to get what I want in the future.		
People who know me well might call me a "fraidy cat" because I won't take chances.		
I'm afraid of my strong feelings.		

Sense of Urgency	Yes	No
I can't wait to solve my problems, even though I know it took a long time for the problems to develop.		
I would say I'm impulsive. I do things without a lot of thinking because I want quick results.		
People tell me I'm impatient because I want what I want *now*.		
I'm anxious because I feel that my problems are so bad they should be changed immediately. They are so bad that I can't wait for my problems to be solved.		
I feel dread about the future. Something bad is going to happen if I'm not careful.		
I frequently do things without thinking them through.		
I feel pressure to make changes to my life.		

Scoring

Number of yes answers	Is DBT for You?
Fewer than 10	DBT is probably not for you. Loan this book to someone else.
11 to 15	DBT has something to offer you.
16 to 24	DBT definitely has something to offer you.
More than 24	Don't put this book down. DBT is what you have been looking for, for a long time.

If your response is yes in at least one question per category, you can have greater confidence that DBT (and this book) will be helpful to you.

How to Use This Book

After reading this chapter, I highly recommend you read chapters 2 and 3 completely before proceeding to subsequent chapters. These chapters lay the foundation for what is to come and demonstrate how DBT is different from other approaches to treating anxiety or depression separately. Chapter 4 is important for people who have poor self-esteem and have integrated their problems into their basic identity. If you have high self-esteem but struggle with mixed anxiety and depression, you can skip this chapter.

Working on chapter 5 (not just reading it, but actually doing the exercises) should precede chapters 6 through 9. Both chapters 5 and 6 are ongoing processes. You will return to them repeatedly in order to change the focus and direction of your life. While working on chapter 5 can be difficult because of your depression and the sense of hopelessness you feel at times, it is an essential process in the recovery from depression and the ability to tolerate your anxiety while you work at decreasing it.

Chapters 7 through 9 are more independent from each other. If you find that your depression and anxiety are so intolerable that can't force yourself to do anything different, then you may want to skip from chapter 6 to chapter 8, returning to chapter 7 later. While there may be a temptation to work on only certain "skill set" chapters (5 through 9), I highly recommend that people with mixed anxiety and depression work through each chapter, even if the emphasis you place on each skill differs because of your individual needs.

This book isn't meant to be simply pleasure reading. You can't just read it from cover to cover and expect your life and your symptoms to change. You have to do the exercises in order to expect results. I have provided worksheets throughout the book and blank duplicates at the end so you can photocopy them and rework the exercises over time. Just going through the motions of completing the worksheets will do less for you than actually using the principles and exercises over and over again as new situations arise, as well as when your symptoms decrease and you're able to fine-tune the principles to your improved condition.

Finally, there is a table called Symptoms and How to Treat Them beginning on page 225. After you have completed all of the exercises and strategies at least once, you can use this table to identify which strategies you need to use (and where in the book to find them) to deal with the specific symptoms you continue to have.

Comorbid depression and anxiety thus present you with extreme challenges, both tension and deflation. Mixed anxiety and depression are confusing because you feel prepared for disaster while simultaneously having no initiative to take any action whatsoever to avoid the disaster. The two sets of disorders together confuse you precisely because they are so contradictory. In the next chapter we more thoroughly examine the dialectics of dialectical behavior therapy and how DBT can help you to make sense of the symptoms that have puzzled you, and offer specific techniques to reduce those symptoms. Your understanding of the dialectical process will provide a new perspective on your problems, and new solutions are a natural outgrowth of your new understanding.

Chapter 2

Dialectics of Anxiety
& Depression

Conflict

It may sound surprising, but conflict is at the core of both anxiety and depression. With anxiety, the core conflict is wanting a sense of safety, but feeling a threat of some type. The threat is typically expressed in your body (your muscles tighten, your heart rate increases, your breathing becomes disturbed, and you feel general apprehension that something bad is about to happen). With depression, the core conflict is a loss of motivation or energy while wanting desperately to feel the joy and enthusiasm that others seem to experience. Conflict between competing needs and urges is what DBT is all about, and a central component of mixed anxiety and depression.

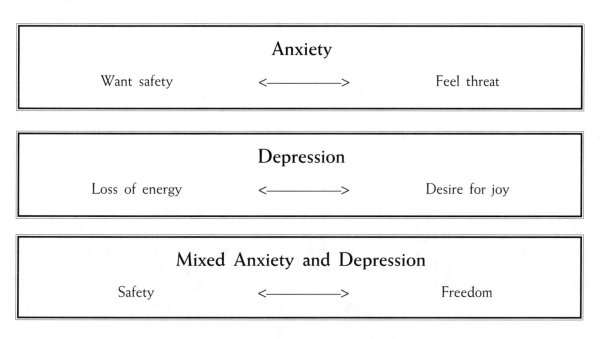

We all experience conflict. You want one thing, and I want something different. But with anxiety and depression, the conflicts are more pervasive, meaningful, and irreconcilable than day-to-day conflicts. With anxiety the conflicts are internal as well as external. Internally, you feel threatened and anxious, but worry that you'll be judged if others see that. Externally, you feel as if others expect and demand things from you that you are incapable of delivering. The same with depression: Internally you feel a sense of worthlessness or inadequacy, and you fear that others will see this and abandon you for your faults. Externally, you feel that the world demands a level of performance of even routine behavior that you don't have the energy to produce. Internally you feel the conflict of needing to feel your feelings while hiding them, and externally you feel that others' expectations and demands of your conflict with your own needs.

DBT Works with Conflict

DBT offers a unique approach to treatment of mixed anxiety and depression because it invites you to identify dialectics, all the competing demands and urges that "power" your depression and anxiety. A *dialectic* is a set of issues that demand different and incompatible responses. For example, you want to feel safe, but you also want the freedom to go places and be around people who could be fun and entertaining. If you experience social anxiety, you can't have both safety and freedom of movement because you only feel safe when you restrict yourself to familiar people and situations. This is a dialectic conflict. Each "side" of the dialectic is equally important to you (safety and freedom), but due to the anxiety, you can't have both. You need to choose to have more of one side and less of the other.

It works the same way with depression. You want to feel good but don't have the initiative to place yourself in situations that could prompt positive feelings. The dialectic (the two sides that require different and contradictory things) could be about hopelessness versus hopefulness. You want something different to happen in your life but believe that whatever you do won't bring those things to fruition. DBT asks you to identify what are called *dialectic failures* (compromises that you've made that generate anxiety and depression) and to "move" along the dialectic differently than before in order to increase your chances of feeling less anxious and depressed.

Dialectic Conflict in Depression

Hopelessness   <———>   Hopefulness

Think of dialectics as opposites that are related. For example, you want to feel comfort and relaxation (on one end of a line between relaxation and tension). You also want to feel the freedom to be in various social situations. But you find that the more you push the envelope of going to new and different social environments, the more you find your anxiety rising. There is thus a dialectic between comfort and freedom, because you either choose to avoid social encounters and thus feel relaxed or choose to be in new and different situations but feel additional tension. As things stand now for you, you have to choose between freedom that brings anxiety or comfort that brings social constriction. Right now you can't have both freedom and comfort, you have to choose between the two ends of the dialectic.

A dialectic is thus like an internal debate you have with yourself. "Shall I choose freedom or comfort?" "Shall I be relaxed but alone, or interact with others but feel discomfort?"

Much of life involves such compromises between competing demands and wants. With mixed anxiety and depression symptoms, the competition and choices become even more frequent and difficult to make. The internal debate with depression adds yet another dimension to the conflict because you have very little energy to make such choices. You often feel paralyzed, unable to jump back and forth between choices along the line of increased social interaction or social isolation, increased freedom or increased comfort. You may indeed feel no freedom to make choices at all, feeling as if nothing you do will make any difference whatsoever. You feel stuck on all dialectics you identify.

DBT invites you to clearly identify the choices you are making, the compromises you're forming between competing desires, and to analyze the outcome of the choices. Even with severe depression, making the choice to stay where you are on a dialectic *is* making a choice. What are the consequences of not making such choices consciously and strategically? Events and feelings seem beyond your control; you feel trapped and manipulated by circumstances that you don't fully understand. What are the consequences of using dialectic analysis to see where you stand now and where you prefer to go? You regain the strategy in life that has been missing, the maneuverability that your mixed anxiety and depression has hidden from you.

Dialectics with Mixed Anxiety and Depression

A dialectical domain is an area of life where you have to struggle to meet two different, frequently competing, sets of needs and wants. It's not wrong or "bad" that a dialectic set of needs and wants exists. In fact, it is normal and expected that conflict exists in life. We have to make compromises all the time. Each time you choose to spend time on your career, you are compromising time with family and friends. Each time you devote yourself to generating cash, you are probably spending less time having fun. Each time you spend energy developing your spiritual self, you are probably sacrificing potential corporal pleasures. You make a choice along a dialectic to pursue one thing and not the other. Below we will explore some of the most frequent dialectic conflicts with mixed anxiety and depression.

Activity versus Passivity

With mixed anxiety and depression the most powerful dialectical conflict is between activity and passivity. Anxiety encourages passivity due to fear: you are fearful of others' judgment of you (that you may come off as stupid and ridiculous in social or business situations); you are fearful of your own bodily response (shaking voice, trembling hands, or the "heart in your mouth" syndrome); you are fearful of being trapped in an environment without escape should your anxiety rise beyond tolerability; and you are fearful of placing demands on yourself that will bring back terrifying tension you had in the past. With such high anxiety, you may decide that the safest thing to do is—nothing. You become passive. You no longer attempt to influence your environment (attend social functions, initiate friendships, make business presentations, take on new projects, go with your children to school functions, date, or do things that could allow you to enjoy your life).

Passivity also figures in depression, but for different reasons. Rather than fear powering your passivity, depression involves the loss of hope. You are unconvinced that being active in shaping your life will make any difference. You're passive due to a sense of incompetence, hopelessness, or lack of energy. Passivity with depression is frequently expressed by sleeping too much, having decreased appetite and thus preparing or consuming fewer meals for yourself, not responding to the romantic overtures of your spouse or significant other, and allowing your mind to space out, so that long periods of time pass with little to no meaningful behavior occurring. Depressed people will sit in front of the television for hours without being able to report what they watched. That's because they weren't actively watching, but were actually passively vegetating in front of the tube.

In the following exercises, you can assess the effectiveness of your current strategies, recognizing that mixed anxiety and depression may be influencing your tendencies in ways that may not always help you achieve your goals. *Do* these exercises—don't just read them. Writing down your responses can help you to take a different perspective on your emotions than those automatic ones you usually react to.

In the following table you'll find specific beliefs that represent passivity (on the right side of the table) or activity (on the left). Which statements would you endorse?

I get things going. I begin projects without a lot of hesitation.	<————>	I procrastinate. I just don't have the critical mass to begin, even when I know I should or want to.
I want to make things different and know that my efforts will eventually pay off.	<————>	I doubt that my energy will result in any substantial changes in my life.
Most of what has been accomplished in my life has been by my own doing.	<————>	Others have provided me with things that are important to me.
Variety and change are the spice of life and I invite them.	<————>	I dread change. Things are bad enough as they are. Change could be worse.
I notice the world around me; it influences me in important ways that I seek out.	<————>	The world frightens me. I need my safe places in order to feel comfort.
I don't let my momentary feelings interfere with my long-term projects and plans.	<————>	My feelings control my life. When I'm anxious or depressed I stop and wait for a better day before proceeding.
I have influence over the course my life takes.	<————>	I'm powerless to control the course of my life.

One important way DBT treats mixed anxiety and depression is to critically examine where you fall in these dialectical domains. The assumption of DBT is not that you should always be on one end of the continuum or the other, in this instance that you should always be active and never be passive. Instead, DBT invites you to consider balance and strategy in deciding where you should fall on the continuum at any particular moment. Balance means that your responses aren't always extremes. Your responses move from one end of the continuum to the other, depending on your goals. The strategy is to change your position on the continuum depending on your goals. So, in this case, your strategy would be to determine how active you need to be to achieve whatever goal you wish to reach. This isn't to say that activity is always the best tactic. Passivity is an acceptable strategy in life when it will result in accomplishing what you want. For example, if you know your boyfriend is in a foul mood and everything you offer right now will be rejected, then being passive and waiting for his negative mood to pass before being active could be an extremely good idea. But, if your girlfriend is in an unexpectedly good and romantic mood and this doesn't happen frequently, in spite of your depression you may wish to strike while the iron is hot. It's a matter of determining the level of action that is appropriate to help you meet your goal.

So bear in mind that I'm not suggesting that activity of any sort always results in a better outcome. In fact, one function of mixed anxiety and depression is a sense of urgency that something needs to be done immediately to terminate your symptoms of anxiety and anticipation of doom (see Tice, Bratslavsky, and Baumeister 2001). This can be disastrous because it increases impulsivity: doing something—anything—just to stop the feelings you're experiencing. Sometimes it's best to try to tolerate the feelings you are having, even if they're strong and negative, waiting for a more propitious time to act. You'll learn more about distress tolerance skills in chapter 8.

For now, take stock of the major ways that you engage in either passivity or activity in your life. Think of the advantages and disadvantages of both ends of the dialectic. How has your passivity successfully protected you from unwanted anxiety and depression? How has your passivity simply served to increase your sense of inadequacy? When you have been active, when has this activity really been prompted by a sense of urgency to do something, almost anything, to terminate what you are feeling in the moment, rather than being a strategy to accomplish something positive in your life that is important to you?

Ways that I've been passive in the past (examples: watched too much television, stayed at home on weekends, kept my cool when someone irritated me):

_____

_____

_____

Ways that I've been active in the past (examples: spent money I didn't have, chose where the group would go for lunch, corrected someone who mischaracterized what I had said):

_____

_____

_____

Ways that I'm being passive today (examples: not telling someone how I feel, not taking my medications as prescribed, not going to stores to spend money):

_____

_____

_____

Ways that I'm being active today (examples: writing in this workbook rather than just skimming it, making phone calls to plan this weekend's social activities, making a decision I've put off for weeks confronting my friend on her betrayal):

_____

_____

_____

This exercise should highlight that being active and being passive each have their benefits depending on your goals. All too often, however, our activity or passivity depends only on our mood and not our objectives.

Self Focus versus Other Focus

People who are anxious tend to either focus too much on themselves (especially how their body is responding) or too much on their perceptions of how others react to them. It is similar with depression.

I'm self-conscious.	<———————>	I'm a people watcher.
I'm introspective and thoughtful about what goes on inside myself.	<———————>	I wonder what others are experiencing and why.
I analyze myself.	<———————>	I analyze others.
I know what I'm thinking and feeling in most situations.	<———————>	I'm finely tuned in to others' feelings.
I try to find out what I want in new situations so I get my needs met.	<———————>	I try to find out what others in new situations are like so I can fit in.
I worry about how I'll fit in with groups of people.	<———————>	I worry if other people will like me.
I'm always thinking about myself.	<———————>	The "other guy" always comes first.
My feelings seem to be the driver behind many of my actions.	<———————>	Other people's feelings come first.

Self-consciousness is frequently a part of both anxiety and depression. "Someone will notice how horrible I feel," you may say to yourself. Depression frequently involves devaluing yourself and elevating others in your opinion. Both anxiety and depression typically involve increased critical or judgmental feelings and can cause you to become more extreme either on the self-focused or the other-focused side. You are more critical of both yourself and of others. This attitude hurts you because it pushes you away from others (making you feel lonely and anxious) and increases your self-doubt (powering your depression).

Dialectic conflicts such as the ones listed above frequently have both advantages and disadvantages to being on one side of the dialectic or the other. Does your anxiety cause you to think that everyone knows your insecurities, even without you telling them? Does your depression make you forgetful of loved ones in your life? Does your self-focus decrease the intimacy you experience with your loved ones? Does your self-focus make you so self-absorbed that nothing interests you except your depressed feelings? Below, write your thoughts about where you fall on the dimensions in the table, judging both the advantages and disadvantages of each side of the continuum.

Ways my self-focus helps me. (Example: I'm aware of my feelings and this tells me what my values are.)

_____

_____

_____

Ways my self-focus hurts me. (Example: I get too caught up in me and lose perspective on what my objectives are.)

_____

_____

_____

Ways my other-focus helps me. (Example: I know where others stand on issues and this helps me keep perspective.)

_____

_____

_____

Ways my other-focus hurts me. (Example: I lose perspective on what my needs and wants are, responding too much to my perception of what others want.)

_____

_____

_____

Trust versus Suspicion

People generally have been great to me.	<————>	People have hurt me.
I assume others will generally do their best.	<————>	Only some people can be trusted.
People don't intentionally hurt each other, generally.	<————>	People do what is best for them.
My friends can keep a secret.	<————>	I keep secrets to myself.
I'm accepted for who I am by my friends and family.	<————>	People will take advantage of you if you let them.
I let many people into my life and care for them.	<————>	I choose my friends carefully.

Both anxiety and depression tend to decrease your trust in your own abilities and worth as well as in the abilities and worth of others. With anxiety you tend to be suspicious of your skills, and with depression you tend to be doubtful of your ability to profit from the companionship and trust of others. Does your anxiety cause you to put unfounded faith in the ability of others to protect you? Does your depression make you trust others so little that you are totally alienated from them? Again, write your thoughts and feelings down about how you currently fall along the trust versus suspicion dialectic. Think of both the advantages and the disadvantages.

Ways I'm trusting of others that I like. (Example: I let others get close to me.)

_____

_____

_____

Ways I'm trusting of others that I don't like. (Example: I let others take advantage of me.)

_____

_____

_____

Ways I'm suspicious of others that I like. (Example: People can't take me for a fool.)

_____

_____

_____

Ways I'm suspicious of others that I don't like. (Example: Perfectly good people get pushed away.)

_____

_____

_____

Transparency versus Privacy

I'm easy to get to know.	<————>	I'm reserved.
People say I'm an "open book."	<————>	People say it's hard to get to know me.
I make known what I want, so people know what they're getting into when they are with me.	<————>	I tend to be quiet and wait until I really get to know someone before I open up.
I'd describe myself as assertive.	<————>	I don't want to push myself on others.
I don't hide what I think and feel.	<————>	What I think and feel is my business and is personal.
I'm a good communicator; people don't have to guess what I'm thinking.	<————>	I keep my cards close to my chest.

With mixed anxiety and depression the above dialectic between transparency and privacy can be very confusing. Anxiety tends to make you feel transparent, and you want to hide. Depression tends to make you want to withdraw from others to increase your sense of privacy and to decrease contact with the world in general. With mixed anxiety and depression, therefore, you may find that you jump from one extreme to the other. Sometimes you may feel totally transparent and embarrassed about it, and at other times you find yourself so concerned with privacy that you don't allow yourself to be in the company of others. With anxiety you therefore perceive more transparency than is the case. You feel as if people can look right through you and see the terror within. Therefore, the tendency is to jump into a privacy mode when your anxiety increases because you do not wish to be so transparent.

Alternately, the anxiety may make you feel inadequate and make you wish that someone else would rescue you from your intense discomfort. In such situations, you may make your anxiety readily apparent to others so that they will take pity on you and intervene on your behalf.

Since these are contradictory tendencies (to be either transparent or private), they can be quite confusing both to yourself and to others.

The same is true for depression. With depression you may either feel that you need to hide your desperate feelings so others will not judge you harshly or that you must display your hopelessness so that others will rescue you from your sense of inadequacy. This, too, can be quite confusing both to yourself and to the others in your environment to whom you express your various emotional strategies of dealing with extreme emotions. (These are permutations on the emotional escape and avoidance strategies so important to the DBT analytical approach to treatment.)

The goal, then, is to analyze the *effect* of your strategy along the transparency versus privacy dialectic. Does your strategy lead you to the goals you want to reach? Does it get you what you want over the long term? Over the short term?

Think about the ways transparency and privacy operate in your life, both the advantages and disadvantages of each, and write them down below.

Ways I'm transparent or open to others that I like about myself. (Example: People know my preferences and tastes.)

_____

_____

_____

Ways I'm transparent or open to others that I don't like about myself. (Example: People see me as emotionally fragile.)

_____

_____

_____

Ways I'm private or unknown that I like about myself. (Example: I can choose what I intend to communicate to others.)

_____

_____

_____

Ways I'm private or unknown that I don't like about myself. (Example: People find me hard to get to know.)

_____

_____

_____

Independence versus Dependence

I enjoy doing things on my own.	<————>	I enjoy doing things with others.
I don't like people telling me what to do.	<————>	I resent having things left for me to do all alone.
I like time to myself	<————>	I enjoy get-togethers with others.
Privacy is important to me.	<————>	Feeling connected with others and having a support system is important to me.
Being self-sufficient is important.	<————>	Being loved and cared for is important.
People can't be trusted	<————>	Having someone I can trust is important.
When I count on someone, they frequently let me down.	<————>	Times when people have been there for me are very special to me.
Listening to a beautiful piece of music or song is fulfilling.	<————>	Sharing time with friends is when I have the most fun.
Having to depend on others is the worst thing that could ever happen to me.	<————>	Being all alone in the world is the worst thing that could ever happen to me.

Depression and anxiety can be displayed on both sides of the independence versus dependence dialectic. Depression can cause you to be so doubtful of the efforts of others that you socially withdraw. Or it can make you feel so inadequate that you become dependent on others to provide a sense of safety. Anxiety, too, can either increase your dependence on others (because you feel unsafe in your own abilities) or make you hide from public view (becoming totally independent of the observations of others). Healthy behavior demands that we jump variously along the independence versus dependence dialectic. Sometimes you should depend on others (for companionship, love, assistance, or advice), and sometimes you should do for yourself such that most of your needs are met without the assistance of others. With mixed depression and anxiety, your tendency is to stay at the extremes. Think about the ways you engage in dependence and independence with others. Write your thoughts and feelings below.

Ways I'm dependent that I don't like. (Example: People see me as inadequate.)

_____

_____

_____

Ways I'm dependent that I accept. (Example: My spouse knows I value him.)

_____

_____

_____

Ways I'm independent that I don't like. (Example: I push people away.)

_____

_____

_____

Ways I'm independent that I accept. (Example: I'm able to survive without others' help.)

_____

_____

_____

Self-Efficacy versus Seeking Help

Doing a project well and getting compliments for it is satisfying.	<————>	Asking for help, getting it, and learning something new is satisfying.
Excelling at a competition (winning a game, coming in fast in a race) is satisfying.	<————>	Being taught a new skill I'll use in the future is important.
Impressing others with my abilities feels good.	<————>	Being surrounded by skillful people I learn from feels good.

Depression tends to decrease your sense of self-efficacy, the degree of competence you anticipate from yourself. You may find yourself asking for help from others when you really don't need it. Anxiety has the same effect. You feel less skillful and want others to do for you. Healthy behavior is being able to identify our assets and skills and use them when appropriate, as well as identify our deficits and ask for the assistance of others when necessary. The difference between the dependence versus independence dialectic and the self-efficacy versus help-seeking dialectic has to do with attributions: Do you see yourself as capable even when asking for assistance? Even if you accept help, do you see yourself as competent to meet your own needs? Try to think of yourself before you felt substantial anxiety or depression, and answer the questions below. Don't let your current feelings of depression and anxiety overly influence your responses.

Skills I feel proud of. (Example: I support myself financially, and I know how to manage my own affairs.)

_____

_____

_____

Things people have taught me that I appreciate. (Examples: My friend consistently reminds me that I'm not in this world alone. My father taught me how to hug and be comfortable with closeness.)

_____

_____

_____

Changing versus Observing

When I see a problem, I go about trying to fix it.	<————>	When I see a problem, I try to understand it.
People call me a go-getter.	<————>	I'm a people watcher.
I'm an active problem solver; I don't just sit back and wait for something to happen.	<————>	I'm a good observer; I don't try to control everything around me.
When I'm upset, I do something about it.	<————>	When I'm upset, I try to see what's going on from all sides.
Pain has never been a problem for me because I do stuff to take my pain away.	<————>	When I'm in pain, I stick with the discomfort long enough to appreciate what the experience is telling me.
When someone else hurts, I try to solve their problems.	<————>	I'm empathic; I try to be sensitive to others' pain.

The changing versus observing dialectic is especially pertinent to mixed anxiety and depression because both sets of disorders tend to make you more observant of what is going on both around you and in the environment. You do less to influence both the environment and yourself. You watch your anxiety symptoms with great intensity but tend not to do the things that will decrease the anxiety. Depression brings the same tendency. You are acutely aware of your pessimism and of your feelings of tiredness and that nothing seems important enough to spend energy on. But you don't have the initiative to change these dynamics.

Mixed depression and anxiety symptoms simply tend to increase your observational power without any focus on how to influence the things that bother you. Alternately, some anxious individuals attempt to control so much of what they experience that it simply adds to their frustration and high emotional arousal. For example, you try to hide your muscle tension, shaking, and misgivings so that no one could possibly notice them. You pretend that you are not experiencing what you are experiencing, and your body rebels. It increases the anxiety symptoms such that they cannot be hidden.

Use the following questions to take stock of your issues regarding observing (simply watching what is going on without trying to influence it) versus changing (attempting to change the things that you don't like).

Ways I try to control and change that I think are positive. (Example: I manage my money well.)

_____

_____

_____

Things I try to control and change that I wish I could just let go of. (Example: Trying to get my spouse to understand why I like a clean house.)

_____

_____

_____

Times I sit back and watch that I think are positive. (Example: Not letting my children's interest in video games get the best of me.)

_____

_____

_____

Times I sit back and watch that I wish I would try to control. (Example: Let my best friend know that her criticisms really upset me.)

_____

_____

_____

Understanding versus Approval

DBT draws an important distinction between the attempt to understand an emotion, a situation, or an event and approving of that emotion, situation, or event. You should attempt to understand yourself not simply for purposes of validation, but because through such understanding you are in a better position to control the emotion, situation, or event. Knowing that you are anxious (being able to identify the elements of your anxiety, such as worry about the future, bodily arousal, or feelings of doom) is completely different than accepting your anxiety as something with which you have to live. Recognizing that your lack of energy, your sense of futility regarding the future, and your decreased ability to sleep are signs of depression is quite different from accepting depression as a natural state of affairs for you to which you simply need to adjust.

Many people confuse understanding with approval. With understanding, we attempt to identify the causes and explanations for why something is the way it is. You may thus understand that because you never received the kind of love and physical affection you wanted as a child, you have therefore never developed the knack of being comfortable with others expressing their love toward you physically. Having such an understanding (that your discomfort with sex or being hugged or otherwise touched by another person is due to early childhood deprivation) is totally different than approval of your intimacy issues (that it is acceptable that you don't like to get emotionally or physically close to others).

Acceptance of an issue means that you *approve* of it, while understanding an issue means that you know why it exists. Most forms of psychotherapy, including the kind of self-analysis you are performing in this book, assume that understanding why you feel the way you feel is necessary but isn't a sufficient condition for change. Understanding why you feel the way you feel can help you to change those very feelings and is thus quite important. However, understanding the connections and causes for your feelings does not imply that you need to simply endure them. You don't have to accept those things that you understand. You can change even those things that are reasonable and predictable given the history of events that preceded them.

I get anxious around new people because I worry what they will think of me.	<———————>	My anxiety is high, so I have to stay away from people. It's just the way it is.
I've been treated so abusively that it's natural that I'm depressed.	<———————>	I must be scum, or else no one would have abused me like that.
I'm afraid of groups of people, and that's why I get so nervous in new situations.	<———————>	People scare me. I'm not comfortable, so why subject myself to that?
I have a lot of negative thoughts, and that keeps me depressed.	<———————>	I'm a malcontent. Nothing pleases me, so why try?
I assume the worst, and that makes me both depressed and anxious.	<———————>	I see what can go wrong. So why try something new?
I lack confidence, so I stay away from challenging activities.	<———————>	I'm not good at stuff. There is no challenge, only failure.

I'm self-conscious, and that makes it hard for me to concentrate and let my knowledge and wisdom show.	<————>	My brain doesn't work right. I have to accept that I'll never amount to anything.
My emotions frighten me, so I try not to feel.	<————>	My feelings overwhelm and destroy me. I might as well destroy them before they destroy me.

Notice that in the "approval" column you accept the issues fatalistically. It gives you a rationale to not try something different. In the "understanding" column you identify the issues but don't accept them as necessarily true for the future. There is room for change and the possibility of different realities in the future.

Now consider how you've understood or accepted challenges in your life.

Ways I've tried to understand myself that really amount to approval and acceptance of things I don't like. (Example: I don't like to be touched because it never happened when I was a child.)

_____

_____

_____

_____

_____

_____

Skill Enhancement versus Self-Acceptance

Things I need to improve	<————>	Things I accept about myself
Problems to solve	<————>	Issues I'll live with

A critical aspect of mixed anxiety and depression is that you tend to blame yourself for your symptoms, whether panic attacks, being fearful of social situations, or feeling sad. Healthy behavior is identifying what needs doing and developing an action plan to make things the way we want them to be. Much of life has painful realities over which you have no control (people we love die, war kills innocents, people starve in a world of plenty, etc.). The same is true for aspects of yourself. If you tend to be an emotionally sensitive person, it doesn't make sense for you to try to become a stoic who only experiences feelings with great effort. Conversely, an individual with great defenses against emotion is unlikely to become an emotionally sensitive person. Your basic tendencies developed over a lifetime probably don't need to be changed in order to decrease your anxiety and depression. You can still be you and not be anxious and depressed. Critically examining things you resist that you should probably accept and identifying the things that bring you pain and that you can influence will increase your probability of being satisfied with life and feeling calm. Use the following exercise to examine the issues that trouble you about yourself and that contribute to your anxiety and depression.

The deficiencies or problems I accept in myself. (Example: I'm emotionally sensitive.)

_____

_____

_____

The deficiencies or problems I do not tolerate or accept in myself. (Example: My emotions are raw and extreme most of the time.)

_____

_____

_____

The above issues I could accept if I wasn't so hard on myself. (Example: I'll never be svelte; just focus on being healthy.)

_____

_____

_____

What I need to do in order to overcome the things I don't accept. (Example: Should spend more time with my significant others.)

_____

_____

_____

The obstacles or barriers to accomplishing the above. (Example: My significant other is angry with me.)

_____

_____

_____

What I've done in the past to solve these problems that failed. (Example: I tried harder using the same strategies that didn't work in the past.)

_____

_____

_____

What I've done in the past to solve these problems that worked. (Example: I changed my tone of voice and gave eye contact.)

_____

_____

_____

Emotion Regulation versus Emotion Tolerance

DBT is about learning to both regulate and tolerate your feelings. That is, you'll learn how to change your feelings or their intensity and learn how to endure unpleasant feelings when appropriate. You have to learn both, because some feelings shouldn't be changed even if they could be. For example, grief is a normal and healthy expression of loss of a loved one. You would lose something important if you learned to shut off this feeling. You will learn an extensive set of strategies later in this book for both emotion regulation and emotion tolerance.

At this point, take an inventory of the emotions you tend to embrace and those that frighten or terrorize you. We mentioned earlier that both anxiety and depression can be anticipatory diseases: you *fear* that a negative event will occur, or that something horrible in you makes you despicable to others. With mixed anxiety and depression the probability increases that you become fearful of your feelings themselves and will do almost anything to not feel what you fear feeling.

On the next page is a list of feeling words. Look at the list, and write the feeling words in the appropriate category (depending on your own particular reactions—there are no right or wrong responses).

Feeling Words

Love	Attraction	Suffering	Exasperation	Gloom
Fear	Tenseness	Infatuation	Hope	Pride
Sadness	Caring	Pity	Grouchiness	Nervousness
Anxiety	Apprehension	Like	Happiness	Thrill
Agony	Compassion	Neglect	Jealousy	Distress
Dread	Surprise	Sympathy	Isolation	Hope
Defeat	Lust	Joy	Resentment	Astonishment
Horror	Apathy	Sentimentality	Anguish	Misery
Despair	Passion	Amusement	Outrage	Bashfulness
Fright	Boldness	Cheerfulness	Depression	Grief
Adoration	Tenderness	Pleasure	Neglect	Impatience
Worry	Shyness	Delight	Loneliness	Hurt
Affection	Insecurity	Rapture	Glumness	Intrigue
Panic	Curiosity	Elation	Sorrow	

A: Feelings you don't care either way about (you could take them or leave them)

_____

_____

_____

B: Feelings you like to have and seek out

_____

_____

_____

C: Feelings you hate to have and avoid at all costs

_____

_____

_____

D: Feelings you dislike and try to avoid, but don't panic over

_____

_____

_____

E: Feelings you wish to increase and have more often

_____

_____

_____

In order to decrease depression, you need to increase activities that bring those positive feelings you seek. As a first gesture toward problem solving, think of activities that formerly brought such feelings. Never mind that recently those activities no longer produce the feelings they used to. Just list them here. You will return to them later in the book, and this exercise will eventually assist you to feel less depressed.

Activities that used to result in the feelings listed under B and E. (Examples: I used to go to social gatherings, ride my bike, watch movies with friends.)

_____

_____

_____

_____

The obstacles or barriers to increasing the above activities. (Example: I wait until I feel like it, and I rarely feel like it any more.)

_____

_____

_____

_____

Now deal with the feelings that you hate to have and would avoid at all costs (those listed under C). What horrible or lasting effect occurs when you experience these feelings? Do people die? Do your loved ones forever reject you? List below the horrible and lasting effects on your life when you feel these feelings:

_____

_____

_____

_____

Now, in the list you just made above, attempt to discriminate between those feelings you prefer not to have, as opposed to those things that are really catastrophic and life-changing events. Which of your hated feelings actually causes you substantial and long-lasting anxiety or depression? Write them here:

_____

_____

_____

_____

_____

This exercise will help you to discriminate anticipatory fear from real consequences of your emotions. So much of what we anticipate is based on fear rather than reality. By discriminating between the two, you are more likely to eliminate artificial barriers to change. You will have considerable practice in the remainder of this book working through these general first observations.

Dialectical Domains

There are many domains around which dialectics, or conflicting demands, play out. Dialectics are found around emotions themselves. When you feel ambiguous (you want two or more opposing things at once), there can be a dialectic. You can have dialectic conflict around your own thoughts or your own values. Dialectics can be found around anticipation, or contradictory behavioral strategies. For example, you may see that your spouse is angry with you and anticipate a verbal attack. In anticipation of the attack, you defensively take the first verbal punch. Your spouse withdraws because they have been hurt. You feel lonely and guilty because you hurt them, so you show affection and concern. This is both anticipatory (your initial approach was to attack before being attacked) and contradictory (first based on attack then based on affection).

With mixed anxiety and depression, frequently the dialectic has to do with the alternating nature of your feelings. One minute you feel fearful and have energy to avoid what you're scared of, and the next minute you feel so deflated that your avoidance is not an action at all but rather a passive submission to your sense of futility about the future. While both behaviors are based on avoidance, the anxiety-generated one has a sense of power and influence about it, while the depressed avoidance is guided by helplessness and has no urgency to it.

Identifying dialectics that bring a sense of urgency is critical because urgency increases impulsive behavior. When you feel urgent, you are more likely to engage in behavior that is self-defeating. In general, urgency is a barrier to good problem-solving skills.

On the other hand, depressed avoidance lacks power, the opposite of urgency. With depressed avoidance you are unlikely to do anything to make changes, increasing the probability that things will stay the same for you.

Possible Dialectics in Mixed Anxiety and Depression

Contradictory Emotions

Anger	<————>	Desire
Depression		Hopefulness
Despair		Inspiration
Deflation		Powerfulness
Resignation		Initiative

Oppositional Thought Patterns

Desire to live	<————>	Desire to die
Feed me		Ignore me
I'm worthless		Don't dare mistreat me
I'm lonely		Leave me alone
I need you		You're worthless

Oppositional Values

People are special to me	<————>	People are disgusting
Things provide meaning to me		Possessions are irrelevant
Money defines my worth		People love me for my cash (which I resent)
I seek spiritual peace		Spirituality screws me up

Contradictory Behavioral Strategies

I can change this	<————>	Trying is futile
I'll reward you		I'll punish you

The fact that you have dialectic conflict does not mean that there is something fundamentally wrong with you. We all have conflict—it's a part of life. What determines success is not being without conflict, but being able to form adequate compromises to the conflicts you do have.

Bring Conflict to Consciousness

Since we all experience conflict, it can become such an automatic and habitual part of life that you no longer notice it at all. Similarly, before reading this sentence, you were probably unaware of the view of your nose between your eyes. Because it is always there, your brain blocks it out of conscious awareness. It is a constant. Since it is constant, you no longer pay attention to it as an important variable worthy of attention.

It's the same with conflict—it's so constant that we can no longer see it. But paying attention can bring you great benefits. The purpose of paying attention to the dialectical conflict is that you may become increasingly aware of the effect of conflict in your life that is promoting your anxiety and depression. Making that which affects you conscious rather than automatic will allow you to have more control over your feelings since you will be more aware of causes.

Types of Conflict

When we examined dialectics, we exposed contradictory emotions, thoughts, values, and behavioral strategies. Dialectical conflicts can be powerful forces behind mixed anxiety and depression. But not all conflicts are dialectical. Some conflict does not involve contradictions, but still produces tension and frustrates your ability to obtain your goals. Below we examine types of conflict that may increase your mixed anxiety and depression. By breaking conflicts down into types, you may better identify the conflicts that power your hurtful feelings.

Self versus Self

When you think of conflict, you probably think of interpersonal situations. You want one thing and another person wants a different thing. Many conflicts are interpersonal, but there are also many conflicts that exist within ourselves. For example, you may want your father's approval *and* want to hurt him due to past events. At the same time, you may have no external conflict or even no contact whatsoever with your father now. Nevertheless, the conflict within you is real, current, and filled with existential pressure.

Self versus Society

Likewise, you can experience conflict with "them," even when "they" are not identifiable. You perceive that society thinks or feels certain things, judges in certain ways, and disapproves of certain things. For example, you may perceive that only certain white-collar workers receive respect in our society, and you're a plumber. As a blue-collar worker, you perceive that you have failed the social test of acceptability. Never mind that many plumbers make more money than many "professionals," or that plumbers frequently have less work stress, don't have to take their work home, and can have just as high or higher quality of life compared to white-collar workers. You discount all of these benefits and still feel slighted by the world. And it's very hard to actively engage this conflict because the people who make these purported judgments are invisible. You can't really spot them because it is not your uncle Joe or father-in-law Larry who has told you that you can never measure up. It is "society." It's "them." They think, feel, judge, and sentence your behavior to consequences, even though they are not actually there in any physical sense. It is a haunting sensation when you feel that they look over your shoulder like secret police and tell you right from wrong, and somehow you always come out looking bad.

Self versus Significant Others

In this case, the conflict *is* interpersonal. You want romance in your life, to be told that you're special and important and loved. You want to be reminded that there is a reason that you're in this relationship. But your boyfriend is quiet and practical. He focuses on what is going to happen today and tomorrow, not on feelings. He doesn't talk about the relationship, he talks about events. You feel disappointed, unappreciated, unloved, and taken for granted. Or, as a student, you have worked hard to write an essay assigned for a class. Pleasing the instructor is important to you. She returns the paper with few comments, no encouragement, and no recognition for the time and intellectual strain you have expended on the project. You feel defeated and insignificant.

Self versus Family

This is a cross between the "invisible" society and significant others. Your mother and father (identifiable, real people) drilled into you as a child that having opportunities greater than they had (more education, more family money, less requirements to work to help out the family), you should soar up the social ladder. You perceive that the entire family (not only Mom and Dad, but the invisible "others") are watching you critically because you're not soaring. In fact, you anticipate they expect you to fail because you're no good. You can't possibly work as hard, be as dedicated, apply as much focus, or be as selfless as your family tells you they have been for you.

Self versus Friends

People you've grown up with provide a point of comparison. Wendy married a handsome professional who is on his way up in society. Mary obtained an advance graduate degree and just obtained her first professional job. Alice just had two adorable twins and her husband seems happy and proud of both the infants and his wife. What have you done? What's wrong with you? How come you have not found Mr. Right or been motivated enough to find satisfaction in a career path?

Self versus Coworkers

You work just as hard as the others but don't seem to have the same chances of promotion. You make the same salary as Jane, but Jane seems to have expensive clothes and always look "right" and more attractive than you. You're nice to everyone, but they seem to be judgmental and mean to you.

Conflict and Your Emotions

Conflict of importance to you, no matter what type, produces anxiety and depression. And, in the spirit of trying to bring conflict and its repercussions to awareness, it's now time to recognize what emotions the various conflicts in your life evoke. When you're more conscious of the roots of these emotions, you will feel more in control and better able to work with them. Look at the list of possible negative emotions below and the domains within which they can occur (the triggers that bring the conflict alive). Begin to identify those situations and thoughts that produce the listed feelings.

Feelings from Conflict

Anger	Frustration	Anxiety	Tension
Sadness	Sorrow	Guilt	Self-hate
Disappointment	Panic	Shame	

Self versus self: For instance, "I've always wanted to be confident, believe in myself, and not be so afraid of the future. I've never been that way. I hate myself because I'm so vulnerable and weak."

_____

_____

_____

_____

_____

_____

_____

Self versus society: For instance, "Society expects me to be thin and tall and to wear all those clothes like in the magazines. No matter how hard I try, I'm short and look pudgy. Clothes just don't fit me right, no matter how much weight I lose. And the weight always comes back. I'll never be acceptable in other people's eyes. I'm both depressed and anxious that they expect this of me, and I feel guilt that I can't fulfill their expectations. I want approval."

_____

_____

_____

_____

_____

_____

_____

Feelings from Conflict

Anger	Frustration	Anxiety	Tension
Sadness	Sorrow	Guilt	Self-hate
Disappointment	Panic	Shame	

Self versus significant others: For example: "My best friend tells me I'm selfish and self-centered and that's why I can't find a mate. I try to understand what others need, but I always seem to miss the mark. I feel tension all the time because I don't know what to do or how to feel. I'm resentful that I'm expected to be someone I just can't seem to be."

_____

_____

_____

_____

_____

_____

Self versus family: For instance, "I want to be left alone, but my wife keeps telling me I'm withdrawing from her and the kids. I feel like a failure. I want to meet their needs. I just don't know how."

_____

_____

_____

_____

_____

_____

Feelings from Conflict

Anger	Frustration	Anxiety	Tension
Sadness	Sorrow	Guilt	Self-hate
Disappointment	Panic	Shame	

Self versus friends: For example, "My girlfriend tells me the reason guys don't like me is that I don't 'put out.' I feel so dirty and hateful when I have sex with guys I'm not sure I love. There must be something wrong with me that I can't enjoy sex like my friends do. I may never have a satisfying relationship. I hate myself both ways: if I have sex I feel dirty; if I say no, I feel unworthy. There is something wrong with me."

_____

_____

_____

_____

_____

_____

Self versus coworkers: For instance, "John tells me the reason I'm not getting promoted is that I haven't learned the fine art of brownnosing. I refuse to suck up to people I don't respect. I won't play that game. It's not fair that my salary depends on how much others like me. I feel powerless and depressed."

_____

_____

_____

_____

_____

_____

_____

There are a number of lessons you can learn from the preceding exercise. First, your feelings have precipitants. Something causes feelings to be provoked or maintained. Second, frequently feelings come from conflict. The conflict may be observable to no one but yourself, but it often relates to conflicting desires. Third, often your feelings are based on presumptions about how you *think* others think. You project, like a movie projector onto a blank screen, your own high expectations of yourself onto others. Finally, by identifying expectations you have or others have (and the feelings those expectations bring), you gain maneuverability. You know more points of intervention: you can change your expectations of yourself, you can help modify other people's expectations of you, or you can accept some conflicts as understandable aspects of living in a world where people have different needs and wants (and that it's not your job to make everyone in the world happy).

Conflict Is a Part of Life

The more you begin to assume that conflict is a part of life, unavoidable and natural, the less sense of urgency you will have in resolving your conflicts. The less you engage in blame and the more you look toward problem solving, the greater your chances of happiness and peace will be. Blame is something those who are depressed understand only too well: culpability, feelings of guilt and remorse, decreased feelings of competence, and the powerful sense that you are wrong. Feeling blame, in addition to increasing depression, also increases your anxiety. You become so tense and vigilant that you often make another mistake, and this increases your tension and negative expectations for the future.

Actually, short-lived blame can be helpful. By accepting some amount of responsibility for your actions, you are also accepting the fact that you have some control over your life and behavior. But with mixed anxiety and depression the tendency is not to accept responsibility and then move on to problem-solving skills. You don't move from blame to action. Instead, you may often get stuck in your feelings of blame and culpability (using it as a method of self-punishment rather than as a cue to cope differently in the future).

People with resilient psychological coping skills accept blame or responsibility for their actions. They understand that they are not perfect, that there is always room for improvement, and that acknowledging responsibility can be a positive thing if they use that information to do things differently in the future.

Dialectical problem solving assumes that you have to compromise. You have to give up something in order to get something else. You have to move from an extreme end of the continuum toward a different position. Accepting blame for a problem then quickly moving toward problem solving can be quite effective. With mixed anxiety and depression, it's only too easy to get stuck in the blame end of the continuum, repeatedly telling yourself how rotten you are, rather than accepting responsibility for something then moving to solving the problem so that it doesn't happen again.

The goal of DBT is not simply to move from one side of the continuum to the other (assuming that your extreme must be wrong, since you feel anxious and depressed). Instead, the goal is to be strategic and analyze how your position on the continuum supports or distracts from accomplishing the goals that are important to you. The goal is thus to shift location on the continuum depending on the effect your position has on your goals.

Contradictory Emotions

Feelings are complex processes precisely because we can experience two contradictory urges and needs simultaneously. For example, we can feel both love and hate for another person at about the same time. We may love how the person is creative, attractive, and stimulating, but hate their selfishness and lack of consistency. It would be easy if the person was consistently negative toward you, because you could simply and without conflict eject them from your interpersonal life. But life isn't so uncomplicated. Those situations that create the greatest strain and stress for you involve contradictory or competing elements (you both want the person in your life and want them to be substantially different than they are). If you eliminate someone from your social circle who previously fulfilled important needs for you, then there is emotional loss. The idea of contradictory emotions thus identifies that we can feel both anger and desire toward a person or situation, that we can feel both depression and hopefulness toward the same problem, and that despair and inspiration do not occur exclusively but can be mixed in the same moment. The more contradictory emotions operating in a situation, the more difficult and complex the solution will be.

DBT thus invites you to look at situations that have been going on for a long time as possibly involving dialectics that need to be resolved. If your situation were simple (you experienced only anger and no desire), then you probably would have engaged in problem solving and resolved the situation without the kind of structure and guidance that DBT offers you. For example, if you hated your job, disliked your coworkers, resented the low pay and poor benefits, and found little attractive about what you did on your job on a daily basis, you probably would seek other employment somewhere else. You would not feel that much conflict. You would quit your job and not feel a great deal of internal conflict about doing it. However, many people stay in jobs that they resent precisely because of dialectics: you may hate your supervisor but appreciate your coworkers, feel that your job is too stressful but worry that other positions will not pay you as well, or resent your commute to work but worry that other companies will not offer the lucrative retirement benefits you currently have.

Dialectics can occur within any set of complicated feeling states and situations. However, with mixed anxiety and depression, the following continua seem to be the most prevalent ones: anger versus desire, depression versus hopefulness, despair versus inspiration, deflation versus power, and resignation versus initiative. The goal or strategy is not necessarily to be on one side of the continua only (for example, to be full of desire, hope, inspiration, power, and initiative). While that might sound great, the reality of the world is that it's full of obstacles, tough choices, and frustrations. While some people attempt to hide from conflict and pretend that it's not there, such illusions of total serenity are likely to crack in the face of typical daily failures and challenges. In fact, sometimes to resign ourselves to harsh realities is the most adaptive thing we can do. If you are in chronic physical pain and the many physicians with whom you have consulted offer no hope of permanent relief from the physical pain, acceptance and resignation that pain is likely to part of your daily life can provide you with greater inspiration about how to cope with your pain while living to your fullest. The goal is thus not to be extremely on one side of the various continua, but to compromise between the two competing emotions in order to reach the objectives you have set for yourself.

Let's look at an example. Sally is angry with her parents because they constantly criticized her for the choices she made as a very young adult. She has found that the less time she spends with them, the less anger she experiences about the past. She now visits them only on major holidays, with periodic telephone conversations in between. Sally finds this compromise—limiting the amount of time she spends with them without totally rejecting them as parents—to be in her best interests, because her anger at them is not total. She still has some desire for contact, and in fact loves her parents, but can tolerate them only in smaller doses. Let's see how Sally might rate herself along the continua in the chart below:

Contradictory Emotions

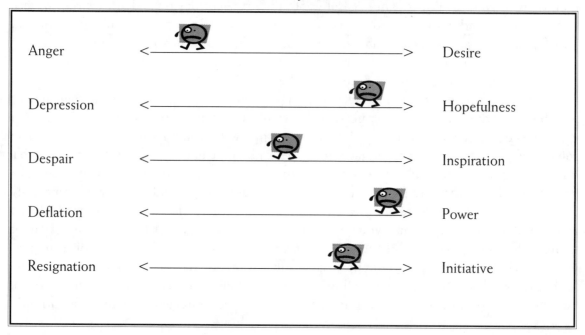

Anger	<————————————————>	Desire
Depression	<————————————————>	Hopefulness
Despair	<————————————————>	Inspiration
Deflation	<————————————————>	Power
Resignation	<————————————————>	Initiative

In the first pair of contradictory emotions, you see that there is a continuum from anger to desire. The more you are toward the anger side, the more you're likely to feel threatened by others, under attack, and in a defensive position toward others. This produces anxiety. The more you're accepting of others (not angry), the more desire you feel toward them. It's a compromise between competing emotions. It is difficult to be attacking someone, verbally or judgmentally, and at the same time being desirous of them and inviting them to come closer to you. You must choose, make a compromise, between feeling and displaying anger and feeling and displaying desire. Whether you like it or not, you're constantly being placed in situations where you must choose to fall somewhere on the continuum each time you feel conflict with someone who is important to you. The strategy you use will either increase anxiety and depression or decrease it.

So it is with your feelings about yourself. The more depressed you feel, the more you blame yourself and engage in negative thoughts and attitudes about yourself, and the less hopeful you are going to feel. Alternatively, if you have hope that things can be different, then you are more likely to take your own deficiencies in stride and to engage in less judgmentalism toward yourself. The more you feel despair, the less inspiration you can simultaneously feel. The more powerful you feel, the less deflated. The more resignation you feel, the less willing you will be to show initiative and do something about your problems.

On the following continua, place an "x" where you feel you fall (in general) at the present time.

Anger	<————————————————————————————————>	Desire
Depression	<————————————————————————————————>	Hopefulness
Despair	<————————————————————————————————>	Inspiration
Deflation	<————————————————————————————————>	Power
Anxiety	<————————————————————————————————>	Peacefulness
Resignation	<————————————————————————————————>	Initiative

Write below how your position on the anger versus desire continuum relates to your goals. (Example: "I'm frequently angry, and that pushes people away from me. I end up feeling lonely and rejected." Or, "I too frequently work hard to obtain the approval of others. I'm too much on the desire end of the continuum, and that makes me feel at the mercy of others. I feel powerless." Or even, "I'm so contradictory. I'm angry, push people away, then feel lonely and give away the farm in order to get people back in my life. It is confusing to me, and I'll bet it is even more confusing to people around me.")

_____

_____

_____

_____

_____

Write below how your position on the depression versus hopefulness continuum relates to your goals. (Example: "I try so hard to hide my depression by being hopeful in my presentation to others that I end up feeling like a fake. I don't believe my hopefulness." Or, "I'm so depressed that I give up hope, then I don't try to accomplish my goals." Or, "I go back and forth so frequently and fast between depression and hopefulness that I don't know how I feel, so I do nothing.")

_____

_____

_____

_____

Write below how your position on the despair versus inspiration continuum relates to your goals. (Example: "My bipolar disorder makes me so full of inspiration that I feel there are no limits. When I act this out, I lose credibility with my family, friends, and coworkers.")

_____

_____

_____

_____

Write below how your position on the deflation versus power continuum relates to your goals. (Example: "I'm so deflated that I feel I'll make a fool of myself no matter what I do. So I do nothing." Or, "I'm so full of myself that I'm constantly in battles with everyone around me to try to show them my superiority. All I really want is respect from others, but my inflated self does not bring me to this goal.")

_____

_____

_____

_____

Write below how your position on the anxiety versus peacefulness continuum relates to your goals. (Example: "I'm so anxious that I believe that peace just is not in store for me, ever.")

_____

_____

_____

_____

Write below how your position on the resignation versus initiative continuum relates to your goals. (Example: "I'm so resigned to my fate of always being depressed and anxious that I've given up trying anything new." Or, "I'm so frozen between resignation and initiative that I get confused, give up easily, and don't sustain my efforts to obtain my goals.")

_____

_____

_____

_____

Forming Compromises

The goal is not to always be, along all continua, exactly in the middle. Anger can be a useful emotion when you are under attack or being threatened. Likewise, being able to take stock of your deficiencies and to recognize areas where you need to improve is an important personality attribute. Recognizing your shortcomings can indeed be a humbling experience (closer to depression than to hopefulness). Too much inspiration and people will call you manic and egotistical!

Instead, the goal is to be strategic and shift to different positions along the continuum (certainly not to always be at an extreme, or even in the middle) depending on your goals and the situation you're in; to be flexible and engage in behavior that creates feelings that help you get to where you really want to go (more on this in later chapters). The goal is to know where you are now and what you're feeling, and to understand the consequences of your current compromises. Your compromises can and should change over time, depending on your current goals and situation. Dialectical thinking involves being able to identify the competing demands of each domain and make choices about how you will compromise one need or demand for another.

If you're in a relationship with someone and they do something that you don't like, you *choose* to either react to your resulting anger or to react to your underlying desire. It's not wrong that you feel anger, just as it's not wrong that you continue to have desire toward someone that you're angry at. It is wrong (or not in your best interest) for you to jump immediately to the left side of the anger versus desire continuum and express your anger with full force if you want the person with whom you're angry to continue to know that you desire them and that they are important to you. The usefulness of your expressions of feelings depends on your goals and wants, not just your immediate feelings. This is the compromise formation. You decide what is in your best interest—in this case, how much to react to your anger and how much to react to your desire. You can't do both strongly. You have to choose how much of each to show according to what will best serve your needs and goals. You must form a compromise.

Previously we reviewed how contradictory emotions create conflicts in our lives. Any kind of conflict demands that compromises be made in order to resolve the conflict. Even if the conflict is all internal (psychological) and does not involve interpersonal relations, compromises must be made. In internal conflict the compromise is precisely between the contradictory emotions explored earlier. Several advantages occur when you consciously make compromises. First, your values become apparent. You must make tough choices between short-term pleasure or pain and long-term pleasure or pain. Second, you force yourself to make choices rather than pretend you can have the best of everything. Third, it forces you to include your objectives or goals in your problem-solving process, rather than simply respond to the feeling you are having in the moment. Lastly, it forces you to accept the reality that in order to gain something you may have to lose something else. Forming compromises is thus an essential component of good psychological coping skills. It helps you balance making decisions based on feelings with basing decisions on goals.

Look at your ratings of your current feelings on page 45. Below, identify the compromises you're making along each continuum. Make a few notes for yourself about the situation you're thinking about so that later you can look back on your writing and remember what you were dealing with.

Anxiety versus Peacefulness

It would only seem logical, you may say, that we all attempt to move from the anxiety end of the continuum toward the peacefulness end. And that is precisely what most people do, at the expense of accepting tension and apprehension that is only too normal in everyday life. There are times when you need to experience your anxiety so that your fear is eventually reduced. In post-traumatic stress disorder or phobias, it is precisely the individual's unwillingness to experience anxiety that creates the disorder and increases subsequent anxiety. Below, consider times when you could have tolerated your anxiety but instead did everything possible in the moment to feel peacefulness instead.

Situation (who, when, where, what). Example: "When I'm with my boss during a sales presentation, I let him do most of the talking. This decreases my immediate anxiety, but it makes me depressed that I'm not more successful on the job."

_____

_____

_____

_____

Compromises I'm making (giving up what, in order to get what). Example: "I'm decreasing short-term anxiety (engaging in avoidance behavior), but increasing my depression (a long-term feeling that makes my life less rewarding in general)."

_____

_____

_____

_____

Anger versus Desire

Most people would rather feel desire than anger. While anger protects you against being taken advantage of, can provide corrective feedback to others, and provides the kind of emotional arousal that makes you active, it also is upsetting. Desire is the opposite emotion. It helps to bring others closer to you by letting them know that they are wanted and helps form the bond between you and others by providing validation that you approve of and want them. The anger versus desire continuum is a common source of conflict for people because frequently you feel both emotions toward the same person, often at the same time. The person with whom you are angry is also often an important person in your life that you don't want to lose. Not just people, but also situations and memories, can cause simultaneous anger and desire (remember our job example above). Below, choose a situation where you felt both anger and desire so you can explore the conflict and later the compromises you were having to make in the conflictual situation.

Situation (who, when, where, what). Example: "John made a fool of me in front of my friends yesterday."

_____

_____

_____

_____

Compromises I'm making (giving up what, in order to get what). Example: "I'm going to suppress the expression of my anger because I'm more interested in making him my ally rather than showing him how he wronged me."

_____

_____

_____

_____

Depression versus Hopefulness

How can you feel both hopeful and depressed about a situation simultaneously? Fortunately, abject hopelessness is rare. While most of you resent the degree to which you feel depressed and hopeless about a situation, the degree of resentment you feel is directly tied to the amount (however small) of hopefulness you feel. Otherwise, you would be totally accepting of your depressing situation (and not seek to change it, because you have accepted it).

Another way to think of the depression versus hopefulness continuum is to think of resignation (acceptance of the situation as it is) versus optimism (having expectation that your situation will improve). Below, try to identify a situation in your life where you struggled with feeling both depressed and hopeful at the same time.

Situation (who, when, where, what). Example: "I don't want to call the kids today to see how they are doing because they're sure to notice how depressed I'm feeling."

_____

_____

_____

_____

Compromises I'm making (giving up what, in order to get what). Example: "I'll call them anyway, in spite of my fears of having my depression noticed. At least I can hope that talking to people I love will remind me that I do sincerely care about others. It will hopefully make me feel less depressed, and then I won't have to worry about having my feelings noticed so much."

_____

_____

_____

_____

Despair versus Inspiration

The despair versus inspiration continuum is similar to depression versus hopefulness, but in this one you're not just depressed, but feel absolute and total futility (despair). The opposite end is not just hopefulness that things can indeed be solved (inspiration) but also energy. With mixed anxiety and depression, the probability that your emotions are extreme increases. It's therefore important that you identify situations where such extreme emotional responses occur and identify the conflict(s) involved and the compromises you are willing to make in order to resolve the conflict. Despair involves lack of energy or drive and lack of belief that anything you can do will affect the situation that prompts your despairing feelings, and consequent suffering. At the opposite end, you have willpower and ideas about how things can be changed and feel the activation necessary to try to implement the ideas.

Situation (who, when, where, what). Example: "I felt totally useless today when my husband asked me how the meeting with the contractor went. I forgot all about it and didn't even schedule a meeting."

_____

_____

_____

_____

Compromises I'm making (giving up what, in order to get what). Example: "I'm going to stop blaming myself and tell my husband that I forgot about scheduling a meeting, thank him for reminding me, and go to the phone right now and leave a message for a meeting tomorrow. My husband is trying to help me, not hurt me. I want this project to go right. I want it for me, not just for my husband."

_____

_____

_____

_____

What compromises do you wish you could make more easily? What is hard to give up that could help you to more easily get what you want out of life? For many people, it has to do with your high expectations for yourself, trying to meet others' expectations and sacrificing your own needs, or unwillingness to sacrifice one end of the continuum for another. Give some thought to these issues, and write them down below. You may be tempted to just read on without doing these exercises, but that would really be shortchanging yourself. Completing these exercises actually helps by making you articulate your thoughts and feelings. Also, your momentary mood state (how you feel now) will influence what you write. By writing now and later looking back on it, you may find that your new and different mood state will make you write something different tomorrow than today. Only by writing down your thoughts will you be able to gain this kind of perspective, a view that occurs over time with different anxiety and depression levels.

Compromises I wish I could make more easily:

_____

_____

_____

_____

_____

_____

Chapter 3

Denying Your Right to Feel

Anxiety is an anticipatory disease. You anticipate that something horrible is about to happen, no matter if the specific disorder you're experiencing is panic disorder, social anxiety disorder, generalized anxiety disorder, or post-traumatic stress disorder. All of these anxiety disorders cause disruptions in your bodily functions. Your muscles tighten up, your heart rate increases, you engage in repetitive negative thoughts about the present and the future, you begin to perspire, and you want to escape these feelings. Depression is also an anticipatory disease. It tells you that your efforts will be futile and that the future is already determined and grim no matter what you do (so you might as well do nothing). With bipolar disorder your feelings are especially confused because you alternate between no energy and hyperenergy. When you have the double whammy of having both anxiety and depression, your anticipation of the future is particularly bleak because you have both intense avoidance of the here-and-now experience of tension (mostly experienced in your body) and a desire to escape the more lingering depression (mostly experienced in your mind).

Mixed anxiety and depression thus has confusing effects on you. There is a sense of urgency to escape your tension, but a sense of helplessness that, no matter what you do, things will stay the same. This is a powerful dialectic: urgency to escape but hopelessness that nothing you do will matter. You are thus hyped up to do something, almost anything, to end the panic that fills your existence, but "hyped down" by feelings of hopelessness. These are contradictory and irreconcilable feelings, and most likely they tend to paralyze you.

The result is often that you feel invalidated, unable to believe or honor your feelings or your thoughts. Your feelings do not accurately predict what you should do: should you do nothing, or do anything, to end your pain? Your feelings and thoughts often propel you in different directions. The result is what Dr. M. M. Linehan (1993a) describes as "active passivity": you feel a sense of urgency and a desire to escape, and simultaneously engage in avoidance behavior (you run away from something you can't precisely identify, thus you're not certain if you have escaped it or not).

Getting Perspective on Emotions

DBT theory tells us that our feelings (or emotions) are an important part of our sensory and data-processing capacity. You have eyesight so you can more easily traverse space, find food and shelter, identify potential sources of threat, and generally protect yourself. Eyesight development was an important part of human evolution and promotes your individual survival, as well as the survival of the species in general. The sense of hearing, too, offers another valuable way of promoting your awareness of the environment and thus increases your survival prospects. Your sense of cold and hot helps you to interact with the environment in ways that preserve your well-being. Your sense of taste assists you in selecting foods, thus increasing your ability to obtain nourishment.

When Americans watched, horror stricken, as the World Trade Center toppled, we knew instantly that something very wrong had just happened. You didn't have to analyze the pros and cons, identify your values and presumptions, or engage in any kind of emotional analysis at all. Why? Your *feelings* immediately told you that it was a dangerous situation of epic proportions, and that massive distress was occurring and would continue to occur for the families involved. You immediately identified with those in the building, projected yourself into their situation, and felt shock. The dangerousness of the situation did not require great thought. You knew it was awful. Period.

Your emotions thus serve as shorthand, as a gigahertz processor able to identify threat, attraction, caution, and attack instantaneously. Such a feature greatly increases your chances of survival. Even when caught off guard, you are able immediately to go into the fight-or-flight response. The feeling instantly sets into motion a series of bodily processes that help you either in the fight to come or in your flight from it. Adrenalin begins surging through your body, preparing your heart to pump furiously, guaranteeing adequate oxygen to the muscles for running away from, or toward, a target. Your muscles tense in preparation for quick movement. Your blood rushes from your extremities and toward your torso in case of injury from attack to your arms or legs. In emergencies, these reactions increase your chances of survival. So emotions or feelings have, over time, developed in our species in order to help us to survive. Feelings are thus the same as eyesight, hearing, taste, and touch. Emotions are senses, a form of information processing, giving you vital data in your quest for survival.

Invalidation of Emotions

Feelings are never wrong. They just are. Okay, you may say, feelings may be senses just like eyesight, but that doesn't mean they're never wrong. What about prejudice? If you feel that another race is a threat, that does not make it so. Correct. Your feelings may not accurately portray reality. You may be attracted to someone who will never return your affections. You may be fearful of someone who intends you no harm. You may feel panic in a situation that is innocuous. The triggering event (the situation or stimulus that you are reacting to) may not turn out to hold the same value that you attribute to it.

But isn't the same true of all of your senses? You may see a cake that looks and smells delicious, but turns out to be stale and revolting when you take a bite. Is the sight of the cake wrong? Was your anticipation of its taste wrong? Would you begin to question the correctness of your eyesight? Probably not. You would most likely say that the cake looked good, but tasted bad. You would not question the data input (the visual appeal of the cake). You would question the cake itself, its ingredients, preparation, or baking. Your sense of vision would go unquestioned, except to tell yourself that what you anticipate, in this case the taste of the cake, may not always hold up to your expectations.

You take for granted that your anticipations or expectations can be wrong, while the sense (taste, vision, tactual feel, hearing, smell) is correct. Why is it different with your emotions?

When you were a small child, you were taught that something was "wet," "squishy," "dry," "hot," "salty," or "smelly." You began to associate the descriptive words with the experiences. A small child, hearing an adult describe the bathwater as "wet" would soon learn the association between the tactile sense of liquids and the word "wet." As you grew older you would learn more discriminating labels, from "liquid" to "soggy" to "soft" and "hard." As a small child, there is such wonder at discovering the world that your more-than-occasional corrections from adults in describing your world didn't matter nearly as much as the excitement at pleasing your parents with a correct description.

Does this same learning process apply to your emotions, as well as your other senses? Unfortunately not. Our feelings are so tied to who we are that we frequently do not differentiate between our feelings and ourselves. Parents tend to focus on their child's emotional response itself, rather than on what's being reacted to. So, when your parent told you not to cry, that you had no reason to be sad, or even that they'd *give* you a reason to cry, they placed great emphasis on your emotional reaction. A toy breaks; you are disappointed, and you cry. Mom tells you not to cry, that you don't deserve to cry, that crying is shameful, and that you should grow up. At that point, you no longer focus on the toy but on your emotions: you feel sad and show your sadness with tearfulness. Mom tells you that you are wrong for feeling sad. You begin to question the appropriateness of your emotions. She tells you to grow up, suggesting again that you are wrong for feeling what you're feeling. Mom could have communicated the same thing by saying that the toy is replaceable or that other toys are equally valuable and fun to play with, or by simply distracting you by presenting a different, unbroken toy. If Mom had focused on the object of your emotions, rather than your emotions themselves, then your learning would be similar to that of your other senses. You would begin to discriminate more reasonably the importance of an event to which you react, rather than beginning to doubt the veracity of your feelings.

While there is great consensus in society that tastes differ (I may like chocolate while you like vanilla), there appears an almost universal assumption that there is a right way to feel and a wrong way to feel. You do not give yourself permission to check out the utility of your emotions the way you give yourself permission to be "fooled" by your senses. You accept that something may look different than it tastes, that an object that looks cool may actually feel hot to the touch, that something that looks pleasing may produce a distasteful sound. You accept discrepancies between your senses. You even accept discrepancies between your senses and danger (that a tiger can look like a playful pet but turn out to be dangerous to you). You tend not to accept discrepancies between your emotions and others' emotions, your emotions and the eventual outcome of an event, or even your emotions now and your own emotions later.

Invalidation and Self-Acceptance

The invalidation of emotions that can begin at an early age makes you question your very self. Rather than evaluate the utility of your emotions, you question how you could be so stupid as to have that particular emotion. There must be something wrong with you if you felt that way.

We are all reasonable people. We problem solve in order to come to desired outcomes. If your emotions are frequently getting invalidated, or if the invalidation occurs around areas that you care a great deal about, then you will begin to compensate. You will begin to look to others to tell you how you should feel. You will begin to see others as right, and yourself as wrong. Obviously this can become quite confusing, especially since emotions (just like taste) vary considerably. If each time you look to someone else to tell you how you should be emoting and compare it to how you actually feel, then each time there is a difference between the two you will increasingly believe that you are wrong—and that there is something wrong with you. Rather than focusing on the object or event that inspires your feelings, you begin to define your essence as invalid and in need of repair. You distrust your emotions, and you begin to distrust yourself. Your confidence goes down, your indecisiveness increases, and, in the worst case, you begin to behave in ways that are confusing both to yourself and to those around you.

Anxiety, Depression, and Invalidation

Invalidation of your emotions could have been external. Others (your parents, your teachers, your siblings, your spouse) may have told you that you were wrong for feeling what you felt. You should not be so anxious, because there is nothing to be afraid of. The reality of your fear, constantly affirmed by your bodily tension, apprehension, and desire to escape, tells you that there is danger. But others tell you that such danger does not exist. Similarly, others may tell you that there is no reason for you to feel depressed. You are wrong to feel despondent, helpless, and inadequate. What's wrong with you, that you feel these things when everyone has tried so hard to make you feel happy?

You may thus have experienced a history of external invalidation, where others tell you that your feelings are wrong. But with mixed anxiety and depression, when you have two sets of incompatible feelings (to do something to escape your anxiety, but to do nothing because your depression saps you of energy), it may not be the environment (all those "others") that is invalidating. The invalidation occurs within. Your feelings tend to invalidate themselves because they are contradictory. Your feelings tell you to do different things. The anxiety tells you to act promptly because there is immediate danger and you need to escape. But the depression tells you to be cautious, that probably anything you do will result in things getting worse for you. Depression tells you to avoid, to do nothing. Your feelings are contradictory and confusing, resulting in you concluding that your feelings must be wrong. You don't know what to do.

You thus begin to question on a primitive level the accuracy of your own feelings and, later, your own being. You should not feel safe. There is no safety. So why seek safety? You must have done something wrong for others to be so disappointed with you. You must be responsible. Your world is transparent, since everyone seems to know your business. If everyone can see inside you, then they see your fear. If they see your fear, then they know your inadequacy. If you are inadequate, then you must avoid others to protect you from their attack. But there is no avoidance, since everything is transparent.

Fear begins to be mixed with urgency to escape the intense feelings. But how do you escape your own emotions? How do you change feelings that are prompted or triggered by so many events in your world? You can't. It becomes an unending cycle of negative anticipation (arousal), fear, avoidance, escape, self-blame, looking to others for how you should feel, noting the difference between how others feel and how you feel, negative anticipation (arousal), fear, avoidance, escape, and so on. It's a conundrum, a paradox, incapable of being adequately resolved. Self-attack (on your self-esteem, your sense of personal power, or even your physical being) begins either in symbolic or concrete ways.

Nowhere is this better exemplified than with childhood sexual abuse. Perhaps a relative, a neighbor, or a close friend of your parents sexually abused you as a child. Such abuse can involve considerable bribing (individual attention, playing games with you, telling you secrets, buying you toys) that "preps" you for the subsequent sexuality. You thus initially feel comfortable and even look forward to the visits of the eventual sexual perpetrator. The sexuality can be sensual and feel good on a bodily level, but violates (invalidates) your expectations on several levels: you know from the secretiveness of the situation that what you're doing with this person is "bad" and will be disapproved of by others, but you seek the continued acceptance and approval of the person because they made you feel special. Eventually, you begin to feel anticipatory anxiety about meetings with the person (especially if the sexual abuse continues repetitively over time). Part of the invalidation is that this person has violated your trust that they will protect you from harm (because they are older and perhaps in an exalted position as family or friend). It is this violation of trust (confusing you as to whether they're protector or predator) as well as the secretiveness of the situation (you've done something bad or it would not have to be kept secret) that is even more destructive than the sexual behavior itself.

Is it your feelings that are wrong (to feel afraid, that this is bad behavior) or the situation? Most youngsters will blame themselves before blaming the adult abuser. So you try to escape from your anxiety and loss of trust, slipping into depression. You try to escape your feelings themselves.

DBT invites you to see feelings as a form of sense, one way of processing the world to make it understandable to you. The feelings you had or have may not actually increase your understanding of the world, but they are attempts at such an understanding, just as vision or hearing function as part of understanding the world, although these senses can be deceiving or misleading. Rather than determining that your eyesight is "wrong," you must look to other forms of information for a more complete picture. If you could look at your emotions this way, as one form of knowing among many, one data point in an infinite array of data, then your attention is returned to the object of your reactions and away from questioning the data collector (your essential sense of self).

Avoidance Doesn't Always Work

Avoidance does not always work. In fact, avoidance often fails to work well at all. DBT assumes that a great deal of emotional pain is caused by disregarding or attempting to avoid your feelings. The desire to escape your emotions is based on the presumption that they will destroy you either by their overwhelming force (especially with anxiety) or by becoming a prompt about your inadequacy (especially with depression). If your feelings came before or after traumatic events, they become associated with those events. Naturally you assume that by avoiding those feelings you can avoid the unwanted event. Yet it is easier to avoid events than it is to avoid feelings.

For example, if Mary makes you feel anxious, then not being around Mary may reduce your anxiety. But what if Mary is also your best friend and you don't want to avoid her? At the same time that Mary causes you anxiety, you love her and want to be with her. But you can't have both, being with Mary and feeling anxiety free. On the other hand, since Mary is your best friend, the thought of not being with her also causes anxiety, because you would miss her. You face a dialectic: being with Mary causes you anxiety, and the thought of not being with Mary causes you anxiety.

While it may be easy to avoid being around Mary (you simply arrange your schedule so you don't expose yourself to her), it's difficult to avoid the feelings of anxiety within you due to missing her because she also gives you periodic joy.

Avoid Avoiding Your Feelings

If you accept your fear and depression as two important pieces of information, just two parts of the puzzle, and begin to use that information rather than attempt to avoid it, your probability of success increases. Thus, one of DBT's primary purposes is helping you to accept your feelings, no matter how painful. DBT asks you to avoid avoiding your feelings, and thus restore the ability of your feelings to provide clues to help you solve your life problems.

In order to accomplish this, you have to drill down into your own history to determine the following: How do you avoid your feelings (what internal and external processes do you use to stop feelings)? What feelings are you avoiding (learning to be more discriminating about the labels and words you use to define your feelings)? What consequences come to you as a result of avoiding these feelings (how do you perceive safety or comfort as a result of engaging in this avoidance, and how does it really work for you and against you)? And how could you do it differently (what can you do to minimize the damage and optimize success)?

Identifying Invalidation

Historical invalidation, when important people from your past told you that your feelings were wrong, can linger years after the invalidating messages ceased. This is due to how impressionable you were when young. When we were kids and young adults, anxiety and depressed feelings were especially powerful because we had fewer psychological coping strategies and rational defenses against our feelings. Think back now to times in your child-hood that brought up strong emotions that were invalidated by adults around you.

Below, write down situations you remember that generated anxiety or depression in you. What was the situation causing the depression or anxiety? In the second column, write the feeling resulting from the situation. In the third column, write how the situation was invalidated (how others expected you to feel differently than you did).

Childhood experiences that prompted or caused you anxiety or depression (Example: I felt afraid of going to school.)	How you felt as a result of the situation (Example: I felt something was wrong with me, because I was supposed to like school.)	Identify the invalidation (Example: I felt anxious, but was told I was supposed to feel good.)

Current situations that are invalidating can have an even more powerful influence over your life. Below, think of situations that prompt both anxiety and depression. What causes your body to show distress (tight muscles, rapid heart rate, jumpiness) *and* causes you to think that your situation is hopeless, saps you of essential energy, and makes you want to do nothing else but stay in bed and pull the covers over your head (even if you resist the urge to do so)? Identify situations that are external, internal, or both.

Current experiences that cause you both anxiety and depression (Example: My wife wants me to have sex with her more often.)	How you feel as a result of the situation (Example: I'm anxious that she will see how utterly uninterested I am in sex, and I feel guilty because of this disinterest.	Identify the invalidation (Example: I'm supposed to feel sexually interested but instead feel disinterest, even though I love my wife. My feelings are wrong.)

Guilt and Blame

A core aspect of dealing with invalidation is learning to manage the fear of your feelings. Fear itself is a feeling and is something that you have probably been taught is wrong. Men should not be afraid. A strong woman is able to push her way through fear. Only inadequate people wade in their fear. DBT tells you the opposite. You must expose yourself to the fear in order to overcome it. *Exposure* means living with an uncomfortable emotion, in this case fear, at least for a short time. In fact, living with it for a short time, leaving it, coming back to it on purpose, leaving it on purpose, then coming back (and so on) is the primary method of reducing fear. If you are willing and able to consciously reexpose yourself in small doses to a situation that causes anxiety and depression, that situation loses its power.

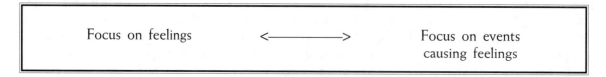

It's much more helpful to focus on the interaction of your feelings and the events prompting the feelings rather than judging the feelings as bad and blaming yourself for having them. In learning to accept and use your feelings, you need to focus only partly on yourself and partly on the triggering events. What is more difficult in emotion management is that frequently what is triggering a feeling is also an internal event, like the emotion itself. Both can be internal events.

Behavior and Feelings

People frequently do not differentiate between a feeling (love, sadness, fear, joy, terror) and a behavior (kissing someone, attempting suicide, avoiding social encounters, running over someone, hitting someone). Behaviors can be wrong. For instance, it is wrong to kill people. Feelings are not wrong. It is not wrong to be angry with someone. Confusing behavior with feelings leads people to be judgmental of themselves and others. But having a feeling and acting on it are two different things. You have been angry with many people, but you've probably never killed anyone. If you do not trust your feelings, and if you confuse feelings with behaviors, you begin to dread your feelings because you assume they lead to behaviors you want to avoid. But feelings do not inevitably lead to behaviors consistent with the feelings. You can see an attractive woman, feel the attraction, but take no action. Attraction does not necessarily lead to infidelity, sexual harassment, or rape. If you think of killing yourself to end your emotional pain, you will not necessarily commit suicide.

You have feelings all the time and engage in no behavior to demonstrate those emotions. Learning to trust that even strong feelings do not have to be acted upon can reduce your tendency to avoid your feelings. Exposing yourself to even intense feelings and then not acting on them (not escaping the feeling, not hitting the person you're angry at, not engaging in self-defeating behavior when you feel badly about yourself) can be a powerful way of developing confidence in your emotional life.

Blame and Guilt

With mixed anxiety and depression, blame (in anxiety) and guilt (in depression) are powerful forces that make you distrust all your other feelings. The result is self-invalidation, where you tell yourself that your feelings are wrong. Secondary emotional responses begin. You start to blame yourself for your anxiety ("It's my fault that I'm anxious") and feel guilt that you're depressed ("I'm guilty of feeling something horrible, feeling no interest in something that I *should* feel excited about").

You may blame yourself because you have withdrawn socially from the family, not leaving them physically, but not participating in conversations with them over the dinner table and when they come home from school and work, and not showing interest in their daily routines. You begin to feel anxious that you're an inadequate parent and spouse due to your self-blame. Then you begin to feel guilty that you are so inadequate. Not only have you accepted blame (responsibility), but then you kick yourself in the pants with guilt over being blameworthy. Rather than focus on the object of your blame (that you need to be more attentive and sensitive to your loved ones), you simply allow the anxiety of blame to propel the depression of guilt. Due to the double whammy of mixed anxiety and depression, you begin to see your feelings as indicators of inadequacy rather than as sources of information about how to cope with the situations that cause the feelings. You no longer trust your feelings as bits of data to inform you about what to do (what action to perform, what set of problems to solve), but begin to use them against yourself.

Below, identify situations that cause you to feel either blame or guilt. In the first column write the situation, in the second column identify your thoughts about the situation, and in the third column describe how those thoughts increase your sense of blame or guilt.

The situation (Example: I'm so depressed I can't force myself to go to work.)	Your thoughts about the situation (Example: I should be able to get to work, no matter how I feel.)	How your thoughts increase blame or guilt feelings (Example: I'm to blame for my troubles because my feelings should not cause me to miss work, no matter what.)

The problem with guilt and blame in mixed anxiety and depression is that these feelings do nothing but make us feel worse. Blame is a form of faultfinding. It does not point to a solution to the problem. Guilt increases depression. It, too, does nothing to help you find a solution to the problem. Review the situations you wrote about in the previous exercise (don't create new ones, use the same situations you used in the worksheet above). In the following worksheet, revise your thoughts about the situation so that they are problem focused, pointing to a solution to the problem rather than kicking yourself with anxiety and depression.

The situation you were in (Example: I'm so depressed I can't force myself to go to work.)	Thoughts about the problem itself (not about you) (Example: I need to get to work even when I feel depressed.)	Thoughts that help you solve the problem rather than increase blame and guilt (Example: I need to stop asking myself if I feel like getting to work and just get moving. Lots of people don't want to work on a particular day, and that doesn't mean that they are bad people.)

Doing the Work

You already feel anxiety and depression. This may cause you to lose your concentration, your confidence, your attention, and your enthusiasm about living your life. You may even feel a little discouraged about working on the exercises in this book. After all, they're demanding. They cause you to have to think, ponder, and reconsider both emotions and thoughts. That's hard work, especially if you're already feeling powerless and helpless. "If I could deal with my feelings as easily as you suggest," you might be saying, "then I wouldn't need this book in the first place!"

With mixed anxiety and depression you are emotionally vulnerable. Every situation can be emotionally and intellectually demanding, not just facing your feelings in written exercises. Emotional vulnerability is developed in at least two major ways: heredity and environmental circumstances. While you have few, if any, ways of controlling your own genetic history, you do have ways of controlling your environment. Even if your early childhood was chaotic, traumatic, and engendered the development of a complex array of brain connections predicting fear and anxiety, you can deal with them. Whether genes or history, you can compensate.

An individual born with a familial history of heart disease knows that they are at increased risk of developing heart conditions and can do something about it. They can't control their genetic propensity for heart disease, but they can control the environment that results in the "penetration" of the genetic propensity. They can control diet, exercise, and health care behaviors that increase their risk.

If some people in your family have had either anxiety or depression problems, you may as a result have many more hardwired reactionary tendencies in your brain that trigger fear than the typical person. You probably recognize that you are more likely to feel anxious, nervous, or fearful than most other people around you. You know from your physical reactions that *hyperarousal* (the fear response) sends adrenaline, cortisol, and other stress hormones into your system on a repeated basis. You may know that you were deprived of the dopamine in your brain characteristic of pleasure experiences. So, now that you know that, you can take compensatory measures. You can plan for the fear response, know that it does not always portend danger, and react differently. You can plan to create experiences that increase pleasure, and thus produce the dopamine that is characteristic of others with a more fortunate genetic and psychological environment.

It is understandable that people with mixed anxiety and depression feel that such planning and psychological work as is offered in this book can seem overwhelming. But if your strategies from the past have not improved your life, doing the same things over and over again is unlikely to result in a different outcome. The good news is that this work is hardest in the beginning and becomes easier over time. Each time you practice the new approaches you'll be learning, the strategies become easier and more natural.

Emotional Hardware and Software

Your physical brain is not as malleable as your learning potential. Your brain will not develop new hardwired pathways as quickly as you can learn from experience. Recent physiological research indicates that your brain continues to develop new hardwired pathways depending on experience well into old age (see Granit 2002 for an excellent summary). But these are not nearly as quickly developed as are psychological learning experiences. So, while you can slowly recondition your brain to react to its new and improved environment, it will be a slower rate of progression than your ability to learn from experience with "software" (learning from emotional experiences, psychologically, rather than relying upon the hardware of the brain to do it for you).

The fight-or-flight response is controlled by *visceral* experience (muscular, bodily processes expressed through muscle tension, heart rate, respiration, perspiration, etc.) and the hardwired neural connections control the *autonomic system* (those bodily systems we normally are not voluntarily controlling, like rate of breath, body temperature, and heart rate). This is the essence of mixed anxiety and depression, both wanting to fight and wanting to flee but not having the energy to do either. While a child genetically predisposed to be vulnerable to the anxiety of a threat response will prepare for danger more easily and readily than other kids, their interpretation of their bodily response will depend on their recent emotional experiences. A person who does not feel threatened for dozens of years will interpret this physical preparation for action (called the *orienting reflex* and consisting of increased attention, a slight surge of adrenalin, and tightening of muscles) as preparation for something interesting rather than something dangerous.

Are dozens of years of feeling safe required for this healing? Well, yes, it can take a very long time for the brain, body, and mind to reorient to a safe environment if you simply let the process take its own time. But you can help the process along considerably. In fact, it can be incredibly speeded. That's what this book is about—speeding the process of recovery. You can reteach your brain and body and undo previous harm. There are no magic-bullet, instantaneous cures. But progressive, hard work using the scientific, spiritual, and emotional healing techniques available in this book will help you. That's what I believe DBT offers and what you'll be learning in the chapters to come.

Chapter 4

There Must Be Something
Wrong with Me

You may have concluded that there is something essentially wrong with you because your feelings are so intense, your feelings hurt you so much, you can't stop your feelings like others seem to be able to do, or your feelings aren't "right," no matter what anyone says. After all, feelings like intense anxiety and simultaneous depression can't be right, can they?

Yet many individuals who conclude "there must be something wrong with me" are saying something more profound than that they simply have an emotional disorder. They refer not just to a chemical imbalance, an emotional disease process that requires medication, but to something much more fundamental. You may conclude that you are broken, fundamentally impaired, different from most others, a freak of nature, totally unacceptable, a disappointment to Mother Nature herself. You may feel deformed emotionally, flawed to the very core. You are shamed by your very existence. And this conclusion is based on your emotional life itself.

The Problem with Emotions

Your feelings may be intense, unavoidable, and out of control. Anxiety makes your body feel as if it is rebelling, too frequently telling you how threatened you are. Your depression makes you feel useless and irrelevant. Your feelings don't mean anything, except that you're existentially broken. Your feelings remind you how different you are from everyone else. "I am not human, I must be something else. An example of how not to be human. An example of worthlessness. A screwup of nature who only looks human. I am fake. I must hide my true nature, my real self, or others will see how truly deformed I am." Such an existence is intolerable. You go from pretense to secretiveness to self-destruction. Mixed anxiety and depression, because such feelings are essentially contradictory (one propelling you to escape and the other propelling you to avoid, with the combination paralyzing you), heightens this sense of shame and guilt.

All the more sad for you precisely because it's a delusion. Such freaks of nature don't exist. There may be many problems to be solved. Some people may experience such intense emotional discomfort that they will kill themselves just in order to eliminate the emotional pain. But no one is fundamentally emotionally flawed. I've met a few who were so morally corrupt and so self-serving that I doubted their worth to society, but in twenty years of clinical practice I've never met anyone who fit the profound emotional deformity assumed by some.

The Stigma of Mental Illness

What tends to make you feel such intense shame about yourself and about your basic validity as a member of humanity? The answer has to do with the intensity of emotions themselves. If you are emotionally sensitive and feel intensely, and your feelings don't accurately predict what you should do or what is going on in a situation, then you begin to doubt your identity, your basic self.

What causes this emotional intensity? Biology can play a large part. Your genetic history simply unfolds to a great degree, in spite of your best efforts to be different from those who preceded you. Severe clinical depression offers a good example. The more relatives you have who themselves inherited severe depression, the greater the probability that you, too, will be stricken with depression. The same with bipolar disorder, where there is an alternation of periods of depression with periods of irritability or mania. Moods shift wildly and without any apparent environmental triggers. You are on an emotional roller coaster, and your feelings don't accurately tell you what is going on or what you should do. The situation is a little like someone who has taken psychedelic drugs. Their vision, their perception, is a cacophony of images and ideas that make no sense. The individual can't rely on their eyesight to tell them what is in front of them or what is going on in the environment. But at least someone who has taken recreational drugs knows, on some level, that it was their drug taking that accounts for their experiences. They try to "ride it out" if they are not enjoying the trip. But the person with an emotional disorder cannot count on riding it out. There is no clear ending point when things will return to normal. And they can't blame it on something external to themselves, like a drug. You, yourself, are the trip. This integration of deformity as a part of identity, this assumption of personal responsibility for dysfunction, creates intense and intolerable shame.

Can you see how different this approach is from other disorders, say medical ones? If you inherit the tendency for heart disease and begin to experience such symptoms, you're likely to feel sad, unfortunate, even angry or depressed. But you probably won't feel shame. You won't blame yourself. You won't feel that *you* are wrong. You'll feel that your heart is in trouble, even fear that your life is in danger (which it may be), but you won't feel ashamed, you won't feel emotionally infected, you won't feel fundamentally flawed and totally inadequate as a human being. You may be scared, pissed off, wonder "why me?" and feel that it's unfair that you have to suffer this heart condition and live a shorter life. You may feel lots of things. But you probably won't feel wrong and bad.

The "there is something wrong with me" syndrome is much more pervasive than most of us would like to admit. Many people feel it but don't articulate it to others. They act as though it were true, even if they consciously have never had the thought in their mind.

Self-blame can only be helpful when the focus is on control: You accept responsibility and thus take some control over your situation. If you have control, then you have influence over the processes and events that lead to the experience you want to change. Since you have control, you can make changes that will improve the quality of your life. If self-blame leads to a "map" of your experience, a map that predicts how to get out of the situation you find unacceptable, then accepting responsibility is a healthy and good process. Unfortunately, self-blame rarely is used in this way. Self-blame typically stops at the judgment itself: You are bad and unworthy. Period. There is nothing but shame and self-recrimination to feel, forever. Hardly a healthy process, since it gets you nowhere. In fact, it hurts.

The Mixed Anxiety and Depression Syndrome

Shame increases intensity of emotions associated with it because you're dealing with two emotions simultaneously: the primary emotional reaction to an event and the subsequent shame experience. There is a reason that the emotional dysfunction characterized by mixed anxiety and depression (sense of urgency, high emotional arousal and sensitivity, slow reduction in emotional tension, distrust of emotions, attempts at emotional escape and avoidance) develops. It doesn't just come out of nowhere. The emotional arousal and sensitivity is designed to "look for" sources of threat. You want to know what it is that makes you hurt so much. This almost constant scanning to find the source of bad feelings is what psychologists call *hypervigilance*, and it's a defensive process. "If only I can identify what it is that makes me feel so lousy, then maybe I'll feel differently." Obviously, emotional escape and avoidance are designed to change the high sense of threat and pain you experience. The sense of urgency is to change things. The slow reduction in emotional tension is the product of prolonged "firing" of the emotional pathways. Like with chronic physical pain, the longer and the more intensively the pathways fire, the higher the probability that the pathways will continue to fire in the future. Once hyperalertness and hypervigilance become a way of life, then it is all the more difficult to change. It is a by-product or residual effect of your chronic coping strategy. Over time, then, you begin to distrust your emotions because they become less sensitive to what is going on in the environment, become less a resource in assisting you to adapt to changing situations, and become more of a self-perpetuating internal process. What was originally designed to protect you eventually becomes the primary enemy itself.

Self-Preservation versus Self-Transformation

The coping process that was originally designed to preserve you, your integrity, and your sense of safety, over time becomes an impediment to change. This is the core of the dialectic struggle in mixed anxiety and depression: the desire for self-preservation versus that for self-transformation. It is unusually difficult to form adequate compromises along this continuum, since it hits at the center of your very existence. It touches your identity, how you see yourself, and is incredibly dangerous (or at least feels that way) because the opposite end of the continuum is change. Self-transformation means that you have to be different, that you have to give up strategies and habits that you have probably used for a lifetime. It means being different, as well as acting differently—and this is scary. It's scary in spite of the fact that your way of being in the world now brings emotional chaos and discomfort. At least these things you know and are familiar to you. While you may scream to yourself that your life is unlivable as it is now, at least it's *you*.

The Anxiety Fear of Change: Engulfment

For some, change brings up all kinds of fear—the fear of engulfment, for example. Here is how the process works: Since your anxiety and depression are so extreme, and you have developed extraordinary defenses against threat (scanning the environment with your emotions and thoughts for sources of threat, current or anticipated), then the threat must be great. Since your anxiety is intense, the threat must be intense. You use the extremity of your anxiety as a gauge of the intensity of threat—high emotions, high threat. But, without your realizing it, a residual effect of chronic tension is the slow return to emotional baseline. Your arousal is high not because there is continued threat, but because you have used this defense so often and so intensively that it has become habit. Arousal and tension are high—the alarm is sounding—not because there is a new or continued threat, but because they have become part of your emotional defense system itself. The "threat circuit" is on dysfunctionally. But the fear is there, and it tells you that if you give up your defense, then the anticipated threat will take over. It will engulf you and possess you like an invading army. The fear of engulfment can be general (something will take you over) or it can be specific (your feelings will take you over, another person will take you over, the situation you're in will devour you). You will lose your sense of "me" and become something else.

"I'm not that bad," you may say. "I'm tense and on edge all the time, but I don't have these fears of being invaded." Great! You have not adopted your psychological defense structure as an essential part of your identity. You have not succumbed to adopting an identity of threat and deformity. You're ahead of the game. You don't have to deal with identity issues, only new techniques and strategies to change the emotional tension and depression you experience on a chronic basis. But for some, it is not just new techniques and old habits that must be dealt with but a pervasive and deep sense that their fear is an essential part of their very being. Whether or not you've meshed your fear with your identity, you may find this book helpful in decreasing your level of emotional suffering.

The Depression Fear of Change: Abandonment

In those who have adopted the identity of dysfunction and those who have extraordinary levels of anxiety, many fears around change are found. In addition to the fear of engulfment, there is the fear of abandonment. By adopting the "screwed up" identity, you assume that family members and loved ones are "connected" to you—the opposite of fear of engulfment, really. Rather than fear that others, or a different self, will take over, you fear that others will leave you. Others stay only because you need help and are weak. If you become strong, then there will be no reason for them to stick around, since you feel you're not such a desirable person to begin with. Others stay with you only because you're so inadequate that you'll fail without them. If you were confident and would be fine without them, others would take the first opportunity to split the scene and be rid of you.

The fear of abandonment is a common fear, and these fears aren't entirely without merit. It's true that if you make substantial changes in yourself and your life, that people will relate differently to you. The entire notion of codependency is based on the presumption that some people enjoy the role of protector and some enjoy the role of needing to be protected. If you define your meaning in life as the ability to do for another, to be the helper and protector, then to lose this need to protect can be devastating. Similarly, if you believe that others are there for you only because of your vulnerability, then to give up that vulnerability potentially means the loss of the reason for the relationship. The meaningfulness of the relationship is thrown into question. Having the most significant relationships in your lives threatened (or at least perceived as in jeopardy) in this way can be even more frightening than the depression, anxiety, and fear that you live with daily. Having to make a choice, to live in desperation or to give up those whom you love, most of us would choose to live life in discomfort rather than destroy meaningful relationships. (Of course, there will always be a part of you that resents the people you love for having "made" you make this choice.)

The unfortunate thing is that all of this is based on fear and depression. You don't know, really, what will be lost and what will be gained by substantial personality change. If a relationship is predicated upon you being weak and needing external support, it's probably not going to be a very healthy or fulfilling relationship for either party. If you become stronger, maybe you will have more to give those who have lived their lives helping you. You will be able to offer something new and desired to others. So change doesn't necessarily lead to the end of the relationship. You don't have to be abandoned. Just as you have developed strong defenses against change, other people have too. Just because they resist your changes does not mean that once you have made the changes that the game is over. New rules, new meanings, and new habits can replace the old ones. The same is true with the fear of engulfment. The reality is that it is psychological, not spiritual or supernatural, forces that bond people together. You cannot be engulfed, no matter how much you fear it. You can allow others to have great emotional power over you, but that's it. You can't really lose "you" all that easily. In fact, it takes a great deal of effort and hard work to change "you."

Feelings and Behavior versus Identity

The essential conceptual difficulty is the confusion of your behavior with your feelings, and the confusion of your feelings with your identity. They are three different and very separate things. Your feelings are emotional responses, a sensory mechanism of sorts. Your behavior is action, the macro steps you take in initiating events (planned or unintentional). This behavior (that which is observable to others) may or may not be related to your feelings. It may be related to practice, habit, or conscious thought. Your identity, the "you" you may be afraid of losing, is a much more complex phenomenon. Your identity is composed partly of all the roles you assume (mother, father, worker, friend, citizen, hobbyist, etc.), the way you perceive yourself, the way you think others perceive you, your values (both recognized and unrecognized by you), your relationship with significant others, your perception of your body, your memories, your thoughts, your behavior patterns, and your feelings. Identity is thus a multifaceted concept. If you change your behavior and feelings, you are manipulating only two among many important elements in the notion of identity. Surely they are critical aspects of identity and can make major shifts in your experience of the world and your experience of self, but still they are only two among many elements. Losing "you" will take a whole lot more than simply changing your most intense feelings and even a large number of your behavior patterns.

What you are "getting" with your emotional pain, I hope, is not the preservation of your sense of identity. But for some, the benefit is precisely that. You have come to identify so much with your emotional turmoil as an essential element of what is you, that to give it up means, subconsciously, giving up your role in life itself.

What I'm inviting you to do is to distance yourself from your emotions. They are only one element, albeit a critical one, of what makes you who you are. The "meta-emotions" (those complex emotions that get at the core of how you understand the world) can be built on faulty foundations. Does that mean the feeling is wrong? No. Like the cake that looks good but tastes bad, it means that you construe the feelings in ways that are not accurate and not helpful to you.

You usually have some evidence that causes you to believe the things you believe. There is usually a grain of truth to even absurd and extreme beliefs. This is one reason why it can be difficult to debunk faulty or untrue beliefs. Look at the list of beliefs below that are indicative of the "there is something wrong with me" syndrome. If you have said one of these statements to yourself, or act as if the statement is true (even if you have never said these words to yourself), then complete the two questions following (what evidence do you have that the statement is true, and what evidence contradicts the conclusion).

"There is something wrong with me."	What evidence do you have? What makes you believe this?	What evidence contradicts this conclusion? What reasons are there to doubt this?
I'm emotionally fragile.		
I'm too needy.		
I'm inadequate.		
I'm different from others in ways that are bad.		
I'm out of control.		

"There is something wrong with me."	What evidence do you have? What makes you believe this?	What evidence contradicts this conclusion? What reasons are there to doubt this?
I don't feel. I seem to be numb compared to others.		
I don't fit in. People can tell there is something wrong with me.		
I'm afraid of losing my mind.		
I've done shameful things. I'm a shameful person.		
I don't know what I feel. I just know I don't feel good.		
People reject me, so there must be something wrong with me.		
People judge me. My behavior is despicable.		
I'm afraid people will judge me.		
I'm afraid of people. I don't know why.		
I'm afraid of me. I don't know why.		

"There is something wrong with me."	What evidence do you have? What makes you believe this?	What evidence contradicts this conclusion? What reasons are there to doubt this?
I don't get along with others. There must be something wrong with me.		
I can't tolerate frustration. I seem to want everything now.		
I can't focus. I don't know what's wrong. I can't think.		
My feelings hurt so much I can't stand it.		
I must have been made differently than others. I seem to react so differently than those around me do.		
I'm so nervous. Everything upsets me. I'm fearful and depressed so frequently—evidence that I'm a damaged human being.		

If you have given this exercise a real work through, then you were able to identify reasons both to justify the statements and to disagree with the statements. Since the beliefs are extreme statements, there is usually ample evidence for and against each. The purpose of the exercise is twofold. First, yes, there are reasons why you feel the way you feel. But there are also plenty of reasons to feel differently. The world is too complex to completely accept any of the above statements.

Even if you don't find yourself questioning the foundation of your identity, this exercise should point toward a significant perspective in DBT: your feelings appear someplace on a continuum, and dialectical thinking is about moving someplace else on that continuum. DBT is about change: changing perspectives, changing feelings, changing thoughts, and changing behavioral habits. Not because they are wrong or necessarily flawed but because they may no longer serve you. DBT enables you to change in order to accomplish your own objectives, to experience the world in ways that are self-enhancing rather than self-negating. The change is to make life more worth living.

Chapter 5

Meaning Making

Nietzsche is quoted as saying "He who has a why to live can bear with almost any how." Meaning making is about Nietzsche's why, while the other strategies of DBT are about Nietzsche's how. With mixed anxiety and depression, meaning tends to shrink. Anxiety causes you to avoid people and situations. The avoidance predicts that you'll miss out on many potentially meaningful situations. Your interpersonal world shrivels. Depression causes you to question meaningfulness itself. Everything seems effortful, and you don't have the wherewithal required to even try to involve yourself in activities and relationships that previously were meaningful. But engagement in meaningful processes reduces depression. Meaning has also been shown to increase your tolerance levels, thus helping reduce anxiety-related avoidance. With mixed anxiety and depression, the creation of meaning is thus especially important.

But what do we mean by "meaningful"? How do you know when something is really meaningful to you and when you are just deluding yourself with values that seem plausible or politically correct? How do you know when you are simply parroting what your parents have told you, what the press has told you, or what you have been trained to say over time by public opinion? Does something called "meaning" really exist, or is it just a concept developed over time to bring you a sense of comfort and place in a world where little really matters?

Psychologists know that when you lose your sense of meaning, when something that previously was meaningful becomes meaningless, the outcome can be depression. In fact, the behavioral definition of depression is "loss of reinforcer effectiveness," meaning that things you used to be willing to work toward, to expend effort and time on, become unimportant to you. You are no longer willing to work hard to gain other people's respect or approval, you give up caring about career success or the accumulation of cash. Your hobbies and former pleasures become demoted in the hierarchy of meaning. If such emotional deflation occurs when you stop defining things as important, then meaning must have a substantial influence over all of us. If it can influence you so dramatically, then it must be powerful force. Meaning does exist, and without it we are predisposed to both anxiety and depression.

But if you have a difficult time defining meaning, how can you influence it? Is meaning something that "happens" without intervention and without conscious effort? Is it bestowed on you by God, or do you create it yourself? Since different people will define what is meaningful in their lives differently, and sometimes there is little to no relationship between what different people find meaningful, how do you go about increasing meaning in your life? And is it important to increase meaning? Can't you just get along with the amount of meaning you now have? Is this yet another thing you have to worry about, that your life is not as meaningful as it should be?

Why Work on Making Meaning?

Your examination of meaning is important because meaning acts as an influential force on long-term feelings. People with a great many things in their lives they define as meaningful can use those things as anchors to keep them from floating off into depression, anxiety, anger, frustration, shame, and many other negative emotions. Having well-defined meaningful things in your life increases your sense of purpose, connection, and commitment to ongoing activities. Meaning transforms "existence" into "life." It turns repetition and slavery to tasks into awe-inspiring devotion. Having meaning means life is worth living, and we are living rich lives rather than simply "getting along."

Seeing Meaning

Language use tells us something about how we traditionally approach meaning in our lives. We talk of "finding" meaning, as if it is something outside of ourselves that we stumble upon. We talk about being "struck" by the meaning in a situation, as if it is an epiphany. Meaning is frequently connected to religious and spiritual pursuits, as if meaning is created by your Maker and given to you as a gift.

If meaning, instead, is a perspective, an attribution, a way of looking at things that is individualistic, then meaning is something inside of you that comes out rather than is given to you. Like love, it's something you create yourself. You can give it away, keep it to yourself, or throw it away. You can receive it, reject it, or ignore it, just like the affections of another person, or you can see it as the most special gift ever given to you. Meaning is a lot like love. It can be multiplied rather than divided. You can love all your children, not just the first one you had. If you have many loved ones, it does not drain or distract from the love you feel for each one. So, too, with meaning. You can imbue much of your life activity with meaning, or you can resent every demand placed upon you as a nuisance.

The notion that meaning is a perspective you take rather than something externally determined does not in any way reduce the importance of meaning in your life. Many people believe that the most meaningful thing in their life is their relationship to God. Does it diminish this meaningfulness to say that this, too, is a perspective? Is there a substantial difference between faith and perspective-taking? I think not. Meaning creates devotion and commitment, the very things that major Western religions seek in their adherents. And devotion and commitment are primary ingredients necessary to overcome mixed anxiety and depression.

So meaningfulness is an attribution, something you give to an experience. It is a reflection of the value you place on that experience.

What Is Meaningful to You?

What is the difference between something routine and habitual in your life, and something that has real and lasting meaning? Some things you do without thinking about them at all, while other things require effort and strain to accomplish. While what is meaningful is fairly individualistic, there are common things that many people find meaningful.

Photographs

A man I once treated suffered from agoraphobia. He was terrified to leave his home and was understandably devastated when it was destroyed by fire. He lost not just a structure, a roof over his head, but his sense of safety in the world. Interestingly, months after his recovery from the subsequent anxiety and panic associated with no longer having the safe place to which he could return, he commented that his house was replaceable. In fact, his insurance money allowed him to replace his older home with a new, bigger, and more elegant home. Most of the objects in his home were replaceable as well. While he had been able to save some of his favorite items that had sentimental value, his comment that he missed his photographs the most was telling. While furniture can be purchased, a home rebuilt, and decorations re-created, the photographs of his family and friends were irreplaceable. As an elder within his family system, he had held the most comprehensive set of photographic memories of family events (the births of his children, the marking of life by holidays and special events). These no amount of money or effort could replace. He had lost the most concrete triggers of memories available, photographs that would remind him of special moments across the course of his own life and the lives of those he loved. He thus attributed meaning to his missed photos since these were irreplaceable and signified his own stance in the family system as family historian.

People

People are pretty much irreplaceable. One friend in one location can fulfill a variety of needs for stimulation, companionship, security, sense of belonging, being cared about, being recognized, being important, receiving feedback, and a variety of other valued functions. One friend can fulfill, to various degrees, some needs, while other friends fulfill others. A small circle of friends may fulfill the same kinds of needs (for recreation, companionship, stimulation), while one or two other friends may fulfill other (even more important) needs, such as feeling loved and cared for. If your most prized friends are lost, you may make new friends to fulfill some of your old needs, but rarely will people report that these new relationships feel the same as those with old friends. Something is lost that can't entirely be replaced in ways that are fully satisfying. The comfort and history that people share with each other helps to define what makes one person fulfill needs in unique ways. A new friend, no matter how trustworthy and stimulating, just does not share in the same way the understanding and comfort you felt with and for the longer-term friend.

Is it just shared history and developed comfort that makes some people irreplaceable in your life? I don't think so. It is the perspective you have taken on the person, the way you allow yourself to think and feel about the person, that makes them meaningful. Perspective taking, that process of looking at things or people with a fresh view, is at the core of how we develop meaning. By paying attention to people in your life, thinking about how they embellish or add attractive elements to your daily experience, people become meaningful People will be more meaningful to you the more you are mindful of the safety you associate with them, the amusement or joy they provide to you, and the needs they meet for you that others meet infrequently, if at all. Your love for them, not just your time together, makes them irreplaceable. And love is something you allow and create, not something that comes along automatically or simply as the result of effort and strain.

Your meaningful relationships are created. You allow love to be nurtured. You "find" a compatible other, but you create the love with that compatible other.

Pets

It's not that different with pets. One pet may have been present and recognized, a fixture within the home, but not entirely loved. When you lose that pet, there is a sense of loss, but not necessarily a great sense of loss. Another pet is not just present, but a truly important member of the household. You know the pet's personality, their habits, their likes, and their dislikes, just as you might know these things about a human friend or family member. You attribute feelings to the pet, appreciate the need of the pet for your companionship, and give value to the pet's expression of affection for you. You take a perspective on the pet as a friend, a relative, a family member. When you lose such a pet, you experience the loss of love, the loss of something quite meaningful and not replaceable. While you may obtain another pet, your relationship with the new pet will not be the same as the relationship with the former pet. While you may enjoy the new pet and find that it meets many of the same needs met by the lost pet, you're aware that it isn't the same as the loved animal. The new pet is different, has a different personality, a different reactionary style. Something meaningful was lost, although you can certainly find new ways of meeting your needs.

Spirit

Spiritual meaning is similar. Your belief in a loving God, a supernatural force that binds us together, or faith in everlasting peace in the hereafter are remarkable expectations. There are absolutely no equivalents for these expectations in the physical realm. They are in a different class, meet different needs, and have different qualities than your relationships in the material world.

What makes one person need to have faith in the spiritual, and another person to demand evidence of the spiritual? What makes one person doubt and another person believe? Are they not both searching for meaningfulness? Are not the questions themselves evidence of the person's desire to acquire meaning? Whether framed as skepticism or faith, both are looking for meaningfulness in the spiritual. Those who neither demand evidence nor struggle with issues of faith, who unemotionally accept that they don't know and who don't try to know, appear not to be searching for meaning, at least on the spiritual level. However, these people may often place extreme importance on finding meaning in more day-to-day ways.

The search for meaning in life comprises an important part of your emotional self. Without a sense of meaning, our lives become flat and without direction. This is depression. Even those who have accepted what many of us would describe as superficial meaning, such as immediate pleasures (alcohol, drugs, sex, and parties), have at least attempted a "working hypothesis" about the meaning of life.

Fear of Creating the "Wrong" Meaning

You may be frightened that you will create the wrong meaning. If meaning isn't something you're supposed to "get" or "find" but that you have to make for yourself, that's a lot of responsibility! We all know people who have chased values that turned out to be rather empty. A shopaholic spends hours at the malls selecting products, purchasing them, bringing them home, admiring them—only to find that the next day or week they are repeating the same process because the objects purchased did not hold their value very long. You may have had what I call "car fever," where you feel compelled to have a nice, new car. You anticipate that the car will make an appreciable (or at least noticeable) difference in your life. And it does—for a short while. Within a few months (or shorter), it feels just like the previous car you had. Only now you have car payments, and the noticeable difference becomes negative as you worry about the additional strain on your budget. People obsessed with having a relationship are no different. You are tired of being single and imagine that if only you had the right relationship, you would feel fulfilled and your life would be noticeably different. But once you are in a relationship, you notice that things aren't all that changed and all your needs aren't getting met the way you thought they would. Then, rather than question the value itself, you question the object. A different boyfriend or girlfriend would make you happy. A different car would make you happy longer.

You may also be frightened that once you obtain more meaning, you will lose it. Even if you find Mr. Right or Ms. Right, they may go ahead and leave you. It won't be permanent. You'll be worse off than when you started, because you'll feel loss and inadequacy in addition to the needs you were trying to get met in the first place.

You may even be afraid that you'll never find the meaning you've wanted. You may be rejected by the object of your desires. You may be found wanting, inadequate, not good enough.

All of these may seem like good reasons to not look, not to invest in the search for meaning. But actually they are simply defenses against fear—fear that you won't find what you're looking for. However, if we accept the presumption that meaning is created, there is no reason to believe that meaningfulness can't be increased.

Creating Meaning in Your Life

So how do you make meaning in your life? How do you create that which you don't fully feel passionately about to begin with? Earlier I mentioned the similarity of meaning to love. When we love something, we value it, think highly of it, think of it often, expect joy or pleasure when we are with it, experience heightened feelings when anticipating being with it, fear losing it, and prolong our time with it. I say "it" because love can be for other than people. Love of country, love of sport, love of a hobby, and love of home are all examples. Many of us have seen people who appear obsessed by an activity. Where I live, on California's Monterey Peninsula, many people are crazy about golf. This is a golf paradise, with some of the world's most treasured golf courses nestled around the bay. Watch an avid golfer, and you will see all the manifestations of meaningfulness. They plan their golf games, watch golf on television, have golf buddies, take golf lessons, compare scores and techniques, frequent golf shops, have golf clothes, join expensive and exclusive golf clubs, and, of course, play golf for hours each week. Homes on golf courses cost tens of thousands of dollars more than similar homes further away. While golf may be meaningless to most of us, to those who invest meaning in this sport, it is next to nirvana.

Did these people develop meaning, stumble upon it, or did they simply create the meaning? People certainly are not born with a golf genetic code that unfolds. There is certainly nothing in the golf game itself that predisposes one to invest hours and thousands of dollars in the game. Like any activity, some who are exposed to it never develop the taste for it. What is the difference between those who do and those who don't imbue meaning in this game? I propose that meaningfulness, like love, is created (typically without conscious planning) by the person. The creation of meaning involves having respect for it as offering stimulation, a challenge, or entertainment, and then practicing those feelings repeatedly. Practice any activity with some attention to it and you'll get better at it.

The Role of Practice

As an example, let's take a look at a negative habit you may practice—anger. If you raise your voice and get more attention and compliance from others than when you speak softly, you are more likely to raise your voice when you want something. Extending upon this, if you yell and scream and the fear response from others increases the chances that you're heard and attended to, then your anger gets you what you want. You are more likely to get angry when others frustrate your needs. Soon, it will take less and less to trigger your anger response. You will have practiced your anger enough that you get really good at it. It comes automatically and without much thought, like other well-practiced skills (typing, riding a bike, driving). Feelings, to a large degree, follow the same laws of learning as do behavior patterns.

So if you practice treating something meaningfully, over time it will become more meaningful to you. Let's take another example—religion. Religious beliefs are practiced by some since childhood. Sunday school may precede kindergarten. Weekly affirmations at church, study groups, reading the Bible, talking to the pastor, priest, or rabbi, and repetition of prayers are all ways of practicing faith. Songs, rituals, initiation ceremonies, and laying on of hands are all ways of heightening the emotional experience associated with the religious beliefs. They are ways of making the beliefs more meaningful to you. Practice is an important aspect of developing meaning, although its significance is typically downplayed as a pedestrian aspect of meaning.

Your religious beliefs, of course, go further and deeper than this. Not only are they well practiced with reverence (though I would argue that this process alone will imbue meaning), but religions offer answers to questions that get to the core of what is meaningful. They offer explanations about the purpose of life, the purpose of suffering, and the purpose of death. Religion offers "purpose" to life, and this belief system based on purpose in and of itself defines meaning. But not all meaningful things in life need go as deep as offering ultimate purpose in life in order to be full of meaning.

So what besides practice can increase meaning? Special attention to it, watching it carefully and respectfully, assists in developing meaning. Reverence or respect, typically taught during the initial stages of involvement, increases the potential meaningfulness. In golf, the pro or instructor speaks of the importance of selecting the right iron, how you handle it, the body posture when using it, and the mental attitude while preparing to hit the ball. The religious teacher instructs in the meaning of symbols and ceremonies apart from any specific doctrine. The place of worship is typically larger than traditional meeting rooms (often with higher ceilings and stained glass windows, with prominent placement of the altar and pulpit), with furnishings that suggest its importance and meaning. In sporting competitions, the Pledge of Allegiance suggests a special quality to the gathering, that the meeting is one of the pleasures afforded by our freedom. Special (careful, slow, methodical, step-by-step rather than spontaneous or haphazard) attention thus breeds meaning.

The Posture of Respect

Just like with golf or worship, posture is important. Parents train their children about proper behavior in the church (not to giggle, to pay attention, to keep their feet off the pews, not to constantly wiggle) not simply due to consideration for others. Parents will insist on behavior in the place of religious worship that they will not enforce at a movie theater or fast-food restaurant. Why? They want their children to show respect for the meaningfulness of the activity they are participating in. The posture for developing meaningfulness is thus serious, watchful, following the model behavior of those around you, and void of sarcasm, doubt, and question of authority.

It is rare in any activity considered meaningful that loud or distracting behavior is considered appropriate. For instance, during the judging of a dog show there is respectful silence. The judges are somewhat set apart from the audience, signifying their special role and reverence by the organization. Publications from professional groups rarely use sarcasm, caricature, or lightheartedness when describing their own activities. The watchful, mindful, serious, and observant stance is taken.

How does this apply to what most would agree is the most potentially meaningful series of events in a person's lifetime, relationship with others? Family life is not supposed to be serious and obedient. A romantic marriage is not based on seriousness. The solemn quality of church is not found in healthy families. But when you stop to think about it, it actually is. During dating, if a partner does not feel they are taken seriously, they will object strenuously. While spontaneity and fun are also required aspects of a healthy relationship, most people will "bail" from relationships where the serious, observant, reverent aspects of relationship are missing. When a child is born to a marriage, there are many of the same qualities of meaning making found in religion and sport. There is preparation: the baby shower, birthing classes, preparation of the crib. There is reverence: selecting a name, holding the newborn infant, weighing the infant, picture taking. The infant is treated specially, with conscious or unconscious attempts to intensify the bond between parents and child (some of these, like feeding, are biologically predisposed to build the bonding process by requiring that the infant be held during breast-feeding). Later, there are rules the child must follow that are different from those held by adults. The meaningfulness of relationships is thus defined by rule-governed behaviors. Some of these rules (how to speak to an adult, how to address an elder, who gives permission and who must seek permission) are designed not just to create order, but to provide and nurture the sense of meaning that family implies. Meaning is thus taught, structured, encouraged, modeled, and transferred from one generation to another. It is not a mystical process that some of you missed when you weren't looking. Meaning is created. It is made up.

Do You Really Need Meaning?

Is having meaningfulness in your life required in order to rid you of mixed anxiety and depression? Probably not. There are individuals who have environments that sufficiently stimulate them, giving opportunities for rewarding relationships, enjoyable activities, and structured routine and habit in ways that make life predictable and pleasant. Such people can have happy lives, but they are more vulnerable to emotional distress than those who have meaning in their lives because they are dependent on the environment for happiness. If the environment changes (people move, people die, job duties become unenjoyable, companions marry and no longer seek out weekend recreational activities with you), these people are more likely to get depressed. Moreover, meaningfulness in your life is a natural antidote to depression and anxiety since it assists you to have a larger perspective on life. You are not as likely to invest all your eggs in one basket because meaning is found in a variety of places.

So engaging in activities and processes specifically designed to create meaning has several important outcomes. It anchors you to the world in ways that make you feel good. It increases your attractiveness to others because you are seen as interesting and complex (while those who have failed to develop meaning in their lives are frequently seen by others as superficial). It increases your psychological complexity because you are connected in important ways to a variety of things. It decreases the tendency to become self-absorbed with your internal (emotional and cognitive) issues. It helps protect you against depression and anxiety by keeping you active, and there is recent evidence that engaging in pleasurable activities and psychotherapy creates the same chemical changes in the brain that taking medications does (Brody et al. 2001; Sackeim 2001). Perhaps most importantly, meaning in your life just feels good.

Obstacles to Developing Meaning

What are the hurdles or obstacles to developing meaningfulness in your life? My experience has been that the same set of assumptions about our emotions that make emotion regulation strategies ineffective also hinder in the development of meaningfulness. If you assume that your feelings are beyond your conscious control, that feelings are somehow bestowed upon you supernaturally, then you are not open to changes in your emotions that are self-regulated. With a deep belief in your powerlessness over your emotional life, you fail to attend to experience that can be emotionally pivoting. Since creating meaning is akin to loving, then objecting that you can't choose to love, that loving is an involuntary process that depends on "chemistry" over which you have no control, effectively stops you from a sincere effort at such creation.

Meaningfulness, like loving, is something we create within ourselves. While one outcome of this inner meaning is that "objects" (a game, a place, a person) become attached and receive your affections, it is not the end goal. We do not love so that we get love. We do not make something meaningful so that we can be meaningful. But, in the end, this is precisely what happens. By loving, it is easier to be loved. By having meaning, it is easier to be meaningful. While these are abstract ideas, the ways of implementing them are concrete and specific. Fromm (1956) tells us that we must practice love, that it takes discipline and concentration, and that since it requires time and practice we must have patience as well as supreme concern (the utmost or highly valued concern) with the mastery of the art of loving. While using our powers of concentration, Fromm tells us that we need to be sensitive to ourselves but not narcissistically concerned with what we may get in return. Finally, Fromm tells us that love requires faith and courage to productively enact or express our feelings regardless of the outcome. We don't love only so that the person will immediately return our affections. Courage is required because, in fact, our love may not be returned. But mature love does not demand a response. Loving, developing meaningfulness, is not tit for tat. Meaningfulness is practiced because it imbues our life with purpose, anchoring us to nature and to others, and provides value beyond what we place into it.

Begin Your Practice

The remainder of this chapter is thus designed to help you to practice bringing meaning into your life. As in the chapters that follow, simply filling in the blanks is not enough. You must practice, concentrate, be disciplined, have patience, show supreme concern, be sensitive to your reactions, have faith, and be courageous. Do the exercises below, knowing that you will need to return to them after you begin practicing mindfulness (that will substantially increase your abilities to be patient, sensitive, disciplined, and observant of yourself and of the environment) in the next chapter.

Specific Paths

The use of mnemonics can help us to remember what we are supposed to do to increase meaning. Mnemonics offer a shorthand way of remembering the steps suggested, even when this book is not in front of you. The mnemonic for meaning making is SPECIFIC PATHS.

Supreme concern. Identify importance, reason, why.

Practice. How can I repeat this in my daily life?

Energy. How can I put emphasis on this? How can I be disciplined?

Concentration. How can I focus on this, making it more than passive?

I. "I," me, not others. What is it that I want to happen in me?

Faith. How can I have faith that this will work, that it makes a difference?

Important. How can I increase the attention and direction of this?

Courage. What can I do when I begin to question or be negative?

<u>P</u>atience. How can I remind myself that this takes time, effort, and energy?

<u>A</u>ttention. Be mindful of it when I'm doing it, not automatic or by habit.

<u>T</u>asks. What are the specific things I need to do? Behavior, not just thoughts

<u>H</u>umility. It's not all about me. I'm imperfect and supposed to be that way.

<u>S</u>ensitive to self. What am I experiencing? How does this feel?

Supreme Concern

As I mentioned before, supreme concern means that you must highly value the activity. You identify what is right and good about the action, object, or process, not arguments against it or your doubts about it. For individuals who are depressed and thus prone to be cynical, negative, or pessimistic, this can be a major obstacle. We know from dialectical thinking that there are always opposing needs, views, or perspectives. Even with fairly universal values such as love, you could identify costs or competing values (such as concern for self, self-preservation, and unrequited love). But in the process of meaning making, you temporarily ignore these. It is a compromise—to give up attention to the negative in service of the positive. Yes, there may be costs or things lost. But to live a meaningful life means you make choices. You form compromises where some things are elevated and others demoted in significance. To pay service to all potential values would behaviorally paralyze you, since there are no perfect compromises where all needs and demands are simultaneously served. You must give up in order get. You create meaning by making some things "supreme." And there is no formula or cookie-cutter approach to what should be supreme. It is the essence of freedom that some of us will choose this while others that. What is important now is that you choose, only for now. Supreme concerns may change over time with differing needs and situations. This does not mean that what was thought supreme really wasn't. It means that you have used your freedom to make life vibrantly changeable.

Supreme does not mean spiritual, necessarily. While we frequently refer to the "Supreme Being," here we use the term differently. We use it to signify value, weight, and heartfelt love. It is not sacrilegious to love that which is provided by a Supreme Being. Judeo-Christian values actually predict the opposite. To value what God has given us fulfills the promise that we will share in God's glory. So don't feel compelled to either include or exclude spiritual values here. Your supreme concern can be given to golf, a pet, a hobby, or any recreation. You are creating meaning, and the force that binds us together is embellished, rather than distracted from by the act. A Supreme Being wants you to lead a meaningful life, a life where much of what you do has importance and significance. Otherwise, your worship and belief in the gifts of life are rather paltry. If you don't appreciate nature, relationships, recreational outlets, career activities, family, friends, and objects that are the products of God's gift, then you have not fully accepted these gifts. So don't feel compelled to list as supreme concerns only those things you think would be endorsed as politically correct or "holy." The goal is to find things that matter to you, not to others.

For those who do not believe in a Supreme Being, don't let the word "supreme" get in your way. It is an abstraction used to signify importance. And, as mentioned above, none of your work on SPECIFIC PATHS needs to be spiritual or religious in orientation.

Obstacles to Identifying Supreme Concerns

Let's get back to the obstacles involved in identifying supreme concerns. Perhaps by engaging in dialectic thinking you can dismiss the underlying negative propensity people with depression and anxiety encounter. Here is a list of possible supreme concerns and doubts or arguments against each.

Supreme Concerns	Negative Thoughts, Attitudes, or Doubts
Honesty	True honesty is unobtainable.
Integrity	You miss important opportunities because your ethics tell you what should or should not be done.
Compassion	Caring about others does little to help them.
Empathy	Understanding others does little to help them. You should help them solve problems so there will be no need for empathy.
Love	You may get hurt, so why bother?
Courage	Let the other guy get it instead of me.
Friendship	You are safer if you trust no one. You're taking a risk.
Peace of mind (security, safety)	It's only an illusion. There is always danger.
Life	You're going to die anyway.
Choice, freedom	Another illusion. In the end, nothing matters.
Companionship	Safety is more important than being with someone. They can always let you down.
Pets	They poop all over the place and destroy things you like.
Family	They will all die at some time, so why attach to them so strongly?
Community	Every community is the same. One is the same as another.
Recreation	It will all end. It's only a temporary diversion from ultimate pain.
Creativity	There will always be a critic. You can't please them all. It doesn't last.
Art	Most people never succeed in the arts, and what does success bring you?
Beauty	Age destroys it. It's temporary. It's up to the beholder (so it's not universal and therefore ultimately unimportant).
Nature	Transitory and difficult to maintain while caring for self. Another delusional value.
Earth	Ultimately not under our control, and why worry about that which cannot be controlled?
Imagination	Just another way of avoiding reality.
Memories	Living in the past doesn't help now or in the future.
Eternal life	Our meager existence is already too long.
Spirituality	We are on our own. Avoiding reality with delusion ultimately leads to disappointment.

Energy	Unnecessary movement.
Purpose	What real important purpose is there? We live, then we die.
Familiarity	Needed by small minds.
Predictability	Brings routine, ruts, and allows people to second-guess you.
Trustworthiness	A fool's delight. You end up getting in trouble anyway.
Loyalty	Falling off the cliff with your buddies is no better than falling off alone.
Justice	All relative. One man's justice is another's punishment.
Acceptance	Another concept for small minds, designed to deny the true futility of existence.
Discovery	We know all that is needed to know. Trying to find out more is just a waste of time.
Awareness	Knowing the bogeyman is going to get you doesn't bring comfort.
Desire to learn and seek knowledge	Catching up with others who are also doomed is no accomplishment.
Being understood	Having people agree with us that things are bad is little consolation.
Self-esteem	Feeling good about being inadequate gets us nowhere.
Success	There will always be someone better who has more and got it more easily.
Accomplishment	Another self-delusion.
Contributions to others	They are not grateful, and they take it for granted. It gets the collective "us" little.
Truth	It's all relative.
Stimulation	Masturbation. A temporary comfort not ultimately important.
Sensitivity	It just opens you up to hurt. Why be a sucker?
Morals, ethics	The meek will inherit the earth. But only after the rest have spoiled it.
Courtesy	Meant for weaklings who can't defend themselves and are trying to not make enemies.

As the list above shows, you can always criticize values, find competing perspectives, and find reasons to believe in nothing. What is useful in terms of meaning making is to temporarily suspend your judgmentalism. For those who tend to be negative (because of the depression), there will be nothing hard about returning later and making something previously important unimportant. Anxiety makes you doubt, to fear what you want because you may not get it. With mixed anxiety and depression, you thus have two obstacles to overcome: with depression, doubt, and with anxiety, fear. It seems to be easier for many people to lose meaning than it is to create it. So let yourself go through these exercises without pessimism. Have the courage to create meaning.

Identify Possible Supreme Concerns

Below is a list of questions to ask yourself. The answers to these questions may provide hints about possible supreme concerns for you. With depression, it's only too easy to say to yourself that nothing matters, and with anxiety, your tendency is to dismiss that these things are possible for you. With mixed anxiety and depression, you will probably do both (dismiss them *and* think they are impossible for you, even if important). Don't let yourself fall into these traps. Be open-minded about identifying the possible importance of issues to you and your life. Read these questions and write down those that represent your supreme concerns.

- How do I spend my time?

- What would I miss if taken from me?

- What creates the strongest feelings in me?

- What upsets me when it doesn't go according to plan?

- What was drilled into me as a child as important?

- What do I most admire or envy when others have it?

- Where do I go when I need comfort?

- What is so essential that I take it for granted?

- What makes me feel safe?

- What makes me feel threatened?

- Is this my value, or someone else's value?

- Do I believe this, or do I think I should believe this?

- Is this the "right" thing to say, or do I truly think this?

- How often do I practice this?

- Does it define who I am and how I wish others to perceive me?

- Does it define a rule I wish to follow in my life?

- Does it speak both to my heart and my head?

- Have I been touched by another when they engaged in it with me?

- Would my world be different without it?

- Is it relevant to those I treasure the most in my life?

- Is it important to how I define success in my life?

- Would it be one of the things I hope I speak about on my deathbed?

- Does it define happiness in my life?

- Does it define fulfillment in my life?

- Does it define meaningfulness in my life?

Below, list some answers to the above questions in order to push through the doubt caused by your depression and the fear caused by your anxiety. The supreme concerns can be things you already have in your life or things that are missing. You should identify both.

_____

_____

_____

_____

_____

_____

_____

_____

_____

_____

_____

_____

_____

_____

_____

_____

If you are having difficulty with the above exercise, look at the list of possible supreme concerns beginning on page 83, as well as the ones below. Check those that are important to you and that you imagine you could adopt as important values if you were not so doubtful and fearful.

Possible Supreme Concerns

_____ Being a good listener

_____ Praying daily in thanks for what I already have

_____ Having hobbies and interests that I routinely enjoy

_____ Being devoted to my spiritual principles and beliefs

_____ Believing in my strengths and attributes (having high self-esteem)

_____ Participating in democracy by social and political actions

_____ Feeling good about my body's physical condition and health

_____ Appreciating of the natural world around me, noticing beauty where it exists

_____ Being kind to people

_____ Helping people in need

_____ Being independent

_____ Enjoying the respect of others

_____ Being well-informed on current events and social issues

_____ Having opinions that are based on facts and knowledge and are well considered

_____ Being able to see both sides of an issue

_____ Being a good mother or father to my children

_____ Establishing relationships with friends based on trust and mutual respect

_____ Having a home that I am proud to share with friends, family, and neighbors

_____ Living my daily life in a way mindful of my values and principles

_____ Being scholarly and well-read

_____ Being surrounded by friends I trust and am not afraid of

_____ Not trying to control so much around me

Practice

Practice is simple as a concept and difficult as a daily reality. Anyone who has ever tried to establish a new habit, even a simple one, understands this. It may be as simple as trying to establish the habit of drinking a glass of water immediately upon coming home from work. There are many expectations upon returning home (pet the dog, talk to your children, read the mail, return phone messages, change your clothes, or simply relax), and integrating a new habit as simple as drinking water can be difficult to sustain. What most people find most successful is to tie or connect a new habit to an old one. Find something that you already do as a habit and make your practice of the new habit follow this one. You may nearly always change your clothes into more comfortable ones upon coming home from work, so making a rule that you drink a glass of water immediately after changing your clothes works. Habits can be simple, like drinking water, or complex, like allowing time for meditation or prayer. The "what" of practice, of course, depends on what it is you're making meaningful.

If this step is skipped, if you don't practice your supreme concerns, you will not make them meaningful. They will be words or ideas only and will not penetrate to the level you seek.

Energy

This means giving the event, activity, process, or concern real enthusiasm. In the beginning, you may have to consciously place this kind of "reverence" on the process. It may seem odd or uncomfortable, just like when you learn any new complex skill (driving, typing, writing an essay or paper). Reverence means to approach the activity with a feeling of deep respect and maybe even a bit of awe. When you practice your concern or value, do it with energy, seriousness, respect, and feeling. Don't make it mechanical or feeling-less. Practice the awe of the simple and routine.

Children have no difficulty with reverence and awe. Watch a child who learns that patting water roughly brings splashes. There is amazement, and each time the splash happens it brings delight. That response of delight, energy, and excitement is trained out of us as we grow older. And it's a pity, since the world's most simple events really are awe inspiring. Somehow, as adults we're expected to be immune to amazement; somehow maturity means not being affected by the predictable. This is a real loss to our psychological experience of the world and one you should attempt to undo. Meaning making with SPECIFIC PATHS can help you do this.

Concentration

Concentration amplifies energy. It means to pay attention while you engage in the activity. Do it like your life depends on it. Do it with focus, watching yourself as you engage. You are attempting to eliminate the automatic nature of much of your daily behavior, the thoughtless way in which you conduct much of your life.

I

This is a reminder that someone is doing the thing. You engage in the target behavior not just to accomplish a task, but to instill a feeling in yourself. Thus, as you engage in the process, place your attention back and forth between the "it" you are doing and your response to it. "I am doing this. I am not doing this for others, to play to an audience. I am doing this for me. Just for me."

Faith

Faith is about trust, not simply blind allegiance. Approach the activity with steadiness, loyalty, and consistency, and be strict with yourself in having confidence. Faith is about not asking for proof, not having to know the outcome before you engage in the process. Faith is engaging fully and without reservation. When making meaning, you don't need to be analytical. You were analytical, making a choice, when you identified your supreme concerns. Don't revisit those choices now. Such revisiting is a defense against full engagement, usually based on fear. It is a form of avoidance, a betrayal of what you are attempting to accomplish with SPECIFIC PATHS, with making meaning. Have faith now. Place yourself in it fully and without doubt.

Important

Make what you are doing important. How? By telling yourself all the reasons you chose the supreme concern in the first place, the feelings you anticipated being able to generate within yourself. Don't be fearful that simply because those feelings you desire have not yet appeared that they won't ever. Remember, meaning is created with practice and engagement. You attribute importance, you make it up. It's not imposed by God or country. Others do not make something important—you do.

Courage

Courage is what we rely upon when those inevitable doubts, the pessimism, the negativity, the judgmentalism, and the resulting fear are generated. You use courage as the source of tolerance. You will submit yourself to these fears, allow yourself to experience them, and push through them in order to have the meaning you seek. Courage is about tolerating the unpleasant, no matter how much you want to give up. And the unpleasant experience is typically fear. You fear that you won't be up to the challenge. You fear that you're not worthy of the meaning you seek. You fear that you don't have the basic stuff that others seem to have. Fear is about giving more credence to your negatives than to your positives. It's about doubt. Courage is about willingness to have the fear, not run away to reduce it. In the chapters on emotion regulation and distress tolerance I will have a lot more to say about dealing effectively with fear.

Patience

Cultivate a willingness to wait. With patience you do not expect quick and easy results. If your supreme concern was easy to obtain, you probably wouldn't have listed it because you would have accomplished it effortlessly without the DBT approach. Patience is testimony to how important your goal is. You're willing to put forth so much, to sustain your efforts over time, because you truly desire it. Be patient with yourself. See this as a long-term effort, not something that occurs miraculously and effortlessly.

Attention

Making meaning is about focus. Don't try to do three things at once. While modern society places value on multitasking (being able to retrieve e-mail messages, listen to the news, cook dinner, and talk to your friend on the phone all at the same time), making meaning is not this forgiving. You have to attend. You watch and observe. You feel and you observe. You pay attention even to the simple aspects of the complex chain of behaviors in which you're engaging. This is mindfulness, another simple concept that is difficult to implement, and so I've devoted an entire chapter to it.

Tasks

Meaning is not found in an object or behavior but in the interaction of self and other or the interaction of self and object. Meaning is found in the relationship to something, not in the something itself. In creating meaning, you need to attend both to the task and to your relationship to the task. Your attention varies, first attending to task, then attending to self, attending again to task, then again to self.

Humility

Humility is recognition that you need not be perfect. You don't have to be the most skillful practitioner in order to have meaning. You can be imperfect, inadequate, fearful, and anxious and yet still create great meaning. You can recognize your deficiencies, you can be realistic, and still find the meaning you desire.

Sensitive to Self

You do this for you, for an internal feeling. It's not for recognition from others, a ticket for entrance into heaven, or .your family that you work for meaning. You engage in supreme concerns for you. To make it work, you need to be watchful of your responses. How do your muscles respond when you do this? How does your stomach respond? What are competing thoughts that interfere with your concentration and energy? You should strive to be sensitive to what is going on inside of you, paying attention to yourself, as well as to the activity in which you are engaging.

In the following chart, write your supreme concerns. What is it that you wish to find more meaning in? Then list all the ways you can possibly think of that you are practicing each supreme concern and the energy you plan to bring to bear during the practice. A few examples are offered, but they are simply to provide general direction. There is no right or wrong response.

Supreme concern	Practice	Energy
Example: To love my wife more fully	Touch her more often. Provide compliments daily. Notice what she is doing for me more often. Help with everyday chores so she knows that what's important to her is important to me also. Provide recreation time with her at least three times per week. Allow time for conversation daily. Talk about feelings (not just chores). Set goals and talk about dreams together. Pay attention when she talks. Tell her she is important to me. Show interest in her pain (not just try to take it away). Make time for eye contact. Find ways she can stimulate me. Find ways to attend to the relationship itself (not just completing daily chores). Take what she says seriously (don't dismiss her).	When I touch her, do it gently and with feeling. Tell her what I feel when I touch her (the warmth, the smoothness of her skin). Tell her things about her I appreciate. I shouldn't have to make them up. When I help her around the house, I won't resent it. I'll help with care and interest for what we both get out of doing it. When playing, I'll try to have fun (not do it out of duty) and express the fun I'm having verbally and behaviorally. When talking to her, I'll listen (not just think about how I'll respond), give eye contact, express interest, affirm her perspective as valid even if it does not accord with my own opinion (I'll look for the grain of truth to what she is saying before I tell her my perspective). I'll ask her about her feelings before I talk about my own. When I express my feelings I'll focus on the positive more than the negative, and I'll try to inspire in myself loving feelings even when I'm feeling irritable, tired, or numb.

Supreme concern	Practice	Energy

Now, take the same supreme concerns you listed above, and write them in the first column below. (Don't choose new ones, but continue to work with your original choices). For each concern, list methods or means you can use to concentrate, why you are doing this for yourself (not for others), and why it's important to you.

Supreme concern	Concentration	I (me, not others)	Why important
Example: To love my wife more fully.	Be careful not to practice this while doing something else.	By loving my wife more fully, I will feel more comfortable at home, I'll look forward to coming home, there will be less conflict in my life, and I'll feel my feelings more often. I'll feel connected to others. I'll have better companionship. I'll feel more stimulated at home.	My kids will be happier to have less conflict in the house. I'll be enacting something I highly value. My behavior will be more consistent with my values.

Supreme concern	Concentration	I (me, not others)	Why important
_____	_____	_____	_____
_____	_____	_____	_____
_____	_____	_____	_____
	_____	_____	_____
	_____	_____	_____
	_____	_____	_____
	_____	_____	_____
	_____	_____	_____
	_____	_____	_____
	_____	_____	_____
_____	_____	_____	_____
_____	_____	_____	_____
_____	_____	_____	_____
	_____	_____	_____
	_____	_____	_____
	_____	_____	_____
	_____	_____	_____
	_____	_____	_____
	_____	_____	_____
	_____	_____	_____

Again, write down your supreme concerns (the same ones you listed before). Now write what you might be able to think about that will encourage you to have faith, courage, patience, and humility, and in the last column what will help you to move your attention back and forth between what you're doing and what you are feeling.

The purpose of refocusing your attention between the task you're practicing and yourself is to help you integrate the experience. By moving your attention from task to self you more easily recognize why you're doing this exercise in the first place: to change your feelings, your experience, and your perspective on life's events. When you pay exclusive attention to the task, you may miss important changes in your feelings simply because you are not attending to them. When you pay exclusive attention to your feelings, you may not allow the task itself to influence you simply because you're not being mindful of the interaction between task and experience. In the last column of the following worksheet shift your focus of attention between self and task often, asking yourself questions that promote attention to the interaction between your body, your feelings, your thoughts, and the tasks or behaviors you are engaging in.

Supreme concerns	What will encourage me to have faith, courage, patience, and humility?	Refocus attention between task (what I'm practicing) and self
Example: To love my wife more fully.	I'm not doing this to get my wife to approve of me, I'm doing this to create more meaning in my home life. Her response to my practicing, my behaviors, is not what this is all about. It may take a long time to undo the insensitivity I've shown in the past. It may take me a long time to reconstitute the respectful person I truly believe is me. I've developed bad habits, and my replacement of these with good habits will take time and effort. I'm not perfect. But I'll be the me I want to be by practicing.	How do I feel when I'm being gentle and observant? How do I feel when I'm listening rather than responding? What does it feel like to express love rather than focusing on the love I'm getting? What makes it hard for me to be attentive? I must allocate time to do these things. I have to think about my goals and my values. Focus on what it is I have to do.

Supreme concerns	What will encourage me to have faith, courage, patience, and humility?	Refocus attention between task (what I'm practicing) and self
—————— —————— ——————	—————————— —————————— —————————— —————————— —————————— —————————— —————————— —————————— —————————— ——————————	—————————— —————————— —————————— —————————— —————————— —————————— —————————— —————————— ——————————
—————— —————— ——————	—————————— —————————— —————————— —————————— —————————— —————————— —————————— —————————— ——————————	—————————— —————————— —————————— —————————— —————————— —————————— —————————— ——————————
—————— —————— ——————	—————————— —————————— —————————— —————————— —————————— —————————— —————————— —————————— —————————— ——————————	—————————— —————————— —————————— —————————— —————————— —————————— —————————— —————————— ——————————

Obviously, writing these things down is just the first step. It provides a map to meaningfulness. The exercises themselves (doing them, not writing about them) create the meaning. Practicing, doing what you have intended, on a daily basis, will lead to the meaning you seek. You will find that developing skills in mindfulness (the next chapter), in emotion regulation (chapter 7), in distress tolerance (chapter 8), and in strategic thinking (chapter 9) will increase your ability to actually do the things you have planned above.

Prompt yourself daily with the mnemonic. What are you doing today that is SPECIFIC PATHS? What are you doing today that is contrary to SPECIFIC PATHS? What do you need to do that will help you increase your SPECIFIC PATHS orientation to life?

Review the SPECIFIC PATHS outline on pages 81–82 of this text at least weekly. Review what you have written in the exercises at least every other week. Make it part of your routine, like checking your phone messages. Prompting, practicing, and remembering your objectives will assist in the creation of meaning.

Chapter 6

Mindfulness Skills

Mindfulness is an important skill for all of us to learn, especially those who have been afflicted with emotional turmoil in their lives. Mindfulness skills involve the ability to attend to the environment. How is mindfulness different than simply paying attention to what is going on? It's not, really, but most of us have had the ability to pay attention trained out of us. Instead, from the time we are children we're taught to categorize, name, and then dismiss what we have seen. The scientific method, which at its roots involves the ability to abstract similarities and differences, use these abstractions to place things into categories, and then work with categories rather than the whole, is without doubt useful and critical to the scientific process. However, it tends to limit experience.

The Urge to Name

Children are taught to name animals, parts of the body, plants, and other objects in their universe. The ability to place an animal in the "cow" category is undoubtedly an important aspect of learning. By using such abstractions, by being able to categorize, we are able to communicate more concisely, to understand the complexity of the world more simply, and to predict and control our world better. The scientific method that encourages us to see similarities and differences is the basis of biological, medical, engineering, and most other scientific discoveries. There's nothing wrong with that. In fact, the method has been essential. But one of the costs of learning to see the world scientifically is that we can lose our ability to see the world with awe and fail to see the individual uniqueness and beauty that the world has to offer. Why? Because our scientific process of classification is about being able to categorize things so that we can dismiss them. Once something is categorized, we aren't usually encouraged to further study it. It's almost as though the categorized thing is "solved," and we are free to move on to the next thing. Once the child knows that the animal is a cow, the parent rarely spends time with the child marveling at the different colors of its coat, the methodical manner it chews its cud, the useful way it wags its tail to dispel flies, the graceful manner that cows cooperate in herd behavior, their relative nonaggressiveness, the thorough manner in which they graze the land, the manner in which they care for their young, or their emotional behavior (that you must spend a great deal of time observing, since cows are rather mute in expressing themselves). Essentially, we are rewarded for naming something. Once we have named it, that's it. We're done. We can put it in a box and close the lid—time to go on to something else.

Why Be Mindful?

Mindfulness skills are about undoing this habit. Now, I'm not talking about undoing your scientific training. I'd just like to encourage you to use it more discriminatingly. There are times to abstract, to analyze and name, and times when a different kind of observation is required. While all of us can profit from learning to observe the environment better, those of us with emotional turmoil can gain even more benefit from it. Why? With emotional intensity (depression, anxiety, panic, despair, fearfulness) you tend to become self-focused. You turn your attention inward, since that is where the "alarm" is sounding. The threat appears to be coming from within yourself, from your feelings, and it's difficult to fully pay attention to what is going on in the environment when you're preoccupied with what's going on inside of yourself. So, high emotional intensity frequently brings a dulling of your observational skills—not due to lack of ability or concern, but due to both habit and training. The training is the scientific orientation, and the habit is due to chronic internal focus of attention from high emotional arousal.

Keen Observation

Mindfulness skills are thus designed to assist you in reorienting yourself. You'll learn to improve your observational skills, to look beyond the naming and categorization you have learned and to be able to see the more detailed aspects of individual events, processes, and people. Besides seeing more of what is going on, there are many substantial benefits to practicing mindfulness in your daily life. Depression and anxiety not only turn your attention inward, thus depriving you of experiences that may occur in relating to the external world, but these strong emotions also function to dismiss the importance of the world in which you live. When depression is strong, you may spend all of your energy attempting to avoid the depression, effectively missing the experience of sunsets, of snow-covered trees in winter, of nature in general, which provides a sense of place and perspective to most of us. In fact, it is this sense of place and perspective that wards off depression for many of us. Moreover, being unmindful of what is going on around you leads to stasis. There are no prompts for change, no triggers that can open opportunities for new and different feelings. You are thus predisposed, through inertia, to continue to feel what you're feeling. Mindfulness skills open the world up again as important, meaningful, and powerful. Through mindfulness skills, you are able to find your place and relationship to the world again, as it was when you were a child.

Reclaiming Your Own Experience

I mentioned in a preceding chapter that individuals with high emotional intensity and slow return to an unaroused state frequently begin to distrust their emotions. Since they themselves appear to feel so differently than others around them, they begin to feel that their feelings are wrong. They may then begin a new, destructive process, looking to others to identify the correct or right way to feel. If others have the right feelings, then you can take your cue from them about how you should be feeling. Mindfulness skills are designed, in part, to terminate this destructive process. You are encouraged to look again to the environment, to put yourself back in the driver's seat again so that you are reacting to your own experience of the environment rather than someone else's.

Avoidance

Alternately, some people find their emotions so distasteful that they will do anything to avoid feeling them. These emotional avoidance behaviors (the opposite of self-absorption, in some cases) create a situation where the person is not attending to what is going on inside of them. Emotional numbness, to them, appears preferable to the emotional turmoil they anticipate if they get in touch with their feelings. Mindfulness skills can allow you to experience your feelings in ways that are not overwhelming but become sources of additional information about yourself.

Creating New Feelings and Thoughts

Mindfulness skills can assist you to have new reactions based upon primary experience. The self-absorption that emotional disorders often encourage is not just regarding your feelings. Self-absorption also involves your thoughts. You form habit-based presumptions about your life, the world, and people. These thoughts are based upon your previous experiences. Since self-absorption involves attending to yourself and failure to attend to the environment anymore, you recognize few new experiences to challenge your beliefs or presumptions. You become self-perpetuating. Your feelings perpetuate the same old feelings, and your thoughts perpetuate the same old thoughts. You are reading this book because you want new, different feelings, thoughts, and experiences. Mindfulness skills form the core of how to accomplish such change.

Kid's Stuff

Finally, mindfulness skills can be downright fun. Mindfulness invites you to look at the world as you did as a young child, to see the awe and mystery in the world that, as adults, we tend to dismiss. Of course, some of us had rotten childhoods and can't remember ever feeling that the world was a wonderful place to be. But mindfulness skills can offer those of us who missed a secure childhood the ability to have some of what was missed as toddlers.

What Is Mindfulness?

So, what are we talking about when we say "mindfulness"? Mindfulness is observing, seeing one thing in the moment. It's watching what is in front of you. Mindfulness is about describing what you see, in small details. It is about enhancing your interaction with the

environment so that you are experiencing it up close. The common habit of naming something dispassionately and dismissing it is not mindful. It is analytical. With mindfulness, you want more than a name, more than categorization, more than simply being able to identify what it is that you're watching. You want to know as much about it as possible. You want to know how your senses react to it. You want to know what it looks like visually, what it tactually feels like, what it smells like, if it makes sounds that you can hear, and what those senses prompt in you. Mindfulness is observing, describing, and participating in something.

While this may sound quite simple, it goes against much of our adult training. When I do couples' counseling, one of my favorite activities is to have each member of the couple practice mindfulness in the office. I present them with a brown bag filled with various objects. I ask one of them to close their eyes, select an object from the bag, and describe it with their eyes still closed. Men especially have a difficult time with this exercise. Many men will name the object ("It's a paper clip") and want to quit. They know what it is, so what more is there to say (what more is there to experience)? Once the name, the descriptive word, is given, it's often difficult for them to continue observing and describing the object. In fact, men will do much better when they select an object that they can't identify. Then they will have an easier time using their senses to describe it. Women, on the other hand, are much better at using their senses. They will be able to say something like, "it's cold, long, metallic, has sharp edges, fits between my fingers, is only somewhat flexible," and so on. And, of course, this is frequently a metaphor for relationship problems. Men are overly practical, wanting to name a problem and then move on, while women want something beyond a simple solution to an issue, often looking for more attention to the senses, to their feelings, and wanting emotional experiences prolonged in the relationship. Attention to task, for men, and attention to process, for women, is frequently at the core of relationship difficulties.

Mindfulness skills are process oriented. The task is not to get someone else to agree about what's being observed. The task is to pay attention, to describe an experience between self and that which is observed.

Both with clients and when I'm training therapists, I use a five-minute video of the ocean. The task is to watch the video mindfully and, at the conclusion, to describe what they observed. The result is always telling. Although everyone sees the exact same video, what people pay attention to and how they relate to it is substantially different. Some people count the number of seagulls that fly overhead, since the birds fly through the video intermittently. Others describe the scene as if they had to reconstruct it for a future film: "There is a large brown rock approximately ten feet from the where I presume the camera is, with a second smaller brown rock to the right of it. Both rocks are approximately twenty feet from where the ocean water comes in. The camera is positioned toward homes on the other side of the bay, and directly beneath the camera is a sandy beach with various seaweed pieces strewn on it." Others react more impressionistically: "The tide was strong, and each time the water came toward the camera I was drawn in. I was reminded of the rhythmic and predictable character of much of life, and it was reassuring to see each new wave thrown against the rocks. The water changed from blue when seen in the vastness of the ocean to white when the water was ferociously pushed against the rocks. The sun was bright, and I wished I were on the beach the day the video was taken." Others have a more difficult time separating themselves from the video, and pay more attention to themselves than to the video: "I knew the waves would sweep me in, would destroy me, so I had to close my eyes in order not to be destroyed."

The world is a complex place, and the number of things to attend to can be countless. Mindfulness is not about trying to capture everything, but about trying to capture more, to stop half-attending to the world and at least periodically notice more. Obviously we can't always be mindful. When we're driving a car it could be disastrous to be mindful. We need to drive defensively, and it is useful to block out all the small distractions that could lead to an accident. We don't want to notice the small objects in the distance away from the freeway since we may run into the car in front of you if you do. At work, we need to attend to our work content in order to earn the paycheck your employer provides you. Most of the time, in fact, we won't be mindful. However, if we are almost never mindful, our world shrinks, and we're deprived of new experience.

Strategies to Develop Mindfulness

Mindfulness, like most important skills, is not learned instantaneously or immediately. It requires practice, and the more you practice being mindful, the greater skill you will have. There is not necessarily one right way of practicing mindfulness, but there are a few ground rules.

Be Mindful of One Thing at a Time

It is difficult to try to be both mindful of something that is happening "outside" and mindful of what is happening inside of you. Be mindful of one thing at a time. Start your practice by being mindful of small things (objects, a view, a photograph) that are not ever changing. Later, as you grow accustomed to this new practice, graduate to being mindful of more complex, changing events (your emotional reaction when something angers you, your way of handling conflict in relationships, your emotional reaction when alone).

Be Nonjudgmental

Mindfulness is not designed to be a problem-solving or decision-making process. (Although you indeed should be able to solve problems and make decisions better once you become more mindful, because your powers of observation will increase and you will become less self-perpetuating. Mindfulness is a simple observational process itself.) One of the easiest ways of dismissing an event is to judge it. If you feel that something is bad, then all you have to do is avoid it. If you feel that it's wrong, then you resist it. Resist the temptation to judge what you are observing as good, bad, right, wrong, appropriate, inappropriate, hurtful, or evil. Just describe what you are observing, without forming a judgment about its ultimate goodness or badness.

Be Mindful of the Moment

Observe what is happening now. So much of our lives are oriented toward the past or the future. We filter our momentary experiences in terms of the impact they will have on us. This filtering is precisely what we are trying to *stop* doing by being mindful. Filtering is about taking things out, dismissing as inconsequential certain qualities or events. The more we filter, the less we see. So try not to filter. See everything, sense everything. With mindfulness you watch the moment, see what is happening now, without regard for what it means about the past or the future. You can always analyze later. Watch what is happening in front of you now, in this moment.

Focus on Your Senses

Be mindful of visual, auditory, tactual, olfactory, and oral experience. What does it look like? How does what it looks like change when you look at it from another perspective? Does your visual experience change the more you look at it? What are other words can you use to name your visual experience? What does it sound like? Does the sound change over time? What does it feel like? Is it cold, wet, hard, warm, soft, mushy? What does it smell like? Do you taste it? Use your senses, not your memories or intellect, to be mindful.

Describe Your Experience

Use words, as many words as you can (even if you are being mindful silently to yourself), to describe what your senses are experiencing.

Using Language

We must take a detour here, because mindfulness is about observation of the moment, and words frequently serve a different purpose. Words, the language we use, are not simply *descriptive* (telling you what you see). Language, the specific words you use, can also be *prescriptive* (leading you in a direction, telling you what you "should" see). One of my favorite undergraduate courses was in semantics. Semantics tells us that words are important not only in describing events, but in suggesting something (both to ourselves and to others) that may not be intended or desired. Especially for those who have had chronic emotional pain, certain words can take on meanings that become triggers for additional emotional pain.

The prescriptive functions of language can be very powerful and unintended. This was demonstrated to me through biofeedback equipment. In biofeedback, electrodes are attached to the skin and pick up electrical energy (minute amounts of it). The typical use of biofeedback is to give more precise feedback to people about their muscular tension so that they can learn to better relax. For example, a person with tension headaches can learn to relax their forehead muscles and thus eliminate the headache. Biofeedback works by picking up small, generally imperceptible muscle reactions. One interesting demastration is to hook biofeedback equipment up to a person's right arm, then instruct them that they are *not* to follow your next direction. If you then tell them "Don't lift your right arm," the biofeedback equipment will pick up clear signals that the right arm muscles are tightening in preparation to be lifted. Why? Because language is prescriptive—it tells us what to do or anticipate doing. The brain processes the words in preparation for action: "lift," "arm," and "right" are processed as potential action sequences. The "don't" is globally processed, since the person does not lift their right arm, but they are prepared to do so. (This is why it's almost always better to tell someone what you want them to do, rather than telling them what you don't want them to do.)

So how is this important to our examination of the function of language and mindfulness skills? When practicing mindfulness, you need to describe the world in simple ways that are not suggestive of anything other than what you're observing in the moment. If you use powerful words that evoke strong reactions in you (such as "depressing," "dark," "overwhelming," "enveloping," "annihilating," "creepy," "out of control," "destroying," etc.), then you are more likely to connect with past emotional trauma or discomfort rather than continue to truly attend to what is going on in the moment. Words serve to measure as well as communicate. If you use strong words, then you are adding to the experience rather than simply describing it.

Mindfulness thus includes attention to the kind of language you are using, even if the language is only spoken to yourself. Even if there is no possibility of confusion in interpretation between people because the language you are using is all internal thoughts (you are practicing mindfulness silently to yourself), language is still important. The language you use shapes your experience as well as describes your experience.

One of the mantras of semantics is "the map is not the territory." This is an important insight. The words you use are maps. They describe what you are seeing. They are not reality. The words are not "it" but a map of "it." In mindfulness, you are trying to explore the territory, and you don't want your maps, your words, to be the primary influence. You want to be influenced by the territory, what is going on that you are observing.

Like in the biofeedback demonstration, you can be preparing to do something, judge something, or dismiss it, rather than describe it. You can be preparing to avoid something, rather than just observe it. Emotion-prompting words, previous-experience-prompting words, and words that demand a particular response ("stop," "awful," "hated," and expletives) serve to diminish mindfulness because they prompt or prepare for action. Mindfulness is not about action. Mindfulness is observation, data acquisition, information input, experience at the most elemental level. It is not analytical, decisional, directive, or action promoting. While improved observational skills lead to improved judgment and thus more adaptive action, mindfulness is simply the observational stage.

Your Observations Are Yours Alone

Most of us seem obsessed with having others have the same "maps" of the territory that we do. We want validation that our views, perceptions, and feelings about events are "correct" and the "right" ones to have. If you get out two maps of the same geography, produced by two different companies, frequently you will find that the maps present the same information in dramatically different ways. Certainly a topographical map will look entirely different from a road map, even though these two maps purport to describe the same territory. And even though they are entirely different, they both can be entirely accurate. Most of you would judge the worth of the map by its ability to allow you to traverse the territory with highly predictive accuracy. If the map shows you how to get from point A to point B with a minimum of wrong turns or detours, then you judge the map to be good.

We don't seem to allow the same diversity in human relationships. Many of us want others to see things exactly as we do. And our primary method of judging if another person is seeing things our way is their use of words. This is a slippery slope. Language is so elastic, with both connotations and denotations, that attempting to have someone truly understand exactly what you're experiencing can be futile and exhausting. Seeking validation through having people use the same words and creating the same map that you have goes beyond the extraordinary when the territory you are mapping is psychological.

One utility of mindfulness is thus drilling deeper than your initial conclusions and judgments about events, and simply experiencing events and describing your experience in simple and concrete words. Others do not have to describe the same experience, nor do you need to insist that others at least acknowledge that your experience is plausible. I may find the cake taste delectable, while you find the cake putrid. Why should I feel the need to defend my taste or feel pressure to have you change your experience to be like mine? While you certainly can insist, in your important and close relationships, that your experiences be respected and that you not be attacked for having your reactions, it's best not to spend much energy comparing your maps to others' as long as your map gets you from point A to point B satisfactorily.

Mindfulness skills are thus not a popularity contest or a method of obtaining group conformity of opinion. Instead, mindfulness skills help you to make more detailed and precise maps that are based less on prejudice and preconceived ideas. Your maps formed with mindfulness are more apt to be driven by the actual territory you're navigating rather than group pressures or emotional reactions. Since you will have so much more information, your maps will be increasingly useful to you.

Getting Active

Mindfulness thus involves surveying the territory, and that means *participating* in the process. Mindfulness is an active process. You must get involved in the survey. Your senses are heightened. You're paying attention, like landing on an alien planet for the first time and noticing all there is to see, touch, smell, and feel. This is difficult if all you can think about is the possibility that aliens are about to attack you. Your survey of the territory is likely to be incomplete if a substantial portion of your consciousness is focused on fear rather than observation of the environment. Self-consciousness similarly degrades your ability to fully participate in what is going on in the environment in the moment. If you're thinking about the past or the future, you're not "here" but "there."

Finally, with mindfulness we're not attempting to prolong pleasant experiences or terminate painful ones. Mindfulness is not about changing the environment or changing yourself. (We will deal with change in subsequent chapters.) In mindfulness you are observing, not avoiding, intensifying, or changing experience.

Mindfulness Skills Training

The mnemonic for mindfulness is ONE MIND.

One thing

Now

Environment. What is happening out there?

<u>M</u>oment. Immediate

<u>I</u>ncrease Senses. Touch, taste, vision, hearing

<u>N</u>onjudgmental. Not good or bad, right or wrong

<u>D</u>escribe: Words. Descriptive not prescriptive or proscriptive

You may wonder how the following exercises are going to decrease your mixed anxiety and depression. Well, with anxiety we become so focused on threat cues that much of the external world gets ignored. When you realize that you're only responding to threat, you can understand how and why your anxiety persists and even grows. Mindfulness will reexpose you to the world, letting you see outside the constant feelings of threat. Your anxiety will decrease over time. Similarly, with depression you simply shut down. You find the world too demanding and complex. But the outcome is the same as with anxiety: you don't have new experiences to decrease the depression by increasing pleasure. To decrease the sense of excessive demands being placed on you by the environment, you simply stop paying attention to the environment. Your lack of attention appears to decrease the demands being placed on you, so this response is rewarded (it feels good, at least temporarily).

Mindfulness Practice: The First Stage

I break mindfulness practice down into three stages in order to increase your chances of success. In the first stage you practice paying attention to simple events outside of you. In the second stage you practice paying attention to more complex events outside of you, and in the final stage you pay attention to your own responses and feelings, as well as what is going on in the environment. By breaking your practice down into these three stages, you are more likely to profit from the powerful effects of mindfulness.

Each day, try one of the following exercises. Don't just try the exercises once. Practice them daily. Spend ten to fifteen minutes in each activity. Attempt to keep in mind the following:

⬥ Before each activity, review ONE MIND and remind yourself of the meaning of each principle. For example, "one thing" means that as you engage in the mindfulness practice exercise you are not doing something else as well. While killing two birds with one stone is efficient in our routine daily lives, it is not optimal in learning a new skill like mindfulness.

⬥ If other things, not happening in the moment, come into your mind, notice them and let them go. For example, if you're listening to music and you become aware that your mind wanders to how you are going to gather enough money to make your mortgage payment this month, simply say to yourself, "I'm aware that I'm worried about money. I'm going to let it go for now. Focus on the music. Listen to the sounds. Attend with my ears. I can do this. It's okay. What do I hear?"

⬥ If an external distraction occurs (the telephone rings, someone comes to the door, your child asks you for something), pause in what you're doing and come back to it immediately thereafter. Remember that you don't necessarily have to be a slave to your phone. It's okay to ignore it and continue practicing your mindfulness.

◆ If you find that your mind is going a thousand miles an hour about all sorts of things, don't give up. Mindfulness is designed to help us concentrate. It is precisely at times like these that practice is helpful. The goal is not to be able to be perfectly mindful each time. The goal is to be able to notice that your mind is wandering and bring yourself back more quickly and easily each time.

◆ First, attend to what is going on outside of you. What are your senses finding? Then pay attention to what is going on inside of you—for just a few seconds—returning your focus to what is going on in the environment. This participative approach, being involved in what is going on, incorporates attending to both the environment and yourself.

◆ Afterward, having finished your mindfulness practice exercise for the day, return to the ONE MIND mnemonic and ask yourself to what degree you were able to accomplish each of the principles.

Mindfulness with Music

Music is a wonderful tool to help you practice mindfulness. Many of us use music to simply provide background noise. You play the music and enjoy it but are doing something else as well as listening. You may be reading the newspaper, cleaning the house, talking on the telephone, or writing checks while you have the CD player or the radio turned on. While this is fine for everyday enjoyment, it is not mindfulness. With mindfulness you want to play a particular selection, sit down in front of your stereo speakers or with your headphones on, and really listen. Perhaps close your eyes, so that the auditory sensory input is better highlighted. Listen to the sounds. Allow it to move you. But always come back to the sounds. Stay with it.

While I happen to enjoy classical music, you don't have to choose classical. I would suggest, however, that you first choose instrumental music rather than music with vocalists. While mindfulness can certainly be practiced with songs with lyrics, in the beginning attempting to stay with both the lyrics and the instruments may be too complex. Better to start either with instrumental music without vocalists or with vocalists using a foreign language you do not understand. Then you are focusing on the instruments and the sound and cadence of the vocalist and will not become distracted with the meaning of the words or the message of the song. Here are some suggestions of pieces to start with:

◆ Samuel Barber's Adagio for Strings

◆ Fantasia on a Theme by Thomas Tallis

◆ "Fanfare for a Common Man" by Aaron Copeland

◆ Henryk Gorecki's Symphony no. 3 (Opus 36), "Lento-Sostenuto Tranquillo Ma Cantabile"

◆ Pachelbel's Canon in D

◆ Bach's Air on the G String

◆ Albinoni's Adagio for Strings in G Minor

◊ The soundtrack from *Mary, Queen of Scotts*

◊ The soundtrack from *The Last of the Mohicans*

◊ The soundtrack from *The Mission*

◊ Sounds of nature (ocean, tropical rain forest, mountain streams, crackling fire, etc.)

Mindfulness with Aromas

Many health-food stores, drug stores, and variety stores sell liquid aromas or fragrant essential oils. Some of these can be a bit expensive, so don't break your budget. You just need two or three scents. If you put one or two drops of the liquid on a piece of paper, the aroma is highlighted. Smelling directly from the bottle is not as effective, as it is too concentrated. While aromatherapy holds that particular scents produce certain moods and health benefits, you are not concerned with those ideas for the purpose of mindfulness. Aroma is an excellent tool to develop mindfulness because there are fewer words involved and thus fewer associations from the past. This will keep you in the moment and in the present. Put one or two drops of one scent on a small piece of absorbent paper. Find a quiet place where you're not likely to be disturbed, and place yourself comfortably in a chair.

1. Slowly move the scented paper close to your nose, just close enough that you barely perceive the scent. Leave it just barely perceptible, for fifteen to twenty seconds. Slowly breathe in. How does the scent change the feelings in your nostrils? What does it smell like? Can you feel the scent deeper than your nostrils (can you feel it in your throat)? Does it have a "taste"?

2. Move the scented paper closer to your nose, but not right up against your nose. Slowly breathe in. How does the scent change? Breathe in five or six times, noticing the aroma and associations to the aroma.

3. Now place the scented paper right up against your nose. Notice how the scent is stronger. Breathe in five or six times. How does the proximity of the scent to your nose change its aroma? Use as many words as you can to describe its scent, as if you were describing a aroma to someone who had never experienced it.

Some of my favorite scents are cinnamon, eucalyptus, lemon, and vanilla.

Mindfulness with Tactile Focus

Practicing mindfulness with our sense of touch can be a particularly rewarding activity, especially for men who have not been given permission to experiment with the sense of touch. Somehow society has relegated tactual sensations to women, and men feel that paying attention to the skin is feminine and thus unallowed. Forget your preconceived notions. You are not, with these exercises, attempting to soften your skin or appear more youthful or feminine. Instead, the purpose is to reawaken a frequently neglected sense. Again, remember ONE MIND. Don't practice these exercises while you're talking on the phone, having a conversation with someone, or planning your shopping list. Find a quiet place in your home, temporarily free of other distractions.

◇ Place a small amount of skin lotion on the back of one of your hands. Don't rub it in yet. Notice how the small pile of lotion feels compared to the area immediately around the lotion. Notice if it is warm, cold, wet, soft, or penetrating. Leave it there for about a minute, noticing the difference between the area on your skin where the lotion sits and the rest of your hand. Now, slowly and gently take a finger from your opposite hand and extend the lotion ever so slightly in circular motion in the surrounding area. (You are not attempting to quickly moisten your hands, but to notice, carefully, the tactile changes between the lotioned and unlotioned areas of your hand.) How does the lotion feel on the finger you're using to spread the lotion? How does the lotion feel as it spreads across the top of your hand? Is it less cold, as you spread it, than it was when you initially placed it on your hand? As you slowly spread the small amount of lotion across the top of your hand, notice the visual change of the moistened skin. Attempt to feel the lotion penetrate through the skin. Use as many words to describe the experience as possible. Focus your concentration. Keep bringing yourself back to the tactile and visual experience of the lotion and your skin.

◇ While you're in the shower or bath, use a small amount of invigorating body shampoo. (Aramis makes a very nice one.) As you rub a small amount of the body shampoo on your hands, notice the feeling on your skin. Slowly, with your eyes closed, begin to rub the shampoo on your face. Feel the tingling. Feel the penetration. As you wash the shampoo off with water, notice the change in tactile sensation. Notice how your skin feels immediately after the water has taken the invigorating body shampoo off your skin. Continue to focus on the progressive changes in your skin as you bathe.

◇ Place a small amount of isopropyl alcohol on your hand. Watch the clear liquid as it sits on your hand. Rub it on the top of your hand. Do this exercise slowly. Smell the alcohol. As you rinse the alcohol off your hands, notice the change in sensation.

◇ Experiment with different lotions, gels, shampoos, soaps, aftershaves, and perfumes. How do the different lotions make your skin feel differently? How do the different scents change the experience? How does a gel feel different than a lotion? How does the same lotion feel different on your hand compared to your forehead?

◇ Purchase several different brands of mouthwash. As you place the mouthwash in your mouth, how does it first taste? As you swish it around slowly, consider how the taste changes. After it has been in your mouth for ninety seconds, how does it taste? How is the sensation different on the inside surface of your cheeks than on your tongue? Can you feel it directly on your teeth? As you spit it out, how do the sensations linger? Where does the sensation leave first, and where is it most long lasting?

◇ Find several small objects (perhaps a small rock, a marble, a small sponge, and some salt or sugar). Close your eyes as you handle each object. Feel its texture, its temperature, its edges, the way it interacts with your fingers and skin. How does it feel different when wet rather than dry? How does it feel different when you grasp it with your fingers, versus when you allow it to roll freely in the palm of your hand?

⋄ Place a small hard candy in your mouth. In addition to the taste, feel the tactual presence of the candy in your mouth. Roll it around on top of your tongue. Place it slightly under your tongue. Roll it against your teeth. Place it on the inside of your lips. Feel it on your gums, on the top of your palate. Notice the accumulation of saliva as well as the taste of the melting candy. Sometimes immediately swallow. Sometimes allow the saliva to accumulate. Notice the temperature, texture, and taste of the candy as it melts. Pay attention to the tactual sense all over your mouth. Prolong the experience, and notice it.

⋄ Take a small bag of sand and grab a handful of it. Slowly let the sand drop from in between your fingers. Feel the fullness of the sand in your hand and how your hand can firmly grip it then allow it to slowly drop back into the bag. Notice how your hand feels as the sand empties. Repeat this many times. Notice the temperature of the sand as it is warmed by your hands. Notice the individual grains of sand. See how some of the grains stick to your hand and others fall. Watch it, feel it, try to hear it.

Mindfulness with Visual Sensations

While visual sensations tend to bring many associations and the possibility of being distracted by our associations and memories increases, visually oriented mindfulness can also be powerfully rewarding since the visual field is so much broader than your tactile or auditory senses. It is important, however, to remember that with beginning mindfulness practice you are not attempting to analyze, control, predict, or have insights. You are simply observing, allowing your eyesight to experience that which is being presented. Again, the more complex the visual image, the more difficult it is to be mindful in the beginning stages.

⋄ Choose a photograph, say the picture on today's front page of the newspaper. First, look at it broadly. Is it in color? What colors can you identify? What is in the foreground? What's in the background? Now attend to the small units of the picture. Scan each area of the photograph. What can you see at the right-hand top corner? What colors are there? What are the objects? What's at the left-hand top corner? What is the relationship of the main foreground object to the background? Is it nighttime or daytime? If there are people in the picture, what are they wearing? See each person's hair, face, neck, and shoulders. Is there an identifiable feeling the person has? Is there action in the picture? Continue to go back and forth between a broad and a narrow focus of attention to the photograph. What would someone who looked at the picture only haphazardly miss? How does the photograph change when it is in bright light compared to dim light? Does the perspective you take on the photograph change your perceptions? Look at it straight on. Look at it from the side. Turn it upside down. What do you notice when the photo is not aligned that you missed when you were looking at it normally?

⋄ Turn on the television, but turn the sound all the way down or mute the sound. Watch the visual images. Chose a program with which you're not familiar. Perform a running commentary in your head, verbalizing what you see as specifically as you can. Try to include as many details as you can, whether they seem important or trivial. Pretend you are an undercover agent witnessing something terribly important, but you're not exactly certain what that importance is. Report everything that you see, so that the person to whom you are reporting will be able to put it together. Do this for three to five minutes, without regard to plot or story line. Describe what is happening in the foreground, as well as in the background. Notice the positioning of the camera, the visual perspective, as well as the action the camera records. Notice the colors, the lighting, and the changes in perspective. Notice all you can.

◊ Rent the film *Contact* with Jody Foster. Watch the very first three minutes with the sound off. Follow the images, and put words to the images. Imagine that you are floating along, experiencing what is being presented on the screen. What do you see? What are those things? Describe them to yourself as if you need to report these phenomena to a scientist who will later make sense of them. You are the scientist's eyes but not their brain. Your task is not to analyze what's going on, just to report it as specifically and in as much detail as possible. Notice the colors, the changes in perspective, the changes in speed, and the floating perspective. (Once the little girl comes into perspective, the mindfulness task is over. Don't watch the remainder of the film yet, please, because it can be used later for a different exercise, explained below.)

◊ Go to a public park and sit on a bench. Attempt to memorize each item in your field of view. Don't pan the area, as if you want the broad perspective, but keep your field of vision straight ahead. Pretend your neck is stiff and restricted, and your eyes can only look forward. From this fixed perspective, notice all the colors. See the ground, see the sky. Identify all the elements in your field of vision, their size, composition, and relationship to each other. See as if your eyes are recording a photograph, a photograph that you must later reproduce as accurately as you can. Describe to yourself, in as many different words as you can, what it is that you see. Close your eyes. Attempt to reconstruct the image in your imagination. Open your eyes. What had you failed to reconstruct in your imagination? Memorize the visual input again. Close your eyes. Repeat the reconstruction in your imagination until you feel you have visualized all the major and minor elements. Spend ten minutes with this exercise.

◊ Take an object that is familiar to you, say, a favorite pen or coffee mug. Look at the object as if you have never seen it before. Look at it from all perspectives. Attempt to see elements of the object that you would not otherwise have noticed. Is it scratched? Does it have bumps on it? Is it discolored in some places? Is it more irregular on some parts than on others? Is it worn in some places?

◊ Look out your favorite window. First turn your attention to the glass itself. Where is it dirty? Where is it clean? How does the window frame the view? What on the outside is moving? What is unchanging? What is big? What is small? What is different from the last time you remember looking out this window? What is exactly the same as the last time you looked out this window? Notice the colors, the movement, and the details. How much texture can you notice? How do the elements stand next to each other? What is the sky like? Is there movement in the sky? Does the light highlight anything more than usual?

◊ Find a small potted plant. Look at the leaves. Attempt to see the veins more specifically than you ever saw them before. Are the leaves fuzzy or smooth? Are the edges smooth or with points? Are some leaves shaped differently than others? Are some leaves colored differently than others? Do the leaves spring from the stems, or is there a more gradual progression? Are new leaves about to burst open? Are there flowers? Notice the main stem, the tributaries, and the ground from which it grows. Notice the plant as if you had to paint it from memory.

⬧ Look up at the clouds. Watch the clouds move in the sky. Watch the shapes. Some may be soft looking and fluffy, while others are smoothed and look like smoke in the sky. How do the shapes change over time? Is there a sharp contrast between the colors of the clouds and the color of the sky? Do they appear to be swept by the air, or do they appear to float? Are they plentiful or only punctuating the skyline? Are some close and others far away? Do they lose their shape? Are they interesting, ever changing, or do they seem simply to be moving away?

⬧ Watch a burning candle. Watch the flame, as well as the accumulating melting wax. Blow gently on the flame, and watch the flame as it adjusts to your breath. Notice the top, the middle portion, and the bottom of the flame. Notice its color, its brightness. Change the other lighting in the room, and notice the changes in the flame. Change your perspective on the candle and the flame.

As you can tell from these examples, you can be mindful of anything. You can be mindful of the pages of this book. You can be mindful of your hands holding this book. You can be mindful of anything in your environment, any time. Mindfulness is thus something you can practice anytime, anywhere.

Mindfulness Practice: The Second Stage

As you become more successful in allowing competing thoughts and memories to fall away from your consciousness as you practice mindfulness, choose ever more complex images, sounds, tastes, and tactual experiences to become part of your mindfulness practice. Below are a few suggestions for practice in the middle stages of your mindfulness practice.

⬧ Rent the movie *Contact* again. This time, view the very first three minutes with the sound turned up. How does the cacophony of sound images change your perceptions? Is it more difficult to attend to the images with the sound up? Do you feel pulled by the sounds to view the visual perceptions in a different way? How do your memories of the sounds affect your perception? Rewind the tape or DVD several times and see if on the second viewing, less distracted by the memories provoked by the sound, you're able to notice more than you did in the first few viewings.

⬧ Listen to one of your favorite pieces of music, whether instrumental or with vocalists. Try to listen to it differently. Hear the individual nuances of pitch, texture, and tone. Don't listen to the words, but to the emotion behind the words. Imagine the musical instruments being played, not the musicians who play them. Imagine the keys being struck, the strings being strummed, the horns being blown. Try to hear it on a different level than you typically do when you listen to it for pure enjoyment.

◇ During a relaxing meal, pay attention to the food as it enters your mouth. Note its temperature, texture, and flavor. Chew a few more times than usual, and note the changes in temperature, texture, and flavor. Feel the food as it goes down your throat. Pause between each swallow, before you take another bite. How does this change your eating experience? Notice the difference in sensation as you drink a sip of beverage compared to solid foods. Notice the food on your plate. Try to feel the heat or cold emanating from the food. See the textures visually before you feel them tactually in your mouth.

◇ Try to look at elements of a room with which you are very familiar. Look for areas in the ceiling to which you normally do not attend. Look at areas of the floor or carpet that you typically ignore as irrelevant. Look at a particular area of furniture that you typically would have no reason to attend to. Pay attention to areas that are normally filtered out as unimportant. Try to see the same old thing in a new and different way than before.

◇ Listen to the engine of your car. Turn off the radio and roll down the window. Is there a rhythm to the sound of the engine? Are there variations? Now feel the weight of your body on the car seat. Is the car seat hot or cold? Is the seat temperature different from the temperature of the air? Feel the steering wheel with the very tips of your fingers, not grabbing or holding it in the usual fashion.

◇ Go to a local candle shop, plant nursery, cosmetic counter, or art gallery. Notice the visual, kinesthetic, olfactory, and emotional responses to these.

After you engage in mindfulness practice, ask yourself the following questions:

◇ Was I able to allow myself to really concentrate and control my attention?

◇ Did I push away nothing and cling to nothing?

◇ Was I able to have other thoughts simply pass by quickly, like images on a merry-go-round, while I looked straight ahead?

◇ Was I full of strain as I practiced, or did I approach it as an observer, with possible delight?

◇ Was I nonjudgmental?

◇ Did I stay in the moment?

◇ Did I use my senses more than my brain?

◇ Was I watchful rather than thoughtful?

◇ Was I observing rather than trying to change something?

Mindfulness Practice: The Third Stage

You will eventually reach a point where your observational skills and ONE MIND come more naturally. After much practice, you will find that you're no longer struggling to allow sensual input to be primary, and memories and feelings from other events will more easily fall to the background. When you feel you've reached this point, you are ready to begin to practice being mindful of yourself. This is, in many ways, the highest and most difficult aspect of mindfulness. Being mindful of yourself involves

◊ Watching your emotions as if from a distance

◊ Watching your reactions to outside stimulation as if from a distance

◊ Watching your emotions and allowing intensification of them by the outside experience

◊ Watching your reactions to outside stimulation and allowing them to be intensified

◊ Watching the intensification of your emotions and allowing them to subside

◊ Watching your intensified reactions to outside events and allowing them to subside

◊ Doing all the above while changing your focus of attention, back and forth, between what is going on inside of you and what is going on in the environment around you

ONE MIND still applies, but now you're being mindful in a more complex way because you are not intentionally controlling the environment and yourself in order to attend. Instead, you are watching a natural interaction of your self with the environment. Being mindful in this way means that you are both allowing yourself to be affected by your experiences and are able to participate or not participate fully (to be swept away or be in command of your emotional process). You are being mindful, or watching, your different ways of being in the world: either controlled by your intellect or controlled by your emotions.

Like everything dialectical, there is no one "correct" way to be in the world. Sometimes you need to be rational, analytical, and controlled, not allowing your feelings to control you. Other times you need to be emotional, to allow your gut feelings and needs to persuade you in one direction or the other. Healthy adaptiveness is the ability to choose which way to be, depending on the situation and your goals. Mindfulness can assist you to combine the two ways of being in the world (rational or emotional) by decreasing fear and avoidance responses.

It is paradoxical but true (as you will see more specifically in the emotion regulation chapter) that by resisting or avoiding emotions, we make them stronger. Paying attention to emotions without trying to resist or prolong them makes them more responsive to the moment, and thus more adaptive to your long-term functioning. Mindfulness is the process of paying attention, of observing, and thus is critical in learning to make friends with your emotions (to reduce your fear of them). While you will learn more specifically how mindfulness assists in regulating your emotions in the next chapter, now what is important is learning how to apply mindfulness to yourself.

In your previous practice, you paid attention to the environment and how the environment affected your senses. Now, in this final stage, you incorporate the most complex aspect of your existence in the world—your emotional response to what is going on. Emotions obviously are more than what we see, hear, taste, or smell. Feelings are a combination of our bodily response, our thoughts, our wants and needs, and the labels we use to describe these responses. (Remember our discussion that labels, or language, have both descriptive and prescriptive functions. Feelings describe *and create* new experience.) With mindfulness, you thus watch your total reaction and your participation with experience.

In this third stage of mindfulness, you must continue to attend to the environmental aspects around you while periodically attending to what is going on inside of you.

1. What are your muscles doing? Are you clenching your jaw? Are your teeth being tightly held together? Are your fists clenched? Are your back muscles tight? Are your leg muscles prepared for action? Is your forehead relaxed? Do your limbs feel light or heavy? Is your tongue pressed up against your teeth?

2. How is your temperature? Do you feel hot or cold? Are your extremities warmer or colder than the rest of your body?

3. Are you perspiring?

4. Has your heart rate changed? Is your heart speeding up a bit? Do you feel adrenalin pulsing through your chest?

5. How is your breathing? Is it shallow or deep? Fast or slow? Are you breathing deeply into your lungs, down toward your stomach, or are your breaths so short and shallow that they never reach this deep?

6. Does your head feel light or heavy?

7. What are your thoughts oriented toward? Are you thinking something bad is about to happen? Are you anticipating something good is about to happen? Are you interested or bored? Are your thoughts light and happy, or are they heavy and prepared for danger or threat?

8. What word would you use to describe the emotion you're experiencing? Are there several words to describe it, or only one? Is the emotion you feel one that leads you to withdraw from or get closer to what is happening?

9. Are you socially comfortable with the bodily, thought, and emotional response you are observing? Would you prefer that others didn't see it? Would you prefer not to have it? Do you wish you could have it more often?

Mindfulness to self means to describe, as specifically as you can, what is happening inside of you. You're not trying to change anything, but just noticing how you feel and describing it to yourself.

Next time you feel an intense emotion (joy, sorrow, frustration, anger, hate, depression, anxiety), rather than trying to influence it in any way, first watch it. Observe it, like you've never had this emotion before and you want to understand it. You want to know its components, you want to be able to reproduce it if necessary in order to know this experience better.

First attempt to watch this strong emotion objectively, as if from a distance. See it as though it has nothing to do with you. Note all the small changes in your body, your brain, and your heart. Then notice what in the environment is producing this response, as if from a distance, dispassionately.

Then watch the emotion itself, considering the label or word you would use to describe the emotion and any action tendency (avoid, attack, approach, withdraw) it implies. Allow yourself to see it up close.

Even if it is an unpleasant emotion, stick with it for at least twenty seconds. Then go back to the events that prompted the emotion. Allow the emotion to recede, if it will. Watch the emotion decrease in intensity, if it does. Then see if you can intensify the emotion by identifying more words to describe it and feeling again how it is experienced in the body and mind. Go back and forth between the objective and subjective perspective (getting closer and further away from the experience) a few times, if you can.

Practicing being mindful of your emotions will eventually teach you a great deal about yourself. Then, by applying emotion regulation techniques, you will be able to influence those emotions with greater ease. The result is that you will feel more in control of yourself, will accept your emotions as useful rather than destructive aspects of your life, and will be prepared to make better decisions to influence the long-term course of your life.

Mindfulness decreases escape and avoidance behaviors, the very processes that make mixed anxiety and depression linger. If you engage in the activities described above regularly, daily, your anxiety will recede because you will have learned to attend to more than threat cues in your life. Your depression, too, will slowly resolve because you will expose yourself to the naturally occurring world that can bring joy and inspiration, and evoke movement, so lacking in the experience of depression. Mindfulness is thus a critical component of the DBT approach to emotional healing. Practice it daily.

Keep a Practice Record

Each day (or each time you practice), record what you did in each category of experience to practice ONE MIND. Habitual ways of responding are difficult to change, particularly something as fundamental as how you pay attention to your moment-to-moment experience. Mindfulness sounds simple but is extraordinarily difficult to implement because it requires that you change how you attend, what you attend to, and how you sustain such specific attention. Mindfulness is a powerful emotional change technique, so much so that six separate articles recently appeared in a single scholarly publication (Dimidjian and Linehan 2003, Roemer and Orsillo 2003). But mindfulness can bring substantial emotional change only if it's practiced. The following practice record can help you determine if you're practicing frequently enough and are using the full range of senses with which you can be mindful.

Date				
Sound				
Smell				
Tactile				
Visual				
Body				
Thought				
Feeling				
Taste				

Date				
Sound				
Smell				
Tactile				
Visual				
Body				
Thought				
Feeling				
Taste				

Chapter 7

Emotion Regulation

Regulating your emotions means to be able to change your emotions. If emotions are always right, you may ask, then why would we want to change them? Anyone who has ever been in deep, unrelenting emotional pain intuitively knows the answer to this question. Because although our emotions may be right, they frequently hurt. It is "right" to feel anger when someone has betrayed you, to feel loss when someone has abandoned you, to feel empty when you lose someone's love, to feel despondent when your important plans are foiled, or to feel shame when you have committed an act of which even you deeply disapprove. But these feelings hurt. And that hurt can linger.

Experience It Then Move On

The most powerful way of regulating your emotions is to have a life full of meaningful activities, as explained in chapter 5. Why? Meaning provides a sense of purpose and direction to your life. There are, however, many other specific techniques and processes that can help you to regulate your emotions. Emotion regulation skills offer a set of psychological coping technologies that can transform hurt feelings. No appropriate psychological technique can change a natural feeling into a different one. It would not be right to change the feeling of depression about losing a loved one into the feeling of indifference. This would be an attempt to truncate your feelings, to deny them. Denial and avoidance lead to even greater psychological disturbances over the long haul. So emotion regulation isn't about making one feeling into another one. It's about changing our emotional state altogether. Rather than reacting to your loss, you engage in techniques that make you react to something different, that bring a more desired state. You change your emotions because they hurt so badly, and you seek respite from the pain.

Is this just fancy footwork, giving avoidance a new name? No, it is entirely different. The difference lies in acknowledgment. You admit the truth that you hurt, you are even mindful of it. But at a certain point you decide that experiencing the anxiety and depression is not getting you where you want to go. You decide that the pain has outlived its current usefulness and set upon a path to change the emotion in this moment.

Let's go back for a moment to the horrific events of September 11, 2001. The news media helped us understand the devastation of the event. You probably saw the planes crash into the Twin Towers scores of times. You saw the skyscraper tumble to the ground nightly for weeks on television. It was a visual and emotional reminder of death and fear. You understood on a level that required little analysis that we were under attack and unsafe. However, the news media did not let up. You saw it over and over again. At first, the images were broadcast continuously for days. After a week or so, they were shown daily. After a month, they were shown periodically. How many times do you have to reexperience a horror before you register it as such? Not many. You don't need constant reminders of your pain. You're not stupid. We had gotten it already. The repetition served to increase terror.

There is a difference between feeling a feeling because it is right or natural, and repeating a feeling in order to increase its intensity. Repetition is a form of practice. When you practice something, you get better at it. Most of you would prefer not to practice your feelings of sadness, anger, rage, depression, anxiety, fear, and shame. They are powerful enough the first time around. You don't need them again and again. Unfortunately, that often is what we do with negative emotions. We practice them and get really good at feeling them.

Moving Away from the Hurt

Emotion regulation is about having available a strategic set of procedures to change emotions that hurt. You don't question whether the emotion you are having is right or not; you simply decide that the emotion is hurtful and that you want to have a different feeling. The current emotion has outlived its usefulness. It no longer brings you adaptive information. Like the media broadcasts of horrific events, it simply repeats the same message endlessly for effect and self-aggrandizement. The emotion itself becomes self-perpetuating and no longer serves a useful purpose. You decide to dispel it, like changing the channel of the television set because the program you're watching is repetitious and without value. This result is entirely different from repression, where you pretend that something has not happened. You don't pretend you didn't see what was on channel four before you turned it to channel five. You make a conscious and active decision to switch your input—to see something different, perhaps something that sparks more adaptive responses. You decide to change your emotional channel. Your input changes, so you have a different picture. The different picture brings a different emotional response.

Emotion regulation skills are thus a set of strategies. They are techniques to feel differently than you currently feel. This is not denial or avoidance. Avoidance is based on fear, while emotion regulation is based upon conscious decision. You decide you want to feel differently because that is in your best interest. It's strategic; it gets you where you want to go. It's planned and intentional, therefore conscious and goal-oriented. By being purposeful, emotion regulation is empowering.

Emotion Theory

Let's briefly review the most accepted theory of emotions (see Lazarus 1991; Eisenberg 2000). By reviewing the theory, you can get a better understanding of how your emotions work and how to change them when you want to. First, on the most elemental level, emotions are biochemical processes. *Neurotransmitters*, chemicals in the brain, either increase or decrease the probability that information will be sent. The information regulates other chemical processes that together produce mood states. A mood is a generalized feeling. When psychiatrists speak of "a chemical imbalance" when describing mood disorders (types of depression), they are referring to these neurotransmitters. It is now well understood that dopamine and serotonin have powerful effects on emotion, perception, and thought.

Biology and Emotions

That we are biological creatures, dependent upon our bodies and chemical makeup for reliable function, comes as no surprise to anyone. Obviously a balance of the right chemicals is required for effective operation of our entire organic system. Some emotional disorders (notably schizophrenias, bipolar disorders, and severe obsessive-compulsive disorder) require direct intervention on the chemical level. Taking medications as prescribed is a prerequisite for recovery. Biology and genetic heritage play an important role in how you develop, and how your experience of the world unfolds.

Biology is probably the most powerful single factor determining *propensity*, which is all about probabilities. If you have two parents who are both depressed, the probability that you too will suffer from depression increases. However, even both parents being depressed does not predict with 100 percent accuracy that their children will all be depressed. In fact, there is less than a 50 percent chance that two depressed parents will produce a depressed offspring. Most people do not have two parents with exactly the same emotional disease. Perhaps one parent suffers from clinical depression, while the other one does not. One's mother may suffer from an anxiety disorder, while the paternal great-grandparent may suffer from a mood disorder. Since the science of mental health has evolved rapidly over the last several generations, it frequently is difficult to determine if a relative had a mental disorder or not. Diagnostic criteria and availability of mental-health professionals have changed radically over the last several generations. Perhaps your relatives were merely said to have had "a nervous breakdown." A nervous breakdown could be almost anything by today's standards.

So biology plays a critical and undeniable role in the development of many mental disorders. However, biology plays only one role. Many children of emotionally impaired parents are perfectly okay. My father was paranoid schizophrenic, but I'm not. Moreover, the propensity for a disorder does not mean that we necessarily must suffer the disorder. What is called the *diathesis stress model* of disease predicts that the environment (stress and strain) has a compelling effect on whether or not you develop a mental disorder that you're genetically predisposed to have.

While you cannot control your genetic makeup, you have great control over your environment. By controlling your environment and modulating stress, you can increase your chances of health and happiness even in the face of biological determinants.

Bodily Cues

So the first factor of emotion theory is neurochemistry and biology. You look at biological risk by assessing your family history. How many of your relatives had emotional disorders, and what were those disorders? A second factor is the body itself. Your brain takes

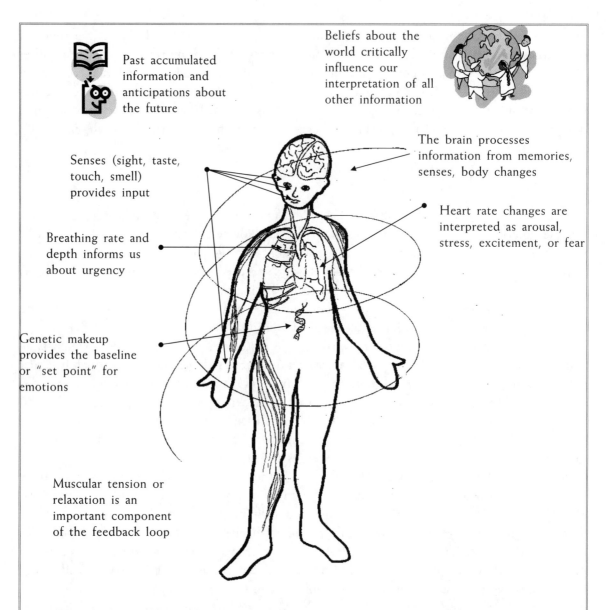

Past accumulated information and anticipations about the future

Beliefs about the world critically influence our interpretation of all other information

Senses (sight, taste, touch, smell) provides input

The brain processes information from memories, senses, body changes

Breathing rate and depth informs us about urgency

Heart rate changes are interpreted as arousal, stress, excitement, or fear

Genetic makeup provides the baseline or "set point" for emotions

Muscular tension or relaxation is an important component of the feedback loop

The Biopsychosocial Model of Emotions

The biopsychosocial model of emotions assumes that each element (biology, psychology, and environment) reciprocally influence each other in establishing our total experience of the world. For example, when our heart rate increases the body can interpret this as a sign of danger, and as a result muscles tighten in preparation for fight or flight. We will be more likely to interpret sensory input (sight, sound, touch, taste) as signals of such danger. We begin to breathe rapidly and shallowly. We remember similar threats experienced in the past, and connect with our assumptions about the world (do we see it as a supportive or threatening place?). The swirl indicates that each component influences each of the others. If we wish to reduce crisis and tension, we can increase body relaxation, shift our input from the environment to those that are supportive, and reinterpret our assumptions and thoughts. The model provides hope for those who suffer from mixed anxiety and depression since it demonstrates the many different levels that change our experience.

Drawing courtesy of Louise B. Barnard, LCSW

cues from your body about what you're experiencing. The face, for example, has more muscles than any other single area of the body. While they are not strong muscles like those in our arms and legs, they are instead exquisitely delicate muscles that can produce hundreds of facial changes. You learn over time, as a child, the difference between a sad and a happy face. You learn how facial muscles express numerous and diverse emotions. You're able to predict both how others feel and how you feel, based upon the reaction of your muscles.

As with our earlier discussion of language (that words both describe and prescribe), our bodily reactions both express and intensify emotions. You feel sad, and your facial muscles express this sadness. Your brain subconsciously processes this muscular change in your face. It notices that your face is expressing sadness. You develop thoughts about your sadness. This is the third factor in emotion theory, cognitive processes or thinking (how your internal, silent dialogue and debate both describe and prescribe emotions).

The body expresses emotion in six major ways: muscle contraction or relaxation, increased or decreased heart rate, increased or decreased temperature, fast or slow breathing (rapid short breaths, slow deep breaths, or normal breaths), perspiration, and dilation or contraction of blood vessels. That's it. There are consequences or other reactions to these processes, such as skin color changes (flushing or paling in response to blood flow changes), sensations of butterflies in the stomach, being sick to the stomach, feeling light-headed, having buckling knees, or feeling like you will pass out. But all of these effects result from changes in the six bodily processes listed above.

What is important in emotion theory regarding the second factor, the body, is that the body is both a receiver of emotions and a sender of emotions; it both expresses emotions already processed and begins a new process of creating emotion. Your brain "watches" your bodily processes. As your heart begins to speed up, the brain says to itself, "Hey, my heart is speeding up. There must be danger. Prepare to fight or flee." The heart reaction both expresses cumulative emotional events (things that bug you over time), thus far unrecognized on a conscious level, and then (once noticed by the brain), serves to recognize the emotion and send it for further conscious processing (you begin to think about it).

Thoughts and Emotions

The third factor in emotion theory, cognitions or thoughts, have their own unique topography. Your thoughts are either interpretive ("What does this mean? How will this affect me?"), judgmental ("This is right," or "This is wrong"), analytical ("What should I do? What is my strategy?"), or ruminative ("Woe is me, here it goes again, the same old thing," repeated several times with no new information produced). Thoughts involve internal language, or self-talk, and as we discussed in chapter 6, language has both descriptive and prescriptive functions. Not only do the words you use in your head describe what you're feeling, they *define* and help *create* how you are feeling. If your thoughts are negative and pessimistic, you are defining your situation as bleak, hopeless, and catastrophic. It becomes a self-fulfilling prophecy: You look for the negative, generate evidence of the negative, and prove your presumption. You can't see beyond what you believe to be true, and eventually you make the negative outcome actually come true. You do this by behaving in a manner that's consistent with your thoughts. Thus, the fourth factor in emotion theory, behavior.

Behavior and Emotions

What is the significance of behavior? You got it—behavior, too, is both descriptive and prescriptive. You enter the bank to cash a check, perhaps a large sum of money for you. You worry that you may be robbed if you carry that much cash. You leave the bank clutching your wallet in your back pocket with your hand. You're looking nervously around you. Your face and body posture scream out how vulnerable you feel. Almost anyone around you can tell two things: you're feeling nervous, and you obviously have something you're protecting in your back pocket. A perfect setup, since you've done everything but place a sign on your back that says "Rob me now, I have lots of money in my back pocket!" This is the self-fulfilling prophecy.

The same process works internally, too. Your brain watches your behavior. The combination of watching your bodily functions (muscles, breathing, temperature, heart rate, blood vessel dilation or contraction, and perspiration), your thoughts, and your behavior tells a convincing story to your brain about how to feel.

History

So feelings are combinations of your biochemical composition, how your body is responding, how you're thinking, how you are behaving, and the fifth factor, your prior conditioning or history. Your history, stored in both visceral (body sensations, including smells, tastes, and arousal states) and memory components, provides powerful influence over your emotions. If you grow up in an unpredictable environment, one moment feeling loved and another moment feeling threatened, then you will find it difficult to develop a stable coping strategy to both defend against threat and still be open to support and love. If you grow up in a consistently hostile and personally degrading environment, then you will develop defenses against intimacy and keep your guard up constantly for threat. Your psychological history, consisting (among many things) of threat, support, encouragement, consistency, protection, rewards, punishments, and modeling of your adult guardians, provides a sometimes rigid set of dispositions that can be as difficult to dismantle as your genetic history itself.

Your Environment and Emotions

But you do not feel in a vacuum. Your feelings are not just the result of your biology, your body, your thoughts, your behavior, and your history. Because history continues, your environment continues to provide new experiences and new contingencies. The last major element of emotion theory is thus the environment itself. Your current world influences you and provides prompts to do this or that, feel this way and not that way.

Ways You Can Change

Emotion theory outlines the major avenues you can use to change your emotions. First, you can change your biology through medications. Second, you can change the prompts your body gives you by manipulating your level of arousal (decrease muscle tension, take slow and deep breaths, allowing your heart rate to slow—thus decreasing temperature and perspiration). Third, you can change your self-talk. You can monitor negative thoughts, accept your feelings without resisting them or encouraging them with internal dialogue, and predict the positive for yourself. Fourth, you can change your behavior, being strategic rather than operating in a reactionary manner or out of habit. Fifth, you can monitor your use of previous coping techniques developed from your psychological history, and be conscious and careful in using only those that help you to obtain your goals. Finally, you can make changes in your environment.

Emotion theory is thus inspiring, because it shows you multiple levels of intervention. There are many ways to influence your feelings. You are not a slave to your body, your mind, or your environment. There *is* hope for change.

Emotion Regulation Skills Assumptions

The following assumptions summarize the approach of emotion regulation and offer you clues about how to approach your work with managing your feelings. Come back to this list if you find that your emotions continue to increase in intensity no matter what you do (you may find that you are violating one or more of the assumptions, and the list may help you back on a more helpful course of emotional recovery).

1. Your emotions serve important purposes. They help you to react quickly, to protect you from threat, to bond you to others, and to add color and excitement to your life.

2. Emotions, in order to serve the important survival and humanistic functions for which they were designed, must be experienced and acknowledged.

3. Avoidance of emotions has paradoxical effects: the more you engage in avoidance and escape from your emotions, the more powerful and urgent the emotions become.

4. Feelings are always right. It is what you do with them and how you react to them (how you think about them and how you behave because of them) that can be hurtful or maladaptive.

5. Feelings are not values. Values are thoughts, ideals, and principles. Feelings are a form of sense, like touch, taste, smell, and sight. They are ways of experiencing the world. They are holistic, residing in the body, mind, and spirit (not just the head).

6. You must first stay with an emotion, allow its recognition and internal expression, before you attempt to move on to a different emotion. You must first "be here" before you rush for "there."

7. Feelings are not exactly the same as action urges. Just because you feel anger does not mean you will necessarily strike out. Feelings prompt actions and increase the propensity for action, but feelings do not necessarily have to be acted upon.

8. You are not your emotion. What you feel is only one (important), aspect of who you are. Your identity, who you are, is not the same as what you're feeling.

9. When you are in high arousal (heart pumping fast, muscles tight, short and shallow breaths, thoughts that you must do something quickly to change what is happening), your emotions are unlikely to provide the most useful and wise advice to you (unless you're under direct and immediate physical attack by a known and identifiable danger).

10. Emotion regulation skills require practice and patience. If emotion regulation were easy, you would not be reading this book. Like all important and useful things, you must work hard and consistently to produce lasting effects.

11. Emotion regulation is not about insight. It's about emotional and behavioral strategies. Don't just think about the exercises in this chapter—do them daily and weekly.

12. Emotion regulation skills are processes. The exercises below are not like throwing on a light switch. Humans developed feelings for survival purposes. Processing the world using emotions introduced variability and unpredictability in the human species, and this in itself increases the probability of survival of the species. It defines our tenacity, creativity, group bonding and commitment, competitiveness, and ability to love and protect one another. Because of this, no one technique or strategy will always work (even with the same person having the same feeling in the same situation as before). Fortunately, there are many techniques. If one does not work this time, try a different one. Go back to one that failed before. It may work this time.

Be Mindful of Current Emotions

While emotion regulation skills are about how to change emotion, it cannot be overemphasized that the first step is to be mindful of your emotions. While in the last chapter you used mindfulness as a way of exposing you to the world anew, here you use it as an acceptance strategy. You pay attention not simply in order to increase your sensory appreciation for what the world has to offer you, but also in order to accept the world and your experience of it just as it is in this moment.

When you're depressed and anxious, it is understandable that your initial reaction is to want to terminate that pain as quickly and effectively as possible. But if you respond to this sense of urgency, what you often end up doing is avoiding. Avoidance has severe and persisting consequences. First, avoidance breeds phobic responses. When you are able to decrease arousal (fear, anxiety, dread, or depression) by avoidance, the avoidance response becomes imprinted on an unconscious level. You will begin to engage in avoidance automatically and without even knowing you're doing it. Second, avoidance becomes anticipatory. Not only do you avoid situations that originally created the panic, but soon you begin to avoid other, related situations as well. First, you may avoid emotional encounters with your father. Then, unconsciously, you avoid emotional encounters with teachers (also authority figures). Then, you unconsciously add supervisors to the growing list of figures to avoid. Soon, perhaps all authority figures become signals of impending danger. You are not able to have a satisfying interpersonal relationship with any authority figure, leaving you feeling powerless to progress in your career and to feel comfortable with all people you see in a higher status than yourself.

It is easy to prevent such emotional phobic responses: avoid avoiding. Be mindful of your current emotions, even the painful ones.

Labeling

For mildly to moderately painful anxiety or depression, allow yourself to label (give words to) your emotions. Look at the list of emotions on page 33 if you are not able to specify what the emotion is. Identify the emotion, identify whether and where you can feel it in your body (muscles, temperature, perspiration, heart rate changes, breathing changes, blood flow changes), what the thoughts are accompanying the emotion, the environmental precipitants (what prompted the emotion), the behavior expressing the emotion (what you do), and what happens afterward (any consequences of the emotion).

Complete the chart below and on the next page in order to practice the breakdown of triggers to your anxiety and depression. Here, choose something immediate and pressing in your life. In a subsequent chapter you will practice longer-term situations that trigger your anxiety and depression.

Identify the emotion (label it)	Example: Shame that I misled my supervisor	_____
How expressed bodily	Back muscles tighten, heart rate increases, shortness of breath	_____
Thoughts about the emotion	I'm a coward who can't face up to my responsibilities. I'll always be a coward.	_____
Environmental precipitants	Supervisor asked me how far along I was in getting in the report.	_____
Behavior	Told her it was almost done when I hadn't even begun it.	_____
Afterward	Feel even more anxious and pressured. Take work home to complete so I won't get caught. Feel resentful that I'm working at home and not paying attention to the children.	_____

Identify the emotion (label it)	
How expressed bodily	
Thoughts about the emotion	
Environmental precipitants	
Behavior	
Afterward	

For severely painful emotions, ones that interrupt your ability to think clearly and logically, it may not immediately be possible to perform the step-by-step analysis given above. Instead, practice simply being mindful of the emotion itself.

Mindfulness of Painful Emotions

The following procedure will help you to desensitize yourself to the agony of intense emotions. Desensitization is the process of removing the fear that surrounds an event, and in this case the event is the experience of your emotions themselves. By engaging in the process below, you can reduce your fear and thus have fewer emotional responses to deal with (for example, dealing only with your depression and not both depression and fear at the same time).

1. Feel the emotion.

2. Imagine that the emotion itself is a wave of the ocean. It comes toward you, but then the tide of emotion recedes. It comes toward you, but then recedes.

3. Imagine that you are on a warm beach, the sun hitting your face and gently warming you. A cool breeze blows past your face, cooling it from the warmth of the sun.

4. Imagine that the emotion itself is a wave of the ocean, but the cool breeze makes the emotion just a little bit lighter and less intense.

5. Imagine you are back on the warm beach enjoying how the dark-blue sky makes the water so blue and how the water turns crystal white as the waves come near the shore.

6. Imagine that the emotion is intense, but only when you look at how large (like the ocean itself) it is from a distance. As you get close, just as the waves becomes less intense as they reach the shore, so, too, do your emotions. As you imagine your body being warmed by the sun's rays and cooled by the ocean breeze, see the emotion as small and less intense.

7. Go back and forth between the images of the ocean, which allow you to feel comfort and steadiness, and the emotion itself, which makes you feel tense and afraid.

8. As you go back and forth between reassurance and fear, feel the rhythmic back-and-forth motion of your breathing. Feel the air as you exhale from your nose, and feel the clean air as you inhale.

9. Imagine the similarity between the rhythmic back-and-forth motion of the ocean's waves and the rhythmic in-and-out motion of your breathing.

10. Pay attention to the emotion itself and how you can increase and decrease its intensity. Note how it can go in and out, like the waves of the ocean.

11. Pay attention to how you can influence your feeling as you pay attention to it, and then turn your attention to both your breathing and the visualization of the ocean and beach.

12. Go back and forth between the imagery and the emotion, again and again, until you're able to feel the noticeable difference between being mindful of the emotion and being mindful of another, more comforting experience.

Getting Perspective

Once you feel you have decreased the immediate intensity of the strong painful emotion, as soon as you can, perform the same analysis of the emotion as you do for mild to moderate emotions. This type of analysis, where you break your emotions down into smaller components, is important for several reasons: It allows you to get out of emotionalism (where all you're doing is feeling intensely), and it interrupts the emotion (even if temporarily) with rational thought. This, in itself, tends to reduce emotional intensity. It also provides perspective. Frequently, when you write things down (as you'll do in the following exercise), they seem less compelling. Finally, it allows you to see more completely the connectedness between your language, emotions, thoughts, interpretations, body, behavior, consequences, and the events that prompted the emotion in the first place.

Below, choose a situation from the past that caused you intense anxiety or depression, and break it down into the components listed below.

Identify the emotion (label it)	Example: Intense anxiety that I made a fool of myself when I went to the party	
How expressed bodily	Head pounding, stomach tense, back muscles hurt, hands shake, face sad, and eyes tearful	
Thoughts about the emotion	I'm such an idiot. I knew I didn't belong at the party. Why did I go in the first place? I should have stayed home where I'm safe.	
Environmental precipitants	Went to company party. I already feel inadequate at work; why did I feel it would be any different at the party?	
Behavior	At the party was quiet. Didn't say anything. I was visibly anxious. Could not think of anything to say. Probably looked like I wasn't having a good time.	
Afterward	Feel more inadequate and socially stupid. Tell myself I'll never go to a company function again.	

Identify the emotion (label it)	
How expressed bodily	
Thoughts about the emotion	
Environmental precipitants	
Behavior	
Afterward	

Primary and Secondary Emotions

Sometimes the difficulty in identifying a feeling is that it is so complex. It's not simple anxiety, simple sadness, or simple depression that we feel. It is a combination of many different emotions that come to be experienced simultaneously. Most of your initial reactions to events are primary emotions. These are the simple, straightforward emotions about an event that hit you first. You feel simple sadness that someone disappointed you. You feel anxiety that you may fail. You feel fear that someone may reject you. You feel depressed that you lost someone you loved. Most of us handle primary emotions well. This is because you don't question the validity of the emotion itself. You tell yourself that it is natural and normal to feel the way you feel. However, many times a secondary emotional reaction rears its head. A secondary emotion is when you begin to feel something about your feeling itself. For example, many people become depressed that they are depressed. You may feel shame that you feel anxiety. You may feel guilt that you feel angry. The first feeling is the primary emotion, the subsequent feeling (based on the first) is the secondary.

Primary feelings are typically reactions to the external world. Some precipitating event caused you to feel the way you feel. You thus feel justified to have the feeling since you can identify an external, worldly event that has prompted the feeling. You may not accept responsibility for this external event, and thus you feel normal for having the feeling, since you are simply reacting to what happened to you. You can handle that.

Secondary feelings, on the other hand, are not so simple. Secondary feelings are reactions to your reactions. You do feel responsible for the feeling because it is an internal response to an internal event. You see secondary emotions as core representations of your identity, of who you are (which they are not—they are simply reactions to reactions). Secondary feelings turn an emotion into a complex set of reactions, less easily identified, accepted, and resolved. You begin to feel overwhelmed as you begin to react to a series of emotions, each reaction increasing the intensity of the original emotion.

The example below illustrates the difference between a primary and secondary feeling. In the example, a woman has a primary emotion (loneliness that her husband is at work all day and she is at home alone). She rates this feeling, on a scale of 1 to 10 (1 being low and 10 being high-intensity emotion), as a 6. In the second example, the woman has both a

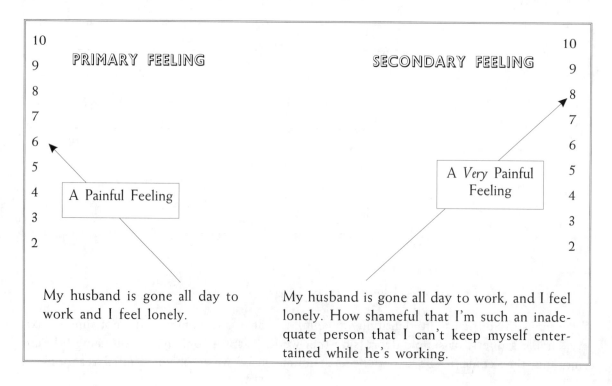

primary and a secondary emotional reaction. She not only feels lonely because she is alone, but also feels shame because she judges her loneliness as a sign of inadequacy. She rates this emotional intensity as an 8. Obviously, it is easier to handle an emotional response that has an intensity of 6 than it is to handle one rated as an 8. With the secondary emotional response, she has turned a painful emotion into a very painful emotion.

Secondary feelings have a powerful influence over your life because they tend to increase the intensity of your emotions. Because of this dynamic, the ability to discriminate primary from secondary emotions provides a powerful coping technique. Although this is not a hard-and-fast rule, primary emotions generally are responses to the external environment and secondary emotions are responses to internal events (your own thoughts, ideas, memories, and anticipations about the future). When you feel a very powerful emotion, ask yourself "What was it that prompted me to feel this way? Is the intensity of my emotional reaction consistent with the intensity of the event that I'm reacting to?" If not, look for secondary emotional responses. You're probably stacking additional emotions on top of your primary feeling.

Let's look at an example. Your wife tells you you're not taking enough responsibility with the children. She says that you let her be the "bad guy" because she generally has to mete out all the discipline. You've developed the habit of leaving punishment to her, as you'd much rather play with the kids in your limited time with them. Your emotional reaction to this confrontation is to feel disregarded for all the work you do, misunderstood about how demanding your job is, and resentful that you're expected to participate in every part of family life *and* earn all of the money for the family. So far, so good. There is a reasonable correspondence between the event that you're reacting to (being confronted with the idea that you're not doing enough) and your consequent feelings of being disregarded, misunderstood, and resentful. However, if your feelings begin to grow over time, turning from slight feelings of being disregarded to feelings of outrage, anger, and speculations about divorce, then you're no longer reacting to the event (your wife's request that you do more disciplining). You're probably having secondary emotional reactions.

Feeling disregarded often brings up, over time or even immediately, intense emotional memories from the past. Many of us felt that our needs didn't matter while we were growing up. We were present in the family, but didn't feel as if our needs were important enough to our parents to influence the course of events. If you felt powerless and unlovable as a child, feeling disregarded as an adult "cues" the set of intense emotions from the past. This is a secondary emotional reaction. If you take the time and attention necessary to tease apart your feelings (those that are responses to the immediate situation, and those that are reactions to the reactions), then you're in a better position to respond to both. Why? Because then you'll be able to respond to your wife's requests and complaints for what they are. You won't punish her with an emotional tantrum that makes her feel as if she can make no requests of you whatsoever. Then, measuring your response to the primary feeling, you can use your feelings as information. You feel disregarded, so you must need additional recognition for what you are doing right around the house. You also may need to distribute your time better, which is what your wife really wants you to do. Then, you can deal with the secondary feelings. You still have feelings of powerlessness and unlovability from your childhood. You can work on activities and processes that make you feel influential and cared about. You can remind yourself that your early childhood feelings are powerful, but you don't need to react to them as if they are ongoing experiences. You acknowledge the feeling, but stop practicing the feeling. Gradually you'll be able to stop reenacting the feeling.

Types of Secondary Emotional Reactions

Though they often feel the same, there are several different kinds of secondary emotions. Take a look at the following list and see if any sound familiar.

1. *Discomfort with your primary emotions.* This occurs when you fail to validate your primary emotions as normal, expectable, reasonable, and even useful sources of information about what is happening to you. For example, if you feel ashamed that you feel needy, depressed, inadequate, or angry, then you have one more feeling (shame) that you have to deal with.

2. *Intense feelings from past events.* Emotional memory is not that different from other forms of memory. When you have an intense emotion, it's stored in memory (you can recall how you felt, on some level associate the emotion with how your body responded to the emotion, and may associate the emotion with what prompted you to have the feeling in the first place). When similar situations occur later, your memory of the previous emotion kicks in. You may or may not be aware of this associational memory, and it may influence your experience of the current situation, typically increasing the intensity. For example, if you dealt with intense fear and anxiety as a child, then simply being uncomfortable or tense now may make the old feelings come back. Why does this happen? You remember the feelings that you've tried so hard to avoid. If you stop avoiding the feeling and be mindful of it without running from it, the old feeling will lose its power and gradually lower in intensity.

3. *Feelings from assumptions you make about your world.* We all make assumptions about the world (what the "rules" are, what comes easily and what comes hard). The assumptions you make can have to do with almost anything: the nature of people, the purpose of government, how groups react to others, the nature of the workforce, or even the purpose of life itself. Some of these assumptions you make are accurate, and some may be inaccurate. Either way, these assumptions may serve to either increase or decrease the intensity of your emotions. If you feel that everyone must approve of you, then each time you anticipate disapproval you'll feel especially lousy. Disapproval never feels good, but if you expect that you should always obtain approval, then what would otherwise be an unpleasant feeling turns into an intolerably strong negative emotion.

4. *Feelings from anticipations about the future.* Anticipation has a powerful role in regulating your responses (both emotional and behavioral) to events. Your anticipation defines your assessment of the outcome of future events. With mixed anxiety and depression, your anticipations may be pessimistic in that you expect that you are helpless and the situations you confront are hopeless. If you expect failure in some form, then obtaining evidence of shortcomings or obstacles to your goals becomes more important and you'll likely have less confidence than when you started.

5. *Feelings evoked about your identity.* If you assume an event says something meaningful about your personality, your worthiness, or your image to the world, then the emotion is likely to be an intense one. For example, if you cry at the loss of a friend and believe that crying means that you're weak, you're likely to start heaping negative secondary emotions like shame and anger on top of that initial sadness.

Let's look at another example. You're invited to a barbecue with friends whom you respect and value. At the barbecue someone suggests that everyone play Trivial Pursuit. You start to feel anxious that you'll look stupid, that your fund of information is deficient, or that your anxiety will prevent you from deploying the facts you do have stored in your head. The anxiety is a primary emotional response to the event (having to play a difficult game). When you are unable to pull up trivia, your anxiety increases. Probably this is a secondary emotional reaction, because you're not just anxious about looking stupid, but also that others will see that you're anxious and are making more of a game than should be made. You're essentially anxious that others will see your anxiety (a secondary emotional reaction of anxiety to a primary emotion of anxiety). The less trivia you are able to produce, the more anxious you become. You're also experiencing anxiety from anticipations about the future. You're anticipating your failure, that others will judge you poorly for taking a game so seriously, and you're anxious that you'll look stupid to people you want to judge you positively. So the primary emotion (anxiety) is present, but so are several secondary emotional responses: anxiety that others will see your anxiety, anxiety that you will look foolish in front of friends, and anxiety that you will lose the respect of your friends.

How can you reduce the secondary emotional responses? From the above list of five types of secondary emotions, you can see clues about prevention and treatment.

Identifying Secondary Emotions

Identifying secondary emotional responses is particularly difficult because they are reactions to reactions, and at times it's difficult to identify the beginning point and the end point. They become so enmeshed that teasing them apart becomes more difficult than unraveling a long electric cord full of knots and twists. A set of strategic questions to begin the untangling follows.

1. Is your feeling a direct reaction to something that just happened? If yes, then it probably is a primary emotional reaction.

2. Is the feeling growing in intensity over time? If yes, then it probably is a secondary emotional reaction. (Or you could be practicing the feeling, where you express the feeling over and over, and each time you express it the feeling intensity increases.)

3. Do you have this feeling more frequently than events prompting the feeling? If yes, then you're probably piling secondary emotional reactions on top of primary emotions.

4. When the event prompting your emotions recedes but your emotions don't recede soon thereafter, then you're probably piling secondary emotional reactions on top of primary emotions.

5. When your feelings drag on, interfering with your ability to concentrate and be affected by new and different experiences, you're probably dealing with secondary emotional reactions.

6. When your feelings are complex and ambiguous, with intense and different feelings occurring simultaneously, then you're probably dealing with secondary emotional processes.

Discomfort with Your Primary Emotions

When feeling discomfort with your primary emotion, first notice your immediate reaction. Acknowledge the judgment of the emotion by saying something like the following to yourself:

"I immediately noticed that I became anxious when he asked me to say a few words to the group. Okay, I'm anxious and tense. I'm telling myself that it's not acceptable to feel anxiety, that somehow I'm inadequate because I feel tense. But anxiety is a natural reaction to being put on the spot like this. I feel my jaw muscles tightening, as well as the muscles in my upper back. My thoughts are filled with anticipation of failure. It's okay to feel fear. It's how I manage the fear that really counts. This fear will not destroy me. I'm aware of the fear and allow myself to feel it for just a moment, then refocus on my task."

Below, I've broken this process down into seven steps. Obviously, the order in which you engage in the seven steps is not nearly as important as engaging in as many of the steps as you can, rapidly and confidently. Your experience may be more back and forth between the steps, with more reassurance thrown in between steps to increase your soothing:

"I'm not accepting that it is okay to feel anxiety. Allow myself to accept the anxiety. Watch the anxiety and identify its components: I feel it in my jaw muscle, upper back, and in my thoughts. Watch the anxiety for a few seconds, and accept it for what it is. The judgment I'm making is that I should not be fearful, ever. Everyone feels fear. It's okay to feel fear, but I blow things out of proportion and react to my fear with fear. I can defeat this. I'm watching my anxiety and feeling it in my body and my thoughts. I've felt this way before, and nothing really happened that was all that bad. I'm doing fine at this. I'm going to stay with my fear for just a minute, and allow it to recede on its own rather than try to force it away. I can do this. Anxiety is not such an intolerable thing. I feel my jaw muscle become more comfortable already. Anxiety is not the end of the world. By watching my emotions rather than running from them, they lose their power. This is not so bad. My feelings are not my enemy, and I'm not going to treat them as if they are."

When you're faced with discomfort over your primary emotions, take these steps:

1. Notice your immediate emotional reaction to the event.

2. Acknowledge the emotion.

3. Identify how you're judging the primary emotion.

4. Dispute that judgment.

5. Be mindful of the emotion (watch it).

6. Reassure yourself that you can tolerate the primary emotion.

7. Stay with (tolerate) the primary emotion for just a while.

Below, perform the mindfulness acceptance analysis on a situation that causes you anxiety or depression. Perform the analysis, as in the example, like you are coaching yourself to accept something that is painful but inevitable and tolerable and that will eventually go away if you accept it for this moment. Remind yourself that all emotions, as well as all situations, are temporary. Nothing is permanent.

Acknowledge the emotion	Example: I'm feeling ashamed that I feel vulnerable.	
Identify the judgment	I don't feel it is acceptable to be vulnerable. I should always be strong and capable.	
Dispute the judgment	Vulnerability is a part of life. While I don't like it, it is not an experience that I must feel shame about.	
Be mindful of the emotion	I feel this shame. It's about inadequacy and not being good enough. I'm paying attention to this feeling of shame.	
Reassure (soothe) yourself	I can take this shame. It won't destroy me, I just don't like it. I can put up with it forever, if I have to—but I don't have to put up with it forever. I will put up with it for a few moments.	
Tolerate the emotion	I experience this shame and feel its full intensity. I tolerate it for just this moment.	

Acknowledge the emotion	
Identify the judgment	
Dispute the judgment	
Be mindful of the emotion	
Reassure (soothe) yourself	
Tolerate the emotion	

Intense Feelings from Past Events

Everyone has issues from the past, unresolved conflicts or those poor compromises between competing and contradictory needs we discussed in earlier chapters. It is not a sign of mental illness that current (primary) feelings trigger other feelings. In fact, it's predictable according to the emotion theory I outlined previously. So, knowing that feelings from the past can interfere with your ability to use your primary feelings as useful sources of information about how to respond to current situations, you can use the four stages of problem solving outlined here. First (and you can see this principle being broadly applied in the dialectical framework of emotional recovery), you must acknowledge the emotions. You notice them, give them labels or words, and try not to repress or deny their existence. You don't engage in avoidance. Instead, you tease apart the emotions. You identify the primary emotion. What is it that you are reacting to in this moment? What prompted this feeling? Feelings don't come out of nowhere. They are prompted by something, either internal or external.

1. Acknowledge the emotions you are feeling. Give them labels.

2. Differentiate the primary from the secondary emotion.

3. Outline your plan to respond to the primary emotion only, in this moment.

4. Set aside a time later that you can be mindful of the secondary emotional reaction when there is no external prompt.

Below, identify a situation where feelings from past significant events seem to reoccur. If you find that there are so many such situations that it's difficult for you to choose just one, don't panic. You can perform this exercise again in the practice sheets provided at the end of this book. If you are having difficulty identifying any such situations, but you find that your reactions to current events are out of proportion to the seriousness of those events, you may wish to work with a psychologist as a coach to perform this task.

Identify the emotions	Example: I'm upset that my friend is ignoring me. I'm feeling lonely, unworthy, and angry that I'm always the person who has to initiate in relationships.	_____ _____ _____ _____ _____ _____
Differentiate primary from secondary emotions	My primary feeling is being lonely that my friend is not calling me or initiating social plans with me. My secondary emotions are the feelings of anger and unworthiness because I feel that others have done this to me in the past.	_____ _____ _____ _____ _____ _____ _____ _____
My plan to deal with the primary emotion	I'm not going to take my anger out on my friend. It is not his fault that others have been passive in my past social relationships. I'm going to react only to the feeling of being lonely by picking up the phone and calling my friend.	_____ _____ _____ _____ _____ _____ _____
My plan to deal with the secondary emotion	My resentment and anger that I'm always setting up social encounters is something I'll be better prepared to handle when I'm not actively feeling lonely. I'll take a look at these resentful and angry feelings when I'm not feeling so alone.	_____ _____ _____ _____ _____ _____ _____

Identify the emotions	
Differentiate primary from secondary emotions	
My plan to deal with the primary emotion	
My plan to deal with the secondary emotion	

Feelings from Assumptions

Practicing different assumptions about the world can be quite difficult, because our assumptions about the world tend to be automatic and thus not easily recognized. Assumptions tend to be hidden, in that you think these things unconsciously and without even knowing that you're doing it. With mixed anxiety and depression, common assumptions are that the world is a risky and scary place, that you're likely to fail in accomplishing your goals, that others are judgmental and critical of your every move, that you're being watched and examined closely by others, and, perhaps most destructively to your ability to function well in the world, that your symptoms are observable and also shameful. Question these assumptions. What if they are not true?

1. Identify the emotion you are feeling.

2. Identify the assumptions upon which these feelings are based.

3. Question how accurate, intense, or consequential the assumption is.

4. Practice different assumptions, and notice changes in your emotions.

Practice questioning your assumptions below.

Identify the emotion	Example: I'm feeling lonely.	
Assumptions	I should not have to be the person who always makes the phone calls, identifies social activities, makes the plans, and invites the guests.	
Question your assumptions	It doesn't mean that I'm liked less because I'm the organizer, it just means I do all of the work.	
Practice different assumption and notice emotion changes	I'm just better at maintaining friendships, at recognizing my social needs, and at taking action to meet my needs. That is healthy and means I'm effective and strategic. I don't have to let my loneliness last a long time. I feel a little better about myself.	

Identify the emotion	
Assumptions	
Question your assumptions	
Practice different assumption and notice emotion changes	

Feelings from Anticipations about the Future

Anticipation about the future is a close cousin of assumptions you make about the world. The difference is only that you do not assume this anticipation is about all aspects of the world, just about this one situation. It is not as pervasive or deep, but in the particular situation you're confronting it increases your anxiety or depression. Identify such a situation from your life below, and attempt to practice a different anticipation. If you believed this new anticipation (which might take some practice over time), how would your feelings change? Notice these changes.

1. Identify the emotion.

2. Identify the anticipation.

3. Question how accurate, intense, or consequential the anticipation is.

4. Practice a different anticipation, and notice changes in your emotions.

Identify the emotion	Example: Fear that I'll be seen as stupid.	_____ _____ _____ _____
Anticipation	If I don't pass the bar exam the first time, everyone will know and think that I'm not smart enough to be an attorney.	_____ _____ _____ _____ _____ _____ _____ _____
Question your anticipation	People won't know when I plan to take the test unless I tell them. Anyway, no one cares as much about whether I pass as I do, so I just need to prepare as best I can and reduce my anxiety.	_____ _____ _____ _____ _____ _____ _____
Practice a different anticipation and notice emotion changes	What I think and feel is more important than what others think and feel. Trying to please others just takes my mind off the real task of study and preparation. Having a certain amount of test anxiety is normal, I just need to manage the anxiety. I'm now paying more attention to the task at hand and less to anticipatory feelings. And that feels better.	_____ _____ _____ _____ _____ _____ _____ _____

Identify the emotion	
Anticipation	
Question your anticipation	
Practice a different anticipation and notice emotion changes	

Feelings Evoked about Your Identity

As I mentioned in chapter 4, when your feelings become intermixed with your perception of self, you tend to overvalue the function and purpose of your emotions. Emotions are senses, data input, not anchors that define who we are and how others will always perceive us. When you become aware that you're mixing your identification or awareness of an emotion with your basic sense of identification (who you are and how others will invariably perceive you), engage in the five-step process below:

1. Identify the emotion.

2. Identify what you are saying to yourself about your personality, your identity, or what you're saying to yourself about core elements of yourself.

3. Question how essential, permanent, consequential, or true the identity statements are.

4. Practice identity statements that are more consistent with what you want.

5. Identify the feelings you would have with greater practice of the desired identity elements.

In the exercise below you have the opportunity to work with aspects of yourself that really generate substantial anxiety and depressed mood. In this exercise you choose to work with aspects of your thinking and feeling that have to do with your self-image and self-esteem. Attempt to pick something that makes you question yourself in this way.

Identify the emotion	Example: Self-loathing	_____ _____ _____ _____
Personality or identity statements I'm making	I'm a habitual liar. I can't seem to tell the truth to save my life. I want to believe my lies so badly.	_____ _____ _____ _____ _____
Question these statements	I do lie frequently. I so badly want other people's approval and acceptance. However, this is not a personality thing. It's a behavior—the behavior of telling lies. I can change my behavior. I was not born with a "lie gene" that makes me this way. I have control over this behavior.	_____ _____ _____ _____ _____ _____
Practice desired identity statements	I want to see myself as a person who is connected and compassionate to other people and who encourages these interpersonal connections by being honest and trustworthy. I want to like myself and my behavior. I want to trust in myself.	_____ _____ _____ _____ _____ _____ _____
Identify feelings I'll have with practice	As I tell the truth more often, I'll feel good about myself. There is nothing wrong with wanting others to like me, but I have to like myself first. When I feel the impulse to lie, I'm going to keep my mouth shut and say over and over to myself, "I am a trustworthy person. I'm honest with myself. I like me."	_____ _____ _____ _____ _____ _____

Identify the emotion	_____ _____ _____
Personality or identity statements I'm making	_____ _____ _____ _____ _____
Question these statements	_____ _____ _____ _____ _____ _____ _____
Practice desired identity statements	_____ _____ _____ _____ _____ _____
Identify feelings I'll have with practice	_____ _____ _____ _____ _____

Dealing with primary and secondary emotions, being mindful of your emotions (both the desired ones and the aversive ones), and engaging in coping strategies can go a long way toward increasing your ability to manage your emotions. Emotion theory tells us that the environment can also have a powerful influential effect on your experience of the moment, so we now turn to increasing positive emotional events.

Increasing Positive Emotional Experiences

Emotion regulation skills assume that you're a responsive person. You respond to what is going on around you, as well as what's going on inside of you. When you have chronic negative feelings, especially anxiety and depression, there is a strong tendency to stop engaging in positive emotional events. You create an external world that is in accord with your internal world. This is obviously unhealthy, since it tends to feed and nurture even more negative feelings. What you end up doing is incubating negative emotions. What you want to do instead is to incubate positive feelings. The inertia is against this, so you have to force or prompt yourself to behave differently, to engage in uplifting experiences even though you do not feel like doing it.

The mistake many of us make is that we wait until we feel like doing something enjoyable. We assume that the mood or feeling should precede the behavior, that once we feel good, then we will be able to have fun. While there is truth to this approach (in that positive moods influence our level of appreciation for events), there is also truth to the reverse proposition. If you engage in enjoyable activities, then your mood will be lifted. Intentionally engaging in positive events with the precise goal of changing your mood can be a powerful coping strategy.

People frequently place artificial barriers in the way of engaging in positive experiences when they feel chronic anxiety and depression. I call these "artificial" because they are created by the person, typically unconsciously, rather than being unalterable aspects of life.

Beliefs That Prevent Engagement in Positive Experiences

"Why should I do anything? I'll just feel bad again afterward."

"I've tried doing stuff I used to like. It just doesn't feel the same as it used to."

"I can't think of anything fun to do."

"I don't have the energy. I would just go through the motions, and that's no fun."

The belief that enjoyable activities produce only time-limited uplifting feelings really begs the question regarding emotion regulation. Of course, *all* feelings are transitory. No feeling lasts forever—nor would you want it to. You want your emotions to be sensitive and responsive to the environment. If you wait until a guarantee of permanence is given, you will be behaviorally paralyzed. The goal is to build more enduring positive emotions, but you have to start somewhere. And you start by creating even short-lived positive emotions. By creating even five minutes of amusement, humor, joy, interest, laughter, or pleasure, you are less likely to assume that your negative feelings are chronic and unalterable. By experiencing variability in your emotions, you are creating a new inertia in a more beneficial direction.

When you start on an enjoyable activity with a sour disposition, this obviously will affect your level of enjoyment. To assume that you will have exactly the same resulting emotion this time as you did before will result in disappointment. So what you need to say to yourself is that you're not trying to produce the exact same level of enjoyment as you experienced previously, or that you assume others who engage in the activity experience, but that you want to experience *some* joy.

Try to see engaging in pleasant activities as an act of emotional creation. Like cooking or gardening, you're setting the stage for later developments (good-tasting foods or a beautiful flower display). Don't look at the activity as the sole strategy for feeling good. It is one among many things that you can do to change your mood.

The belief that "I'm just going through the motions" is probably the most difficult with which to deal, and it gets at the heart of being mindful. If you are just going through the motions, then you're not participating in the activity mindfully. This destructive belief can be undermined by practicing mindfulness while engaging in the activity.

Guidelines for Increasing Positive Emotional Experiences

1. Pay attention to the activity. Be mindful. Watch each element of what is going on like you have never experienced it before.

2. Be engaged. Actively participate. Let other thoughts and ideas that are not related to what you are doing fade away. Focus your energy and concentration on the enjoyable moment.

3. Pay attention to the now. Don't think about when it will end or how long it will last.

4. Pay attention to the feelings in the moment. Don't compare them to previous feelings, anticipated feelings, or ideas about how others might feel when they are engaged in the activity.

5. Don't wait for a particular level of satisfaction or enjoyment to appear before you further engage in the activity. Be mindful of the now.

Pleasant Events Schedule

Can't think of anything fun, amusing, or interesting to do? The following list is a modified version of one created by Douglas J. MacPhillamy and Peter M. Lewinsohn in 1981. It also might prompt you to notice things that have already happened, that you fail to be mindful of, that could bring amusement if you let them.

1. Being in the country
2. Wearing expensive or formal clothes
3. Making contributions to religious, charitable, or other groups
4. Talking about sports
5. Meeting someone new of the same sex
6. Taking tests when well prepared
7. Going to a rock concert
8. Playing baseball or softball
9. Planning trips or vacations
10. Buying things for myself
11. Being at the beach
12. Doing art work (painting, sculpture, drawing, movie-making, etc.)
13. Rock climbing or mountaineering
14. Reading the Scriptures or other sacred works
15. Playing golf
16. Taking part in military activities
17. Re-arranging or redecorating my room or house
18. Going naked
19. Going to a sports event
20. Reading a "How to Do It" book or article
21. Going to the races (horse, car, boat, etc.)
22. Reading stories, novels, poems, or plays
23. Going to a bar, tavern, club, etc.
24. Going to lectures or hearing speakers
25. Driving skillfully
26. Breathing clean air
27. Thinking up or arranging songs or music
28. Having an unusual beverage
29. Saying something clearly

30. Boating (canoeing, kayaking, motorboating, sailing, etc.)
31. Pleasing my parents
32. Restoring antiques, refinishing furniture, etc.
33. Watching TV
34. Talking to myself
35. Camping
36. Working in politics
37. Working on machines (cars, bikes, motorcycles, tractors, etc.)
38. Thinking about something good in the future
39. Playing cards
40. Completing a difficult task
41. Laughing
42. Solving a problem, puzzle, crossword, etc.
43. Shaving
44. Having lunch with friends or associates
45. Being at weddings, baptisms, confirmations, etc.
46. Using mouthwash mindfully
47. Playing tennis
48. Taking a shower
49. Driving long distances
50. Woodworking, carpentry
51. Writing stories, novels, plays, or poetry
52. Being with animals
53. Riding in an airplane
54. Exploring (hiking away from known routes, going somewhere new)
55. Having a frank and open conversation
56. Singing in a group
57. Thinking about myself or my problems
58. Working on my job
59. Going to a party
60. Going to church functions (socials, classes, bazaars, etc.)
61. Speaking a foreign language

62. Going to service, civic, or social club meetings
63. Going to a business meeting or convention
64. Being in a sporty or expensive car
65. Playing a musical instrument
66. Making snacks
67. Snow skiing
68. Being helped
69. Wearing informal clothes
70. Combing or brushing my hair
71. Acting
72. Taking a nap
73. Being with friends
74. Canning, freezing, making preserves, etc.
75. Driving on the scenic route, mindful of what you normally don't see
76. Solving a personal problem
77. Being in a city
78. Taking a bath
79. Singing to myself
80. Making food or crafts to sell or give away
81. Playing pool or billiards
82. Being with my grandchildren
83. Playing chess or checkers
84. Doing craft work (pottery, jewelry, leather, beads, weaving, etc.)
85. Putting on new makeup
86. Wearing a new perfume or cologne
87. Fixing my hair differently
88. Designing or drafting
89. Visiting people who are sick, shut in, or in trouble
90. Cheering, rooting
91. Bowling
92. Being popular at a gathering
93. Watching wild animals
94. Having an original idea

95. Gardening, landscaping, or doing yard work
96. Shopping
97. Reading essays or technical, academic, or professional literature
98. Wearing new clothes
99. Dancing
100. Sitting in the sun
101. Riding a motorcycle
102. Just sitting and thinking
103. Going to an elegant cocktail lounge
104. Seeing good things happen to my family or friends
105. Going to a fair, carnival, circus, zoo, or amusement park
106. Talking about philosophy or religion
107. Gambling
108. Planning or organizing something
109. Smoking a cigar
110. Preparing an exotic meal
111. Listening to the sounds of nature
112. Dating, courting, etc.
113. Having a lively talk
114. Racing in a car, motorcycle, boat, etc.
115. Listening to the radio
116. Having friends come to visit
117. Playing in a sporting competition
118. Introducing people who I think would like each other
119. Giving gifts
120. Going to school or government meetings, court sessions, etc.
121. Getting massages or backrubs
122. Getting letters, cards, or notes
123. Watching the sky, clouds, or a storm

124. Going on outings (to the park, a picnic, or a barbecue, etc.)
125. Playing basketball
126. Buying something for my family
127. Photography
128. Giving a speech or lecture
129. Reading maps
130. Gathering natural objects (wild foods or fruit, rocks, driftwood, etc.)
131. Working on my finances
132. Wearing clean clothes
133. Making a major purchase or investment (car, appliance, house, stocks, etc.)
134. Helping someone
135. Being in the mountains
136. Working on job advancement (being promoted, given a raise, or offered a better job, accepted into a better school, etc.)
137. Hearing jokes
138. Winning a bet
139. Talking about my children or grandchildren
140. Meeting someone new of the opposite sex
141. Going to a revival or crusade
142. Talking about my health
143. Seeing beautiful scenery
144. Eating good meals
145. Improving my health (having my teeth cleaned, getting new glasses, changing my diet, etc.)
146. Being downtown
147. Wrestling or boxing
148. Hunting or shooting
149. Playing in a musical group
150. Hiking
151. Going to a museum or exhibit

152. Writing papers, essays, articles, reports, memos, etc.
153. Doing a job well
154. Having spare time
155. Fishing
156. Loaning something
157. Being noticed as sexually attractive
158. Pleasing employers, teachers, etc.
159. Counseling someone
160. Going to a health club, sauna bath, etc.
161. Having someone remember what I previously said
162. Learning to do something new
163. Going to a "Drive-in" (Dairy Queen, MacDonald's, etc.)
164. Complimenting or praising someone
165. Thinking about people I like
166. Joining a book club
167. Being nice to someone who was mean to me
168. Being with my parents
169. Horseback riding
170. Protesting social, political, or environmental conditions
171. Talking on the telephone
172. Having daydreams
173. Kicking leaves, sand, pebbles, etc.
174. Playing lawn sports (badminton, croquet, shuffleboard, horseshoes, etc.)
175. Going to school reunions, alumni meetings, etc.
176. Seeing famous people
177. Going to the movies
178. Kissing
179. Being alone
180. Budgeting my time

181. Cooking meals
182. Being praised by people I admire
183. Impressing a superior
184. Feeling the presence of the Lord in my life
185. Doing a project in my own way
186. Doing "odd jobs" around the house
187. Crying for myself on purpose
188. Being told I am needed
189. Being at a family reunion or get-together
190. Giving a party or get-together
191. Washing my hair
192. Coaching someone
193. Going to a restaurant
194. Seeing or smelling a flower or plant
195. Being invited out
196. Receiving honors (civic, military, etc.)
197. Using a different aftershave
198. Having someone agree with me
199. Reminiscing, talking about old times
200. Getting up early in the morning
201. Having peace and quiet
202. Doing experiments or other scientific work
203. Visiting friends
204. Writing in a diary
205. Playing football
206. Being counseled
207. Saying prayers
208. Giving massages or backrubs
209. Meditating or doing yoga
210. Seeing a fight
211. Doing favors for people
212. Talking with people on the job or in class

213. Being relaxed
214. Being asked for my help or advice
215. Thinking about other people's problems
216. Playing board games (Monopoly, Scrabble, etc.)
217. Sleeping soundly at night
218. Doing heavy outdoor work (cutting or chopping wood, clearing land, farm work, etc.)
219. Reading the newspaper
220. Doing something "out of character"
221. Snowmobiling or dune-buggy riding
222. Being in a body-awareness, sensitivity, encounter therapy, or "rap" group
223. Dreaming at night
224. Playing ping pong
225. Brushing my teeth
226. Swimming
227. Standing up for what I believe
228. Running, jogging, or doing gymnastic, fitness, or field exercises
229. Walking barefoot
230. Playing Frisbee or catch
231. Doing housework or laundry; cleaning things
232. Being with my soul mate
233. Listening to music
234. Arguing
235. Knitting, crocheting, embroidery, or fancy needlework
236. Petting, necking
237. Amusing people
238. Talking about sex
239. Going to a barber or beautician
240. Having house guests
241. Being with someone I love

242. Reading magazines
243. Sleeping late
244. Starting a new project
245. Giving in when I don't want to
246. Having sex
247. Going to the library
248. Playing soccer, rugby, hockey, lacrosse, etc.
249. Preparing a new or special food
250. Bird watching
251. Shopping
252. Watching people
253. Building or watching a fire
254. Winning an argument
255. Selling or trading something
256. Finishing a project or task
257. Confessing or apologizing
258. Repairing things
259. Working with others as a team
260. Bicycling
261. Telling people what to do
262. Being with happy people
263. Playing party games
264. Writing letters, cards, or notes
265. Talking about politics or public affairs
266. Asking for help or advice
267. Going to banquets, luncheons, potlucks, etc.
268. Talking about my hobby or special interest
269. Watching attractive women or men
270. Smiling at people
271. Playing in sand, a stream, the grass, etc.
272. Being with my husband or wife
273. Having people show interest in what I have said
274. Going on field trips, nature walks, etc.

275. Expressing my love to someone
276. Slowly eating my favorite candy bar
277. Caring for house plants
278. Having coffee, tea, a coke, etc., with friends
279. Taking a walk
280. Collecting things
281. Playing handball, paddleball, squash, etc.
282. Sewing
283. Remembering a departed friend or loved one, visiting the cemetery
284. Doing things with children
285. Beachcombing
286. Being complimented or told I have done well
287. Being told I am loved
288. Eating snacks
289. Staying up late
290. Having family members or friends do something that makes me proud of them
291. Being with my children
292. Going to auctions, garage sales, etc.
293. Thinking about an interesting question
294. Doing volunteer work; working on community service projects
295. Water skiing, surfing, scuba diving
296. Receiving money
297. Defending or protecting someone; stopping fraud or abuse
298. Hearing a good sermon
299. Winning a competition
300. Making a new friend
301. Talking about my job or school
302. Reading cartoons, comic strips, or comic books
303. Borrowing something
304. Traveling with a group
305. Seeing old friends
306. Teaching someone
307. Using my strength
308. Traveling
309. Going to office parties or departmental get-togethers
310. Attending a concert, opera, or ballet
311. Playing with pets
312. Going to a play
313. Looking at the stars or moon
314. Being coached
315. Making a scrapbook
316. Working on my photograph album
317. Going to a coffeehouse/bookstore
318. Surfing the Internet
319. Using programs that came with my computer I've never used
320. Writing a short story
321. Renting a videotape
322. Going to a store that sells things I've never previously had interest in
323. Test drive a car I know I can't afford, just for the experience
324. Go house hunting, even when I'm not in the market
325. Wear frilly undergarments to work
326. Get rid of junk I've collected but don't enjoy any longer
327. Browse a pawn shop
328. Watch the history station, or another channel I never view
329. Get on the Internet and research a culture I know little about
330. Design my dream home, even if I know I'm not interested in building
331. Go to a pet store
332. Plan an extravagant vacation, even if I know I'll never take it
333. Imagine being someone else I admire
334. Imagine being an astronaut exploring other worlds
335. Flirting with someone
336. Visit a chat room
337. Go to a cosmetic counter and smell fragrances
338. Go to an electronics store and look at gadgets
339. Go to a local park and watch small children play
340. Watch a provocative documentary
341. Read literature reviews
342. Read a book on social graces and manners
343. Become a pen pal to someone in prison
344. Play a video game
345. Write a letter to someone you have not seen in years

Mindfulness and Positive Experiences

One of the most difficult aspects of emotion regulation is allowing yourself to experience uplifting or pleasant emotions when your "baseline" emotion has been a painful one. Remember our list of criteria presented early in the book for what dialectical behavior therapy is designed to treat: high emotional arousal, in other words feeling intensely, with slow return to emotional baseline (an emotional level of intensity that is being jacked up by ruminating on events that produce emotional pain or engaging in behavioral or mental processes that allow emotional pain to linger). It is mindfulness of our current primary emotions with strategic behavior designed to increase positive experiences (consciously producing pleasant experiences to attend to) that can break the recurring emotional suffering cycle.

What frequently happens is that you have a series of emotionally painful experiences, predicting high emotional arousal. As you saw in our initial examples, these experiences can be a few traumatic experiences or "small" painful experiences occurring infrequently but consistently. Since you have not developed effective psychological coping skills to deal with the depression and anxiety, you begin to engage either in avoidance of your emotions (which increases anxiety and fear along with the pain) or rumination on your emotions (which increases depression, shame, and self-loathing). The cycle of emotional suffering is thus that you attend to only painful affect or engage only in anticipatory escape from your emotions. The cycle can only be broken by changing one or both of these two processes (stop trying to escape and start trying to attend to pleasant emotions).

Trying to stop avoiding your emotions, what psychologists call *escape conditioning*, can be a difficult process. Once you begin running away from something frightening, it can take powerful courage to stop running, turn around, and face the thing that you run from. Moreover, since in this case what you are actually trying to escape is your own emotion, it is a slippery slope indeed. Each time you engage in the escape, avoid your emotions, and the anxiety decreases somewhat, the avoidance response becomes stronger because it was somewhat successful in reducing your fear. It's a totally unconscious process—you don't realize at the time what you're doing, and you don't plan to do it. Just like a phobia gets stronger each time you move away from or avoid the feared object, so too it is with "emotional phobias," where you become so fearful of your fear, depression, anxiety, shame, anger, or guilt that you will do whatever necessary to avoid experiencing it. You develop the habit or strategy of specifically *not* paying attention to your current primary emotion, and instead have both your moods and your behavior regulated by the secondary emotional experiences (typically fear and depression) that are at the center of the avoidance and escape tactics you're now trying to undo.

So, being mindful of your current pleasant experiences can take conscious effort, probably will not feel natural, and in fact may feel quite awkward in the beginning. It will go against the grain of the attentional strategies you have habitually been using. (That is why, in the previous mindfulness chapter, I suggest you start with simple tactual, olfactory, and auditory experiences and slowly move toward more complex emotional experiences.)

Mindfulness as a technique is specifically designed to encourage attention to the moment. While being mindful of positive experiences, what you're attending to is happening *now*. You are not thinking about the past or anticipating the future. Even though your underlying emotion may be sadness or fear, you pay attention to the event that you are engaging in. Slowly, by being mindful, your underlying emotion will shift from the secondary emotions you were feeling to the new primary emotion based on the experience of the moment.

What to Do

Follow these steps to help you increase your mindfulness of pleasant experience:

1. Choose a positive experience to engage in, and do it even if you are not in the mood or anticipate that it won't be the same as what you want.

2. Be mindful of the current event. Be in the now. What is happening in the environment? What are the sounds, sights, and tactual sensations going on resulting from what you're doing now?

3. If you find yourself beginning to attend to something else (thoughts not based on your current experience, memories from the past, your underlying mood that is unrelated to what you are doing now), gently refocus on your attention to the moment.

4. Don't judge your emotion. Don't compare it to the past or to what you want it to be. Just pay attention to it.

5. Constantly bring yourself back to the environment, to what you are doing.

6. Don't be serious, be attentive. It doesn't have to be hard or effortful; you just need to pay attention.

7. Finally, allow yourself to be affected by the experience. The resulting feeling need not be powerful, strong, persistent, or meaningful. It just needs to exist. Allow yourself to have emotions based upon what you're doing now. Respond emotionally. You don't need to act on the emotion, to make any decisions, or to engage in any problem solving. Just allow your feelings to be influenced by what you experience.

8. Afterward, don't judge your emotions. Just identify them. Give labels to the emotions you created by the experience. Be mindful of the emotions and sensations you experienced by paying attention to the now.

Mindfulness to Negative Emotions

Early on we saw how many of life's emotional difficulties relate to conflicts between irreconcilable emotional demands, and that emotional health involves making compromises between these competing demands. It should be little surprise then that much of dialectical behavior therapy involves seemingly contradictory interventions, as the intervention is designed to change elements of conflict at both ends of the dialectical pole. Mindfulness to positive experience involves reducing avoidance in general and reducing secondary emotional processes. On the other hand, mindfulness to negative emotions involves increasing attention to negative emotional processes. While in the previous exercise you attempt to pay attention to something different, to produce a new emotion, in this exercise you attempt to do the reverse: pay attention to the painful feeling and, paradoxically, observe the pain itself decrease.

Dialectical behavior therapy thus involves interventions both to change emotions through new emotional experiences and to directly confront emotional pain in order to diminish it. We want to move away from avoidance of emotions on two fronts: to increasingly be sensitive to experience that produces emotions and to increasingly experience present emotions that inappropriately linger. By doing both, by making emotions more responsive and by making lingering emotions less extensive, we are able to return emotions to their rightful place as sources of information that allow us to adapt to changing life demands.

Few rational people want to experience pain. We all want to feel good. However, many of us take the pleasure principle too far. You want to feel good all the time, to never feel pain. Unfortunately, life (even the good life) is not so forgiving. Pain is part of life. In fact, pain encourages you to enjoy life and to appreciate joy even more. Fundamentally, pain is unavoidable, so you need to accept it. By accepting your emotional pain, you don't prolong it. It comes, you experience it, and it leaves. It is the escape and avoidance responses, the attempts to avoid experiencing it at all, that make it linger.

Being mindful of your emotional pain is thus a strategy that allows you to reduce the pain. By reducing the fear that surrounds negative experience, the intensity of the pain is slowly but predictably reduced. Mindfulness accomplishes a number of objectives:

⋄ It reduces emotional anticipatory processes (fear and anxiety).

⋄ It increases your sense of mastery and competence over your emotions.

⋄ It increases your confidence that emotions are useful and necessary parts of life.

⋄ It allows you to more fully experience all of life, without unnecessarily and artificially attempting to be blind to the meaning that inheres in loss and disappointment.

⋄ It makes you more responsive and responsible to changing life events.

⋄ It reduces the lingering effect of negative emotions (emotions become responsive to painful events, but leave when new positive experiences occur and positive emotions replace painful ones).

Thus, while it is rational and normal to want to not feel bad, you engage in the following exercises because you understand the greater, long-term good that will occur in your life. You do it even though it is hard, and even though you really don't want to do it.

What to Do

Here are the steps to take to increase your mindfulness to painful emotions. Try to remember that, though these steps may feel uncomfortable at first, they will help you decrease the unnecessary negative emotional reactions you've learned.

1. Pay attention to your emotions, even when they feel bad. Pay attention mindfully. Don't do two things at once. Watch your emotions as if you had never before experienced them. How is each emotion expressed? Is it in your body (can you feel it in the pit of your stomach, in your muscle tension, pressure on your chest, feeling hot or cold)? Is it filled with thoughts (interpretations, assumptions, appraisals, judgments)? Does it make you feel like doing something (an action or urge to attack someone, run away, hide, stomp your feet, or scream)?

2. Stick with the emotion, paying determined attention to it, even when you're sick of it and wish it was not there. Stick with observation of the emotion for at least three

minutes, even after you think you have observed all of the possible components of the emotion.

3. Don't block the emotion, suppress it, grow or intensify it, or attempt to push it away. Don't change the emotion (by attempting to either shrink the emotion or amplify it). Just watch it.

4. Attempt to identify if there is more than one emotion occurring. Attempt to tease apart primary from secondary emotions. Pay attention to the primary emotion and let the secondary emotion be less attended to. Visualize, pretending that the two emotions are separate visual entities. Close your eyes and see the primary emotion as a bright white glow in the distance, and the secondary emotion as a dull brown glow in the distance. Pay attention to the primary emotion, and let the secondary emotion be in the far distance.

5. After three to four minutes, if you have not found the primary emotion reducing in intensity on its own without your effortful suppression, then begin to experience the primary emotion as a wave. Imagine or pretend that the essence of your emotion is like the ocean's waves. They come toward you powerfully, then after cresting they recede and actually move away from you. Experience the emotion coming and going, being close and far away. If the emotion is particularly powerful and you can't easily make it recede, try shifting your imagination from the emotion to a pleasant scene. Take ten seconds to view the emotion, then concentrate for twenty seconds on a vision of being at an expensive resort by a beautiful swimming pool, with the sun warming your body and a gentle, cool breeze bringing contrasting temperatures. Allow yourself to feel the relaxation that accompanies the pleasant vision, then return to the experience of your painful emotion. Go back and forth between the two until the intensity of the emotional pain is reduced.

What you are trying to do in this exercise is called *counterconditioning*. Through experience we have learned that we can avoid negative emotions by avoidance and escape. You have conditioned yourself. The above exercise, if repeated frequently enough, will countercondition (undo that conditioning). It will undo the connections or pathways that create the urgency to escape or avoid your emotions. By engaging in the above exercise over time, the fear, sense of urgency, action urges, and shame surrounding your emotions will dissipate—leaving only the primary emotion. Obviously it is easier to deal with one (even intense) emotion than it is to deal with a complex set of emotions that have been intertwined together through conditioning.

Taking Opposite Action

Since our feelings are always right, many of us feel compelled to act on our emotions. If you're depressed, you feel entitled to stay home from work, pull the covers over your head, and wallow in your depression. After all, that's what you feel like doing, right? If you're angry at someone, you feel justified in calling them up and telling them off. A few insults traded back and forth make you feel even more vindicated that your anger was justified in the first place. If you are fearful, you feel it's only logical that you avoid that which you fear. Why date men if you know because of your relationship with your father that you will only feel controlled and ridiculed by them? The tendency to act in accord with your emotions is powerful.

But, as we saw previously, even though the emotions you have are right, you frequently don't like them. You don't like that you feel depressed, so acting in a way that encourages the depression to grow is counterproductive. While anger has many beneficial roles in life, anger can also become cancerous. The more you express your anger, the more you push others away from you (reducing intimacy and a sense of safety with others, and creating reciprocal animosity where others wish to hurt you in return). Fear and shame are the most pernicious, since they tend to grow like weeds and spoil other venues that otherwise could provide joy in your life.

The primary strategy in emotion regulation skills is thus to be strategic in deciding when to act on your emotions, when to do nothing, and when to do the opposite to what your emotion propels you to do. You separate out your feeling from your behavior. They are two different things. Accept the feeling as it occurs, and decide if you wish to grow, retard, contain, or eliminate the emotion. Your behavior will have a powerful influence over how the emotion is regulated. Generally, acting consistently with the emotion will encourage growth of the emotion. Acting contrary to the emotion will reduce the intensity of the emotion.

If you're having a difficult time accepting the judiciousness of acting opposite to the way you feel, then you are not adequately separating your emotion from your wants. You may feel depressed, but you want to feel good. You engage in behavior opposite to depression in order to serve your desire to feel better. You may ask if this flies in the face of being true to your feelings. Aren't you being "fake" by pretending to be one way when you really feel another way?

When you are in a hurry to get somewhere, is it fake to stop at red traffic lights? This is not behavior consistent with being in a hurry. Most of us recognize that to obey general laws is more important than satisfying your temporary needs and wants. And if you get stopped by a police officer, you will be even more late than if you obey the traffic laws. The difference between denial and suppression is important here. You are fake when you pretend you are not depressed and you actually are. This is denial of your emotions. Suppression is when you recognize that you're depressed but consciously choose to engage in behavior designed to make you feel a different feeling. You temporarily suppress the experience of your depression in this moment and attempt to create a new feeling that will substitute for the old one. If successful, you will not have to suppress your original emotion long, since you will have engaged in behaviors that will replace the negative emotion. You can suppress an emotion only so long, so suppression should always be accompanied by behavioral strategies to increase other, desired, feelings. The traffic light analogy is thus designed to show the utility of responding to principles that get you where you want to go over the long haul, rather than responding haphazardly to your immediate urges and desires.

What to Do

The following list contains general principles and strategies that will help you take action opposite to your painful feelings.

1. Acknowledge the feeling you are having. Don't deny your feeling. State to yourself as clearly as you can what this feeling is.

2. Make a list, mentally or on paper, of all the reasons you have for wanting to feel differently. This should increase your motivation and courage to act contrary to the feeling you have now.

3. Remember all the various ways the feeling you are wanting to create is expressed. How is your behavior influenced? What is your approach? What is your voice tone? How persistent are you? What does your body language say? What feedback does your body give you?

4. Once you set out to engage in the opposite action, do it fully and faithfully. Half-hearted or sarcastically inspired actions will backfire. You are not trying to be manipulative or sneaky in any way. You are trying to create a feeling. Do it enthusiastically, in spite of the feeling you are resisting.

5. Give it an adequate trial. Don't give up in the initial stages because you don't immediately feel differently. You probably won't feel differently immediately. It will take time, repeated attempts, and perhaps a variety of different avenues of pursuit in order to work.

6. Again, don't compare your feeling to the feeling you have had in the past when engaging in the same action. Don't judge the feeling. Just feel the feeling in the moment.

7. Move your attention back and forth between the action you are engaging in, the feeling you are trying to create, the reasons you want to feel that way, and your current emotion.

8. Predict the positive. Take an optimistic attitude about the long-term usefulness of these strategies. Engage your hope.

Examples of Taking Opposite Action

Here are some ways you might take opposite action. Use this list when you're stumped for an action to take or as inspiration to create opposite actions of your own.

Emotion and Action Tendency: Lethargy

I don't want to do anything. I have no energy. Anything and everything takes effort. I want to just sit and do nothing.

Taking Opposite Action. I'll make a list of things to do, preferably simple things that are easily accomplished and that are short-term. I can do small things, like vacuuming my bedroom, washing and putting away the dishes, tidying up, and so forth. I won't ask myself if I want to do these things now, and I won't wait for the energy to come. It's important to just do them and anticipate how I'll feel once I've accomplished my short list. I'll focus on performance and the doing, not on my current lack of energy. I'll focus on how I'll feel in accomplishing my tasks—my future feeling rather than the current feeling.

Emotion and Action Tendency: Social Withdrawal

I don't feel like interacting with anyone. Listening to others feels like it would take monumental effort that I don't have. People will see how depressed I feel, and I don't want them to see me now.

Taking Opposite Action. I can call someone I have not talked to in a long time. I'll make a list of things I can discuss with them that have happened since we last talked. I'll also list things I can ask them. I'll be sure to express my interest in them, making them feel included and loved. Giving to others can make me feel better. I'll express enthusiasm and interest in them in my tone. Remember, not everything is about me. Make the call—don't put it off. Once finished, I can pick another person and make another call.

Emotion and Action Tendency: Fear of Failure

I'm afraid of turning in a project to my supervisor. I'm afraid of being discovered as a fraud and an incompetent.

Taking Opposite Action. I'll make a list of all the reasons I have to turn in the project immediately. I can dispute the negative thinking and anticipations I have. For example, the negative thought "I'm incompetent, and my project will show that," could be disputed with "I've had this job for five years, and my supervisor has never told me I'm incompetent yet." I'll remind myself that perfection is not the goal, that performance is the goal. By turning in the project and having my supervisor give me revisions to make, I'm on the way to completion. It will be useful to separate out my behavior (working on the project) from my feeling (fear). I'll tell myself that I can work *and* tolerate my fear. Fear is not a new feeling. I've tolerated it before, and I can tolerate it now. I will engage in the work behavior, notice the fear, take deep breaths, and reassure myself of my ability to handle the fear and produce work simultaneously.

Emotion and Action Tendency: Fear of Rejection

I don't want to ask anyone to go to the movies with me. They have their own life, and I don't want to look needy and inadequate. If they say no, I'll feel even worse. So I'll protect myself by not trying. Feeling lonely is better than being rejected.

Taking Opposite Action. Of course I don't want to be rejected. Who does? It's normal to feel a fear of rejection, but being social and working toward a happy life is even more important. I'll acknowledge my fear but act courageously. Besides, it's not needy to want a companion on a social event—it's normal. I am normal. If they say no, I'll feel disappointed and work with my feelings of rejection. It won't be the end of the world. I'll feel worse if I allow my fears to control my life. I'll make a list of three people to invite. If all three say no, I'll go by myself and "lick my wounds" after I enjoy the movie. I'll call these people now, because the anticipation is always the worst. The more I delay, the more my fears will grow. The more I act, the less the fears will be.

Emotion and Action Tendency: Guilt

I made fun of my friend yesterday when she was expressing herself. If she had done that to me, I would have been extremely insulted. But if I apologize, she'll know how sensitive I am and may try to get back at me. I should just keep my mouth shut and not make matters worse. I feel so guilty that my behavior does not represent my values.

Taking Opposite Action. I do feel guilty, and I am guilty of making fun of someone I like. My guilt is justified, but I'm tired of feeling guilt. I'm going to call her and apologize, tell her exactly how I feel about my own behavior, and let her strike back if she wants to. I can deal better with hurt than with guilt. And I'll like myself better, even if I get hurt. I'm going to do it now, before I chicken out, and I'll feel so much better about myself no matter how the phone call turns out. I'm going to confront my guilt directly then not obsess over it.

Emotion and Action Tendency: Shame

I feel shame that I don't have a romantic partner. I'm ashamed that I don't have a companion and I'm tired of going to parties alone.

Taking Opposite Action. I need to acknowledge my feeling of shame but remind myself that it's normal and acceptable to want to have a companion. Having wants and needs doesn't necessarily need to lead to feelings of shame. I must be attacking myself for not always having my needs met. I'm going to continue to go to parties, because I *can* have a good time if I allow myself to experience others and not be so self-absorbed. I'm going to go to most parties that I'm invited to, remind myself that there is no shame in being single, and use the principles of acting opposite in order to decrease my shame and increase my ability to have fun at social events.

Emotion and Action Tendency: Depression

I feel sad most of the time. It is not fair, and I don't know why I must struggle with depression when others don't have to. I feel sad even when my environment doesn't make me feel sad. I'm sad at work, sad at home with my family, and sad when I'm with my friends.

Taking Opposite Action. Yes, I'm sad and depressed, no question about that. But I'm self-absorbed. I'm not allowing my competence and contributions at work to get through to me. I'm so absorbed in my own thoughts at work, I don't let others really influence me. Same at home: I don't enjoy the small stuff my children do, I don't appreciate what I have that many others would be envious of, and I don't really listen to my friends when I'm with them. In my head, I'm thinking about myself. I'll do the opposite. I'll pay attention to others, pull my thoughts away from myself, focus on the positive, focus on how I can help others feel good, and focus on amusement and pleasantries rather than sadness and heaviness. I'll fight it when my attention turns to my sadness. I'll use the principles of acting opposite and keep it up for a few weeks before I evaluate if it's working or not.

Emotion and Action Tendency: Anger

Everyone annoys me. Everyone is so self-centered. I have to keep my guard up or others will eat me alive. I'm tired of living like this, but my anger is real and growing.

Taking Opposite Action. I'm angry because people don't treat me the way I want to be treated. Acting opposite to anger is being calm and accepting. So I'll have to work on reducing my arousal, using deep breathing, self-soothing, and positive thoughts about others. I'll have to treat people with respect even though I've felt disgust and anger at them in the past. I'll have to treat others as if they've treated me exactly the way I wanted them to in the past and as if they were trustworthy, even though I've had serious doubts about this in the past. I'll focus on the feelings I want to create (calm and acceptance) rather than being so strategic in trying to protect myself from others. I know this is going to be really hard, but I'll keep it up consistently for several weeks before I decide if it's working.

Emotion and Action Tendency: Feeling Inadequate

I always put myself down and verbalize negative things about myself. I do it verbally to others and inside my head to myself as well.

Taking Opposite Action. The opposite of putting myself down is complimenting myself. It will be hard, but I'm going to talk to others about what I do well, what I'm proud of, and what's important to me. I'm going to remind myself of what's going right, rather than what's going wrong. I'm going to show confidence rather than discouragement and inadequacy.

Emotional Opposites

Acting opposite to your current emotion is difficult not only because it goes against the grain of your current experience and habits, but also because people frequently confuse emotional opposites. The opposite of hatred is not love, it is indifference. Hatred is an active emotion—it propels you toward immediate action. Indifference is an inactive emotion because it has no impulse to action. With hatred you are attentive to the person or event you hate, you are "attached" to it, while with indifference you are unattached and couldn't care less. You need to attend to this active-passive dimension when implementing taking opposite action. If the current emotion is active (you feel a sense of urgency to do something), then the opposite will probably be inactive (you will decide to do less).

With fear-based feelings, you will need to *approach* whatever you're afraid of. You will need to interact with the feared event, be exposed to that which you're afraid of, not pretend that you love it. With guilt and shame, you will need to approach (apologize, make amends, accept your imperfections), accept or reject (make a decision if the feeling is consistent with your values), then let it go. Guilt and shame are lingering feelings, passive but persistent. You will need to be active, action-oriented, and then terminate your interaction with the event or process. With sadness or depression-based feelings, you need to be active, because depression tends to make you passive and inactive. Anger-based feelings tend to be active and bring a sense of urgency, so you need to be soft and gentle, patient and uncontrolling with whatever's making you angry.

Taking opposite action is fundamentally about creating new feelings rather than masking ones you don't like. It is therefore important that you choose opposite action that you're intent on making work. Don't choose to do something you have great misgivings about or would otherwise abhor doing. Think about your long-term emotional objectives: what is the feeling that you're trying to create for yourself?

Remembering Your Skills

Mnemonics are good way to cue new behavioral strategies and avoid use of old coping techniques that may not have worked so well in the past. For emotion regulation skills, try EMOTIONS.

<u>E</u>xpose yourself to emotions

<u>M</u>indful of current emotions

<u>O</u>utline plan to deal only with primary emotion

<u>T</u>ake opposite action

<u>I</u>ncrease positive experiences

<u>O</u>utside precipitants?

<u>N</u>otice what's going on

<u>S</u>econdary emotions dealt with later

"E" in EMOTIONS reminds you that experiencing or exposing yourself to emotions will allow you to stop escape and avoidance tactics that don't work over the long run but that many of you are tempted to do. "M" reminds you to be mindful of your emotions in ways that do not escalate or attempt to truncate your emotional experience. "O" tells you to outline a plan to deal only with your primary emotion. The instruction here is to engage in problem-solving techniques, to chart a course of action consistent with your goals and what you find meaningful and important. "T" is for taking opposite action, a reminder that you can influence your feelings with your behavior. "I" is for increasing positive experiences, a reminder that your environment can start new, different feelings. You are not a prisoner of your emotions. "O" is for outside precipitants. What might be causing this feeling to come at this particular time? Feelings don't come out of nowhere. Try to understand what in your thoughts, body, or environment may be triggering this emotion in the current moment. "N" is for noticing what is going on. Be aware of your breathing, your heart rate, your temperature, your action urges, your thoughts, your expectations, your fears, and the internal language you're using to describe the emotions you are experiencing. Be observant and vigilant about your experience, don't just react to it. "S" for is secondary emotions. If your feeling is escalating over time or is out of proportion to the immediate situation you are confronting, then you're probably engaging in a secondary emotional reaction. Don't try to deal with all of your secondary emotional reactions at this point in time. The intensity of your primary emotions are enough to deal with now. Deal with all the secondary emotional reactions later, when you are calm and poised for strategic behavior that is self-enhancing.

Six Steps to Feeling Better

Emotion regulation coping skills thus involve six major components:

1. Understanding your emotions, being able to observe and describe them, and understanding the function or role the emotions play (or played) in your life

2. Allowing exposure to your feelings in ways that allow reduction of avoidance and escape strategies

3. Using counterconditioning procedures that reduce the sense of urgency surrounding painful emotion

4. Increasing positive experiences, so the balance between painful emotions and pleasant emotions shifts in the positive direction

5. Increasing mindfulness to current experience so that your emotions shift more rapidly, and old emotions linger less

6. Developing these coping skills and increasing your competence in using them so that your emotions are an important but not controlling factor in your life

By consistent practice and application of these principles and procedures, emotion regulation skills allow you to influence, appreciate, and experience your emotions as powerful sources of information. You stop killing the messenger and have another set of resources to help you lead the life you want.

Below, practice EMOTIONS by completing the chart with examples of your mixed anxiety and depression.

Expose yourself to emotions	Example: I'm terrified. I'll let myself feel this terror.	
Mindful of current emotions	My heart is racing. I feel like I'm going to die. I'm afraid others will see this terror.	
Outline plan to deal only with primary emotion	Fear is the primary emotion. I'll use deep breathing and mindfulness to deal with the fear and leave the shame that others may notice to deal with later.	
Take opposite action	I'm going to smile and have a nice swing to my gait. I'm going to act as if I'm happy and carefree, even though I'm feeling terror.	
Increase positive experiences	In fact, I'm going to turn on my favorite music CD and listen through my earphones. In my head I'm going to sing along to the pleasant music.	
Outside precipitants?	My supervisor is about to come in to give me my annual performance evaluation. I know this terror is caused by things that I fear. I'm not making it up. It is normal.	
Notice what's going on	As I take opposite action I find that my anxiety is going down a little. I can handle this.	
Secondary emotions dealt with later	So what if my supervisor knows that I'm afraid? She can't fire me for that! I have rights just like everyone else. It's not a crime to feel anxiety.	

Expose yourself to emotions	
Mindful of current emotions	
Outline plan to deal only with primary emotion	
Take opposite action	
Increase positive experiences	
Outside precipitants?	
Notice what's going on	
Secondary emotions dealt with later	

Emotion regulation is thus about accepting your emotions as valid and acceptable responses to events. Emotions are never bad or wrong. However, you frequently don't like them and want to change them. You change them by being mindful to them (the opposite of avoiding them), analyzing their role and effect on you, taking perspective (getting the bigger picture), separating primary from secondary emotional reactions, decreasing your judgmentalism regarding your emotional life, increasing your positive emotional experiences on a daily basis (and being mindful of those experiences), and using new behavioral coping skills by engaging in EMOTIONS. But what happens when you can't, or shouldn't, change the emotion you experience, and it lingers? We now turn in the next chapter to distress tolerance, the set of skills involved in putting up with feelings we can't change.

Chapter 8

Distress Tolerance Skills

Pain, both physical and emotional, is a part of life. There is nothing we can do to successfully avoid all depressing experiences or anxious situations, and there is good reason not to. Just as physical pain is an internal alarm system that something is going on that needs immediate attention, so too is emotional pain a form of feedback that there is something going on to which you need to attend. In fact, people who are born with physiological defects that prevent them from feeling physical pain frequently do not live very long. They bleed to death without even noticing. They experience burns so severe that their body cannot repair itself. The normal bumps and bruises of childhood that sensitize us to be careful of the environment are missing for such individuals. I have seen many mentally retarded individuals who are so insensitive to physical pain that they need others to keep a close eye on any possible signs or symptoms of disease or injury. These disabled people have never learned what the signs of pain mean, and therefore don't take corrective action. Furnaces and the sun burn them badly without them noticing it. The body has a lot to teach us about the beneficial effects of feedback. People in chronic physical pain will tell us emphatically that the alarm system of the body no longer serves a useful purpose, and they would disable it if they could because there is nothing they perceive they can do to make their lives less painful. Pain becomes not just an alerting system that something is wrong, but a constant reminder that life holds less joy than previously.

Depression and anxiety (emotional pain) are no different. It is normal to feel sad when you lose something important to you, to feel despair when the loss is of a loved one, and to feel fury when someone has taken something from you that you assumed was rightfully yours. Temporary, acute emotional pain is thus tolerated by most of us. You tolerate it because you know it will end. You tolerate it because you accept it as natural and expectable. But mostly you tolerate it because you expect to feel different in the future. You can see the light at the end of the tunnel and expect to feel good again in the future.

But what happens when emotionally painful experiences keep the pain going over long periods of time? What happens when your pain feels so bad, for so long, that you feel you can no longer endure it?

When the Pain Doesn't End

DBT presumes that emotional pain is a form of information, like all the other senses (Linehan 1993b). However, any sense can become so overwhelming that you choose not to experience it any longer. We choose not to relive a painful event because once processed, there is no new information available. Once you fully see something and understand as many elements of it as possible, there is no longer any useful information to be had. This applies to all of our senses: hearing, taste, touch, sight, and smell. Once we have taken in the information, once we have been alerted to the environment, then to reexperience it brings no new adaptive capabilities.

Is the message here to avoid your emotions once you know they hurt? No. DBT invites you to accept (experience, pay attention to, and stop resisting) emotions. You're now aware of the distinction between avoidance, where you actively attempt not to feel at all, and denial, where you pretend and tell yourself that your feelings are not what they are, but are something totally different. Both of these processes bring more pain in the long run because they are false. You really do feel depressed, and if you use a defense mechanism built on an inaccurate foundation you are asking for trouble. If you feel petrified to feel your anxiety and design coping mechanisms to run away from it, in the end you are only increasing it. Running away from the bogeyman does not really decrease your fear of him—it increases it.

The dialectic with distress tolerance is between acceptance and avoidance. DBT helps you to pay attention to your emotions, even if they hurt. Don't resist them, try to always push them away, or even summarily disapprove of painful emotions. Relax while you experience even pain, and the agony surrounding the pain can disappear. While it may seem paradoxical, sitting with your pain for a time can decrease the intensity and duration of that pain.

Let's take a look at John, who has social anxiety disorder. He is petrified of having to talk to people he doesn't already know. Even going to the store and having to interact with clerks to obtain items he needs creates an intense dread from which he desires escape. His social anxiety is so intense that it has limited his career advancement. He just can't bring himself to deal with the public or work with others comfortably. He stays in his cubicle at work then goes home to his apartment. He feels imprisoned by his own feelings of dread, rumination, and constant anticipation that he is going to make a fool of himself in front of others. By the time John graduated from high school he was also feeling depressed. He stopped wanting to go places, and he looked forward to very little in the future. Now, as an adult, his sleep is fitful, he has lost weight, and he has even lost his sex drive. John has made compromises in his life, but not ones that serve his best interests. His solution is to reduce his anxiety by avoiding all situations that prompt it. He compromises interpersonal relationships (not having many, because new people make him feel vulnerable), compromises environments (having a rigid routine that does not bring him to unfamiliar places), and compromises desire (shutting down wants and needs that might cause him to challenge his defensive maneuvers).

Effective Coping

Distress tolerance offer a different approach. While emotion regulation skills (chapter 7) are strategies to create new and different feelings (so that there is greater balance between positive and negative experiences), distress tolerance skills are almost the opposite. You learn to pay attention to your pain in ways that do not increase it (mindfulness), you learn to self-soothe in order to increase your confidence in experiencing your emotions (decreasing avoidance and denial), you learn distraction skills that involve acknowledgment, you learn to improve the moment (a variant on emotion regulation skills, in that you are attempting to substitute a bad feeling for a better one, if just for a moment), and you learn critical thinking skills that can increase your emotional pain tolerance.

Distress Tolerance Skills

1. Mindfulness of pain in order to decrease it

2. Self-soothing skills

3. Distraction skills

4. Improving the moment (respite)

5. Increasing pain tolerance through critical thinking

Dr. Marsha Linehan thus describes distress tolerance skills as "crisis survival strategies" designed to "get through bad situations without making them worse" (1993b, p.97). I use her mnemonic for distress tolerance in its entirety because Dr. Linehan so successfully outlines behavioral and psychological techniques that work. And she creates a very easy way to remember the primary principles of distress tolerance: ACCEPTS, IMPROVE.

Mindfulness and Distress Tolerance

Mindfulness skills are an integral aspect of distress tolerance skills. If your goal is to reduce distress, you may ask, then why would paying even more careful attention to distress be useful or ever suggested? Didn't I just say that once an emotion no longer brings new or useful information, we shouldn't repeat it to ourselves? And earlier I even warned against practicing or rehearsing an emotion, as this makes us get "better" at it. If you're mindful of your emotional pain, won't you be practicing that emotion and thus increasing it?

Remember, DBT is a set of strategies that assumes that much of emotional pain and prolonged suffering involves inadequate compromises between competing and at times contradictory needs and urges. Here, the dialectic is between accepting the mixed anxiety and depression and ridding yourself of it. The more you engage in any extreme along the dialectic continuum, the greater the possibility that you are forming an inadequate compromise.

Dialectic Conflicts in Distress Tolerrance

Accepting the anxiety just as it is	<————>	Totally ridding yourself of the anxiety
Rehearsal of anxiety, making it grow	<————>	Denial and avoidance of anxiety, prolonging it
Overlearning the depression response, increasing its probability in the future	<————>	Increasing fear of depression, adding secondary emotional responses that increase distress
Noticing so much about your anxiety that you become oversensitized to it	<————>	Noticing so little about your anxiety that you become undersensitized to it

Richness of Feeling

The goal is to form compromises that optimize your chances to reach your goals. Obviously you don't want to prolong pain. Unfortunately, this frequently means that you must be willing to expose yourself to this very pain precisely in order to not prolong it. Bereavement offers an excellent example. When you lose a lifelong companion, you should feel sadness and loss. Why? Because these feelings measure as well as define meaning in your life. Without attachment, love, need, anger, disappointment, anticipation, or any of the varied emotions you can have, how meaningful would life be? Without our emotions we would be more like plants or statues than human beings. Even our pets have these feelings. How many of you would bother to have a dog or cat that didn't care whether you ever came home? How many of you would tend to animals that seemed unmotivated to promote either their own well-being or that of others? Life would be rather dismal without the color, excitement, and meaning that your feelings bring.

But, at first glance, most of us would probably say we only want to feel good. If, in the dialectical continua above, you always choose strategies on the right side of the continuum (you try to rid yourself of all pain, you avoid and deny pain at every turn, and you minimize your experience of pain on any level), you will become undersensitized to all emotions. Why? Many experiences bring a variety of sensations. When you love someone, they inevitably disappoint you at times. When you hate someone, you are attached to him or her in the passion of your feeling. Even very event-oriented experiences, such as riding a roller coaster at an amusement park, involve a variety of emotions. You feel exhilaration at the anticipation of anxiety; you both look forward to and have a small amount of dread about the experience, which is exactly why some people seek it out. No one has yet discovered how to filter out all negative emotion without simultaneously filtering out joy and all its variants. So you must accept emotional pain, or you give up feeling good as well.

Nowhere is this better expressed than with panic attacks. Panic is when adrenalin flows excessively in the body. It activates your muscles, preparing you to run or attack. Your heart rate increases dramatically. You begin to breathe shallowly and quickly. You may perspire, as the body prepares to cool itself off from physical exertion. Blood rushes through your body as the heart furiously pumps oxygen to cells throughout the body. People having panic attacks feel that they are about to die from a heart attack, or at least that they will pass out and be humiliated. Once someone has a panic attack, the probability of having another one increases. It is the fear of the panic that makes panic disorder such an anticipatory disease. The fear of the fear itself causes that which you fear to actually happen.

The behavioral treatment of panic disorder is thus to assist you to form better compromises on the continua we looked at earlier. The goal is to accept your bodily responses, to decrease the fear that you will die or be humiliated because of your body. By embracing the idea that you can tolerate your anxiety, the fear of the fear is reduced, and the probability of another attack decreases. As you become sensitive to your body you can see the signs of anxiety earlier, and it's easier to calm yourself with low to moderate anxiety than it is with high or extremely high anxiety. But you shouldn't become so highly sensitive to your body that you interpret every change as signal that another attack is coming. It's a balancing act, being both sensitive to your body and yet not overly vigilant. By moving from one side on the continuum to the other, you are more skillfully prepared to adjust your sensitivities to the situation at hand. You are more adaptable and less prone to error. Mindfulness of your distress is thus, paradoxically, actually a method of reducing pain.

Reduce or Accept Anxiety and Depression through Mindfulness

The basic mechanics of mindfulness skills are the same no matter what end you're seeking. With emotion regulation, you use mindfulness as a way to heighten your exposure to new and different experiences that can substitute better feelings for ones you are currently having. In strategic behavior skills (chapter 9), you use mindfulness to help you analyze the environment in order to better predict the course of action you should take in a particular situation. In distress tolerance, you use mindfulness in order to reduce secondary emotional responses and in order to validate the meaningfulness of situations that you confront. This is acceptance. The mechanics (how to be mindful) are the same, but the purpose differs.

We typically spend so much time trying to avoid feeling bad that it may feel foreign to pay specific attention to painful emotions. The procedures below break the mindfulness process down into small components, encouraging you to expose yourself to pain in order to better tolerate it. Certainly this may seem contrary to your natural tendency, but exposure to fear (experiencing it) reduces it.

1. Pay attention to your emotional pain. Where can you feel it? How is it expressed in your body? Do your muscles tighten up? Can you feel pressure in your head and neck? Do you feel hot or cold? Does your heart rate speed up?

2. Pay attention to your internal dialogue. What are you saying to yourself? What are you reacting to, and what does that mean to you? What are you saying to yourself about the future?

3. Pay attention to your language. What words are you using to describe your feelings?

4. Pay attention to your action urges, even if you are not acting on them. Do you feel like running away? Being violent with someone? Crawling in a hole to hide and burning your birth certificate?

5. Pay attention to your behavior that actually expresses the feeling. What are you doing? Crying? Screaming? Shaking? Sulking? Criticizing someone else? Withdrawing?

6. Pay attention to your tendency toward judgmentalism. How are you judging this process as bad, wrong, unfair, or undesired?

Now, be mindful, with the strategies we discussed in chapter 6 (ONE MIND) even more keenly in mind. Remember what the mnemonic stands for.

One thing

Now

Environment. What is happening out there?

Moment. Immediate

Increase senses. Touch, taste, vision, hearing

Nonjudgmental. Not good or bad, right or wrong

Describe. Words, descriptive not prescriptive or proscriptive

1. Focus on only One thing. Don't ruminate on the million things others have done to you to make you depressed. Focus only on one thing, the depression itself. Focus on the emotion itself, not everything that surrounds it.

2. Consider the Now. How are you experiencing this emotion in this moment? Not how you felt yesterday and the day before, but just now.

3. Focus on the Environment. Is anything happening outside of you that is prompting this emotion in this moment? Or are you responding to memories, wants, and past events? If so, refocus to the Moment, what is happening in this immediate second, both inside and outside of you.

4. Increase your senses. Experience your immediate senses in the now. What are you touching, tasting, seeing, hearing? Are you replaying what you saw and heard from the past? Are you really in this moment?

5. Take a Nonjudgmental stance toward what you are being mindful of. Describe your emotion to yourself without all the imperatives and action urges. Watch the emotion without dread or threat. Just for this moment, feel it up close and don't try to change it one iota.

The more skillful you become at being mindful of your emotional pain, the more you'll find that the intensity and frequency of the pain are reduced (Overholser 2000). Why do I say this? Emotions are frequently so variegated, containing so many secondary emotional responses, that by simply attending to the moment without struggling with the emotion makes it tolerable. By teasing out your experiences, taking them one bit at a time, they are less overwhelming. By reducing resistance and judgmentalism, by not "tugging" at them or running from them, you are no longer growing them. They dissipate.

If you do not find, with a little practice, the intensity of the emotional pain reducing, go back to the desensitization procedures we outlined in emotion regulation (chapter 7), where you expose yourself to the pain and then expose yourself to something else more pleasant. Go back and forth between the pleasant and the unpleasant. This exposure to your emotions should help a great deal. If you continue to have difficulty, seek out a psychotherapist who has been trained in DBT. They should be able to coach you through this desensitization process. However, it is essential that you eventually learn the application of this process. Once you learn the strategy, you can then apply it on your own to future situations without professional coaching.

Self-Soothing

Self-soothing is the process of calming yourself down, speaking to yourself lovingly and reassuringly. While most of us learned how to be soothing to children, we rarely are able or willing to be soothing to ourselves. Think of how you soothe a child: you provide physical comfort (hugging them and placing them on your lap after a fall or mishap), you provide verbal comfort (most often by simply reassuring them that everything is going to be alright and that you understand that they hurt), and most importantly you validate them (by simply recognizing that they are frightened, in pain, or emotionally hurt, and letting them know it's okay to feel that way and that you want them to feel better).

Why is it acceptable to almost all adults to provide soothing experiences for children, oftentimes without a second thought about it, and frequently unacceptable for most adults to do the same things for themselves?

Most of us make critical assumptions about what it means to be an adult, to be grown-up and mature. Mature people somehow don't need simple soothing after an "ow-ee." In fact, many people assume that grown-ups shouldn't have "ow-ees." You should somehow be impervious to all the stresses and strains of daily living. This assumption of adult imperviousness is so firmly rooted in many people's minds that it is never specifically articulated. You believe it, even though you never actually say it to yourself. Sad, since children typically express what all humans need and want, just in more visible and less shrouded ways. While adults typically aren't as frightened when they trip and fall, other types of "falls" don't necessarily transform over time into inconsequential events. And why should they? When a friend puts you down a bit at a social gathering, it hurts in the same way that dropping your sucker on the floor did as a child. Why should you not be able to obtain the same comfort and soothing you received as a child when you're hurt as an adult? Especially when the hurts are powerful, soothing and comfort are powerfully effective in making a difference.

Another adult assumption that prevents people from soothing themselves involves the conception that only others should provide soothing. You might think to yourself, "Why should I have to soothe myself? Others should be giving me soothing! If I give it to myself, it's not as meaningful. Others should provide comforting words. I'd feel silly giving them to myself. What am I? Some friendless freak who has to do everything for myself?"

Obviously, if you take this approach to its extreme, you would be totally dependent on others for meeting your needs and at the mercy of their whims and desires—not a good place to be. Ideally, you have internalized the adults who provided support and nurturance when you were a child. If so, you naturally and spontaneously say the same kinds of things to yourself that your important adults (typically parents, teachers, grandparents, and other extended family) said to you as a child. However, when you have a history of invalidation (when those from whom you sought support and nurturance provided conflicting or even negative messages), you may have internalized maladaptive values. "I'm only worthy of validation when someone else gives it to me. I don't deserve soothing because I want it. It's a gift from others."

More damaging still, another adult assumption is that you're unworthy of soothing at all. Not only do you reject self-soothing, you reject soothing provided by any source. You feel unworthy of such good feelings. Because you hurt so much and so often, you *must* be undeserving. You get what you deserve, right? Judging from your past experience, you may say something to yourself like, "I must not be worthy of good feelings because I've received so few." But think about it—this reasoning is circular. You didn't recieve adequate soothing in the past, so now you believe you don't deserve it. Therefore, you don't accept it when it's offered, leaving you with no soothing—which turns around and confirms your belief that you're not worthy of soothing. Psychologists call this *emotional reasoning*. In logic they call it *tautological*.

Finally, another adult assumption is that the soothing is short-lived. You may say to yourself, "So what if I feel better for the moment? The pain will return, it always does." We've dealt with this before. Emotions are intended to be temporary, transitory, and fluctuating. No feeling, good or bad, should last forever. You should be influenced by your experience. Creating experiences that make you feel good, even temporarily, thus should be sought after rather than avoided. Engage in self-soothing, even if it feels weird in the beginning. Perhaps you are just out of practice (unfortunate, since this means that you have somehow suffered extended periods of invalidation rather than soothing). The more you practice it, the better you will get at it. Give yourself permission to feel good. Self-soothing is just that, you helping yourself feel better. You self-soothe by focusing on your senses and your thoughts.

Thoughts

Self-soothing thoughts come in three major classes:

1. *Validation:* It's okay that I hurt and that I want to feel better.

2. *Reassurance:* I can handle this pain, even though it hurts and I don't like it.

3. *Perspective taking:* I felt this way before, so I know I can handle it. The feeling did not last forever last time, and it won't this time either.

With validation you're reminding yourself that your feelings are right and justified, but that you don't want to have them any longer. You're separating out the way you feel from issues of "deserving." You're not telling yourself that you must be deserving of the depression as a form of punishment. Instead, you're telling yourself that your feeling is simply that, a feeling. Perhaps there is no purpose to your suffering. You may be reacting to a situation that you feel is horribly unfair and unjust. It does not matter. You don't buy in to the notion that your suffering says anything fundamental about your personality or your identity. You simply validate that the feeling you're having is there, and that you want to change it. You thus first accept the pain for what it is, an emotional sensation, before you go about changing it. You acknowledge, identify, and validate the pain, then move on.

Reassurance gets at the core of self-soothing. Like the child who needs comfort and to be told verbally or behaviorally that "it's alright, you're okay," you similarly reassure yourself. Tell yourself, unbashfully and unapologetically: "This, too, will pass." "I'm okay, I just hurt." "Of course this is painful to me. I'll survive." "Of course I don't like this experience. Who would? But I can handle it." "This feels awful. I don't like it. But I can take it." "I'm okay, I'll survive, but I hurt." "I'm doing okay. I can take this pain for now. I can comfort myself through this."

Practice some self-soothing below. Identify situations where you experience mixed depression and anxiety and then write self-soothing statements that help you to cope with those situations.

Name the feeling you are having	Acknowledge and validate the pain	Write self-soothing statements you can use for the situation
Example: I'm depressed that I feel like I can't leave the house and anxious about the thought of having panic symptoms if I do leave the house.	I feel a sense of helplessness and being out of control. I feel urgency to escape this feeling. I feel as if I'm going to explode from the inside out. I hurt, so of course I'm afraid of leaving the house.	It's great that I'm feeling strong enough to consider leaving the house again. For so long I didn't even try. I have greater faith that I can handle my panic. I can get through this. I'm getting stronger every day.

Perspective Taking

Perspective taking involves looking at more than the moment at hand (Rusting and DeHart 2000). Unlike with mindfulness, where you attempt to focus only on the now, on this moment in time, with perspective taking you look beyond what you feel immediately and compare it to the past and to the future. You may feel deeply depressed in this moment, rageful now, despondent in this instant, hopeless and urgently seeking escape from your emotion right now. But you can think of times, yesterday or a few weeks ago, when you felt very differently. Perspective taking thus involves comparison and a longer time frame. The intent is not to minimize how you feel now (telling yourself that you don't feel what you know you're feeling), but to compare it to your other previous feelings and anticipated future feelings so that you don't lose the perspective that all of your emotions shift and change over time. Tell yourself something like, "Yes, I feel frantic now, but yesterday I felt calmer. I can develop that calm today." "I feel hopeless now, but yesterday I had a good telephone conversation with a friend that made me feel connected. I'll feel less hopeless in a bit." "I feel worthless now, but when others compliment me I feel better. I always feel better when I work on recognizing my strengths." "My anxiety feels intolerable right now, but I know when I get in the hot tub my muscles let go, and I feel less like crawling out of my skin."

Practice perspective taking below by writing down situations that disagree with your general conclusion about yourself or your situation.

Identify the situation and your feeling	Write about situations that evoke a different perspective
Example: I'm never good enough for my partner. I always seem to do something wrong. Sometimes I just feel like killing myself, the situation is so hopeless.	My new boyfriend told me last weekend that I was fun to be with. He told me many times that I'm attractive. He likes my cooking. He continues to seek out my company and calls several times a week. I guess I can't always be a bad partner to him. My hope for this relationship is high, so I can't give up hope in myself.

Vision

While self-soothing with words or language can be powerful, your five senses can also be enormously helpful. What can you hold in your vision that provides respite from your immediate emotions? In distress tolerance workshops we use videotapes of dancers, ballet, art museum tours, nature videos, and beautiful art books to demonstrate the kind of visual material that you can easily use at home to relieve painful feelings. Focus your vision on beauty. It may be a beautiful bouquet of flowers, looking out at the stars at night, watching fish swim gracefully in an aquarium, lighting a candle and watching the flame flicker, observing the lapping of small waves in a swimming pool, or anything that brings a sense of awe and comfort. Be mindful when using vision to provide comfort and self-soothing. Are you watching something you find beautiful or simply standing in front of something while you turn thoughts constantly around in your head? Go back to the image of an adult soothing a frightened or hurt child. If the adult simply snatches them up and gives them no attention, the child will not be reassured. Why would you feel any differently? Give attention to visual images that provide comfort. Get out of yourself, and see something with care.

Below, write down objects, experiences, or views that can help you to feel soothed. Try to pick items that are accessible to you (either in your home, neighborhood, or library, or at a friend's house) that you can readily draw upon when you feel anxious or depressed. Do this exercise now, even though you may not feel especially tense or depressed in this moment. It's easier to generate such lists when your feelings are not so intense rather than when the anxiety is so high that it is hard to concentrate or the depression is so strong you feel little motivation or hope to initiate new behavior. So make your lists now; don't just skip over this section.

Visual Experiences That Soothe Me

_____   _____

_____   _____

_____   _____

_____   _____

_____   _____

Hearing

Sound can provide incredible comfort. Listen to a CD or tape of nature: waterfalls, brooks, ocean waves, wind in forests, or birds. Get out your favorite record, CD, or tape that you remember as comforting, beautiful, and awe-inspiring. Listen to a vocalist, instrumental music, or a concert that you find captures your attention.

Below, write down sounds that are soothing to you. Again, try to pick things that are accessible to you so that you can readily use this strategy to soothe yourself.

Sounds That Soothe Me

_____   _____

_____   _____

_____   _____

_____   _____

_____   _____

Scent

Find a single flower that has a scent that you enjoy. Go to a cosmetic counter and enjoy the various perfumes, colognes, and toiletries that smell differently than ones you're used to. Walk near a restaurant and enjoy the aromas coming from the kitchen. Go to a health-food store and smell the various aromatherapy products.

Think of aromas that you find pleasant, that bring positive memories, and write them below.

Aromas That Soothe Me

_____   _____

_____   _____

_____   _____

_____   _____

_____   _____

Taste

Go to an ice-cream store and sample their various flavors. Go to a farmers' market and sample the various vegetables and breads. Go to a deli and sample some of the dishes. Prepare a dish you haven't made in a long time. Suck on a slice of lemon. Place a small ice cube in your mouth. Flavor your coffee or tea. Use mouthwash, and feel it in every part of your mouth. Put a very small amount of spice on your fingertip and place it gently on your tongue.

Identify tastes that you find soothing and pleasant, and write them below.

Tastes That Soothe Me

_____   _____

_____   _____

_____   _____

_____   _____

_____   _____

Touch

Hold an ice cube in your fist briefly. Take a bubble bath. Let sand fall through your fingers. Let your hand gently comb a lawn. Rub lotion on your hands and arms. Splash cool water on your face. Rub marbles between your hands. Pet your pet. Hug someone. Write below as many things that you remember touching in the past that felt pleasant, made you feel comfort, or brought pleasant memories or sensations.

Touch That Soothes Me

_____   _____

_____   _____

_____   _____

_____   _____

_____   _____

Use all of your senses to soothe yourself. Pretend you have never seen, heard, tasted, smelled, or touched the thing before. Treat it as a totally new and different experience. Alternatively, try to remember the first time you ever experienced that thing before. Be mindful of the experience. Allow yourself permission to be comforted.

Practice soothing yourself. Write down things you can do in each section and make certain you do some of those things each week.

Soothing When Depression and Anxiety Are High

It's an excellent habit to expose yourself to self-soothing on a regular basis, since this will decrease the probability that you will slip into depression. It also redirects your attention away from your own body, which can decrease anxiety since you're not constantly watching your body in an anticipatory way for signs of stress (the self-fulfilling prophesy). It's especially important that you soothe yourself when your anxiety and depression increase. The next time you feel without energy, just want to sleep to make the world go away, or feel like your body couldn't possibly be any more anxious, choose some of the soothing items you listed above and engage in them. Do them especially when you are experiencing intense emotional pain.

Soothing yourself can involve all of your senses. Especially when you experience intense mixed anxiety and depression, it's important that you use all of your senses to soothe yourself. The following exercise will encourage you to do just that. Use the table below (and the similar one at the back of the book) when you feel desperate, hopeless, helpless, or paralyzed by the intensity of your emotions. You'll find that soothing yourself really does make your emotions less intense and more tolerable. When one sense doesn't work to decrease your agony (say, thinking reassuring thoughts), perhaps another sense will reduce your desperation (aromas that remind you of comforting situations). Engage in these soothing strategies each time you feel intolerable emotion, not just once as you work through this book.

Thoughts. What can I think about that will make me feel reassured?	
Vision. What can I look at that will make me feel good things?	
Hearing. What is pleasing to the ear? What can I listen to that soothes me?	
Smell. What aromas make me feel good?	

Taste. What can I put in my mouth that makes me feel great and prompts fond memories?	
Touch. What can I touch that will invoke feelings that are so different from my pain?	

Distraction Skills

Distraction allows us to attend to something else besides our painful emotions and thus increases our emotional pain tolerance (Gross 2001). Just as with self-soothing, we can use a variety of different strategies to increase our psychological coping skills. Dr. Linehan's ACCEPTS mnemonic is an easy way to remember the different strategies you can deploy when necessary (1993b).

  Activities

  Contributing

  Comparisons

  Opposite **E**motions

  Pushing Away

  Thoughts

  Sensations

Activities

The first step of the mnemonic reminds you to get involved with a project. While typically the last thing you want to do when you feel depressed or anxious is take care of all those little tasks around the house you've put off, this is precisely the time to do them. Not only will you feel better by getting the laundry done, vacuuming the floor, doing the dishes, and so on, but you will also redirect your attention away from your emotions, away from yourself, and away from the memories that prompt the negative emotions. Write a thank-you note to a friend or acquaintance, put together an array of items to give to charity, or engage in a hobby. What you do is not nearly as important as that you do *something*. Get moving, engage in a task. Simply having your body moving and active is important.

Contributing

This is another way to decrease the self-absorption that intense emotions often bring. Self-absorption not only means that you are attending to little else besides your feelings and the events or processes that are prompting them, it also means that you tend to lose perspective. Contribute to others. Get involved in a community project (a park cleanup project, a beach beautification program, an elder visitation program, an inner-city assistance program, tutoring students or adults, or fund-raising for programs you deeply believe in). Join a board or committee of a program you support. Get involved in a political campaign or cause. Agree to distribute materials, stuff envelopes, or write letters of support to the local newspaper. Give of yourself in ways that make you feel good about your efforts and the causes you support. It will increase your confidence, your sense of competence, and the meaningfulness of your life. This, eventually, will increase good feelings and decrease bad feelings.

Comparisons

Making comparisons is another method of perspective taking. How is your life different from those of others born in third-world or developing countries? How would your situation be different or the same if you lived in a nation at combat? How might your relationships with others be different if you were born mentally retarded? Compare your situation and your feelings to those of others who perhaps have more physical disabilities, less income, or less education. Alternately, how might your situation be different if you were born rich? What if you were born into royalty? How would your feelings be different if you were in the immediate family of the president? If you were a butcher, rather than a plumber? What would the differences be? Comparison helps you to get out of the little cubbyholes you have placed yourself in, broadens your perspective, gets you more in a thinking mode rather than a pure feeling mode, and assists you to see that there will always be people better off and worse off than you.

Comparisons also invite you to examine your appraisals of the situation. "Is how I'm interpreting this situation really correct? I feel bad, but maybe that's because my thinking about a situation is inaccurate. Maybe others don't think I'm foolish, immoral, or stupid. Perhaps when all the emotions calm down, I have not lost the relationship I value so highly. Maybe my story won't be flashed on tomorrow's news headlines. While my feelings are accurate reflections of the anticipations I'm having, what if what I anticipate is wrong?" Project how your feelings would change if your appraisal of the situation were inaccurate. Keep perspective. Reserve judgment. Deal with what you know to be true, and question possible alternatives to what you anticipate. Maybe you're right about what you fear is going to happen. But compare your feeling to other possibilities. Not only can it provide comfort in the moment, but also it will decrease the chances that you engage in impulsive behaviors that promote your negative appraisals. "Are there things I can do to prevent my negative worry from coming true?" In chapter 9, you'll learn about what you can do to prevent your negative worrying from coming true.

Opposite Emotions

You may remember this strategy from chapter 7. Engage in an activity that will produce an emotion quite different from the one you currently have. If you feel tired and sluggish, go for a short jog or rapid stroll. If you're feeling bored or useless, read an adventure book, watch a comedy movie, or turn on a drama. If you are feeling depressed, watch a horror movie and change the depression to temporary, controllable anxiety. Any change in emotional state reminds you that all feelings are temporary. Prove to yourself that you can let the environment affect you. Invite in experiences that are influential and that prompt different emotions.

Pushing Away

Many of you are already quite familiar with this technique from childhood. For some, it is the main strategy they use when their feelings are intense. Refuse to think about what angers you. Visualize the person who has upset you, then make them shrink visually as if you had magical powers to do so. See them shrink so small that you can hardly see them in the distance, then watch them disappear. Take your feelings of being small and worthless, and visualize yourself growing visually. Take your anxiety and imagine being able to package it up in a box and put it on the top shelf of your most cluttered closet. Imagine that your anxiety is a ball and toss it far away in a distant field. Push away the emotions, as if you have a force field from *Star Trek* shimmering around you. The emotion cannot get in, no matter how it tries.

Thoughts

Thoughts can provide temporary respite from intense emotions. Do things that engage your mind. Do a crossword puzzle, balance your checkbook, put together your yearly budget, go through your junk mail, read the manual to a recent electronic product you bought, read magazines. Occupy your mind with something else.

Sensations

This item involves another strategy of creating new input. Take a hot bath. Take a cold shower. Smell something pungent. Put on your favorite perfume. Review the stimuli from the chapter on mindfulness for other ideas of sensations to which you can expose yourself.

ACCEPTS reminds you to accept other input and experiences the world has to offer. Don't expose yourself repeatedly to stimuli that keep the same old feelings going. Practice distraction skills. Practice ACCEPTS.

On the following worksheet, write your potential responses to each item.

Activities. What can I do now to distract myself?	_____ _____ _____ _____
Contributing. What can I do for others?	_____ _____ _____ _____
Comparisons. How am I better off than some? Worse off than some?	_____ _____ _____ _____
Opposite Emotions. What can I do to feel the opposite of what I'm feeling right now?	_____ _____ _____ _____
Pushing Away. Don't let the emotion in. Protect myself from it.	_____ _____ _____ _____
Thoughts. Think about something else. Engage my mind.	_____ _____ _____ _____
Sensations. Expose my senses to something else.	_____ _____ _____ _____

Improve the Moment

Dr. Linehan's IMPROVE mnemonic (1993b) invites you to use emotion regulation strategies to feel something different. It's a reminder that each moment is an opportunity to feel a different feeling, to have variety and responsiveness in your life.

Imagery

Meaning

Prayer

Relaxation

One thing at a time

Vacation

Encouragement

Imagery

The first item of the mnemonic means using your memories of visual events. *Imagery* is when you project a mental picture, as if you were using a movie projector to project images onto your closed eyelids. Imagine yourself walking through the most beautiful forest on a warm summer morning. Imagine the tall trees, the various shades of green leaves sparking with the rays beaming down from the sun. Imagine the smell of the earth, the trees, and the fresh forest air going into your lungs. Imagine that with each breath the visual image becomes more colorful and vivid, as if you are really there. Imagine what it would feel like to walk quietly among the trees, as if this is your private forest, grown for your exclusive enjoyment. See the bark on the trees, the leaves on the ground, and the beauty of nature surrounding you. Use this imagery, and remind yourself how your body would feel in such peaceful and magical surroundings, not having to think about, plan, or respond to anything other than the setting you visualize.

Use imagery that is comforting to you, imagery from tranquil and inspiring previous experiences that you've had. For you it might be the ocean, a lake, a mountain cabin, a favorite overstuffed chair in a previous home, the kitchen of your best friend, a childhood vacation spot, or an expensive resort where well-mannered servants cater to your every whim.

Play forward the visual images, staying with them for as long as it takes to reexperience the kind of peaceful and relaxed bodily and mental effects you remember when you were really there. Let irrelevant thoughts come and go. Don't use effort to push them away, just imagine that you look the other way. Don't let distractions upset the mood you want to set for yourself by using the imagery. The more you use this technique, the better you can get at it. Distractions will become less of an issue with your greater skill in using imagery.

Meaning

Meaning is always the foundation of good mental health. Go back to chapter 5 on meaning making and review what you wrote there about what is important to you. Remind yourself of all the important things, people, and places in your life. Don't allow your emotions to make you so self-absorbed that you forget the existing meaning in your life and the meaningfulness you are creating. Are there any ways that your current depression speaks to what is meaningful to you? Does your anxiety heighten the importance of what you find meaningful? For example, if your current pain is humiliation that you made a fool of yourself in front of others that you admire, then your humiliation is an example of how highly you treasure your relationships with others. It is a reminder that you need to pursue your meaningful relationships. It is a painful reminder of your connection to others.

When your emotional pain is intense, reread chapter 5. Read your responses beginning on page 86 of the chapter. Remind yourself, in affirmative terms, what you want (not just what you don't want).

Prayer

Prayer can be a powerful method of reducing self-absorption, increasing meaning, and offering strength and courage in the face of fear. People with deep religious convictions already know this. If I may be so presumptuous, however, I would like to offer a few suggestions about *how* to pray, even for those who consider themselves believers in a Higher Power. Pray in order to be closer to your Higher Power, in order to communicate with God. Don't treat God like a vending machine, asking for deliverance from this or that. Don't ask for things. Don't make requests. Instead, commune. Repetition of well-known prayers (Our Fathers, the Rosary, the Serenity Prayer) can make us feel closer to our Higher Power.

Prayer has been shown through scientific study of brain wave patterns to have the same effect as meditation and deep relaxation exercises of very skillful practitioners of such techniques (Kabat-Zinn 2003). Thus, for those who have ideological difficulty with the notion of prayer, practice meditation.

Prayer serves the goal of acceptance. You accept your pain, you stop struggling with it, and it dissipates.

Relaxation

Relaxation can help with distress tolerance because it provides bodily relief of tension. Remember our brief tour of emotion theory in chapter 7? Recall that you can change emotions by intervening at any of a number of points: behavior, body, environment, or feelings. Since each of these major systems interact with each other, by relaxing the body, the brain accepts that threat is lower. Our emotions will eventually follow.

There are a number of quite effective bodily relaxation techniques. One is called *progressive muscle relaxation* (Jacobson 1938) and relies on the "pendulum theory." Sometimes we're able to relax simply by paying attention to our muscular tension and inviting it to let go. However, when many muscles are very tight this can be a challenge. As with a pendulum, when you pull it very far in one direction and then let go, it will swing fully to the opposite direction. Your muscles work the same way. With progressive muscle relaxation, you tightly flex each muscle group as hard as you can for fifteen to twenty seconds and then abruptly let go of the tension. You do this one muscle group at a time, starting at the head (forehead, eyes, jaw, neck) and moving toward the toes (right shoulder, left shoulder, upper back, chest, lower back, right arm, left arm, right hand, left hand, stomach, right leg, and so on). First, you tighten the muscle group for fifteen to twenty seconds, then abruptly let go and pay attention to the increased blood flow and immediate release of tension you feel, and then go on to the next muscle group. If you do this successfully, you should feel a tingling or warm sensation in the area of the body you just worked on, since you are tightening muscles sharply. This paradoxical procedure of tightening in order to loosen really works. With practice, your skill in using this technique should increase and you should get better results over time.

Deep breathing is an additional way of encouraging bodily relaxation. Under stress, our breathing tends to become more rapid and shallow. Deep breathing is consciously reversing this process. Take slow, deep breaths. Pause a second to two seconds between each inhale and exhale. Pay attention to the air as it enters and exits your nose. Feel your lungs inflate and deflate. Feel your chest and lower belly rise and fall with each breath. Say something soothing to yourself, such as "relax," "calm," "tranquil," "peaceful," or "quiet" with each breath.

Do stretching exercises, get in a hot tub or Jacuzzi, massage yourself, soak in the bathtub, sunbathe, or sit in your favorite chair with soft music and soft lighting. Do whatever allows your muscles to relax, your skin to feel good, your breathing to be gentle, and your spirit to be soothed.

One Thing in the Moment

This idea is familiar to you from mindfulness practice. Focus just on now. Watch your physical sensations. Stay out of your head. Don't think—notice.

Vacation

Take a small vacation from the routine. Most people think of a major one- or two-week get-away when they think of vacationing. However, stress researchers have found that a typical vacation has stress-reducing effects that last no longer than the vacation itself, and certainly no longer than two weeks. Even a monthlong vacation in France will reduce your stress no longer than two weeks once you return to your normal day-to-day existence. So, for our purposes, think of vacation as very short-term and easy things you can do to get away from it all. Visit a friend across town for a few hours, and don't talk about your problems. Go to the mall, just window-shop, and have lunch someplace different from your normal routine. Spend the afternoon in your backyard with a good book. Light a candle, put on music you typically don't listen to, and make yourself an exotic beverage to sip on. Go to a nearby hotel, order one drink, and spend the afternoon or evening in an elegantly furnished lobby. Go to a nearby park and be mindful of the children playing and how it feels to be outdoors. Find something local, inexpensive, unobtrusive, and that does not require lots of planning or stress to participate in. If you have not been to the movies in a long time, go. If you always go the movies, this time go to the park. If you rarely entertain guests, have a small dinner party. Have a picnic, barbecue, or just serve dinner on the floor in front of a good home movie. Do something slightly out of the ordinary.

Encouragement

Encouragement is critical. Be optimistic; predict success. No technique, no matter how powerful or potentially effective, will work if you use it with doubt and misgivings. I'm not asking you to lie to yourself. If you know that spending your day in the backyard with a book wasn't appealing even when you weren't feeling depressed and it still doesn't sound good to you now, then engaging in that activity just to prove that this DBT stuff doesn't work is not helpful. On the other hand, depression and anxiety are often anticipatory in nature. Your expectations are of doom and gloom. However, when you actually engage in the behavior you feel differently than you expected. If all you want to do is moan, pull the covers over your head, and hope that somehow you will magically feel differently in the future, then you're likely to be disappointed. Approach each of these techniques with hope, encouragement, and an expectation of success. Look for small changes in your feelings rather than "light-bulb" epiphanies that immediately transform you. Instead, say to yourself, "I'm going to do this because doing more of the same is unlikely to make me feel differently. I'll feel better just for trying something different and breaking my routine."

Practice IMPROVE and write your ideas here.

Imagery. What can I "see" in my mind that will be reassuring, pleasant, and invoke great memories?	
Meaning. Review what I wrote on pages 86–87. Which of these things can I do, remember, or remind myself of when I'm depressed or anxious?	
Prayer. How can I develop my spiritual or meditative power in this moment of depression and anxiety?	
Relaxation. What relaxation technique can I more faithfully practice?	
One thing at a time. What gets in the way of me really focusing? How can I stay on track better?	
Vacation. What small vacation from the ordinary can I take today, or at least in the next couple of days?	
Encouragement. What can I say to myself that will inspire hope and make me more positive?	

ACCEPT and IMPROVE your day, each day. Practice the principles. They don't work with halfhearted periodic efforts. They must be applied daily, always. Think of behaviors that you can do in your mind, things that you can do at home and even at work, in the car on the way to errands, and when interacting with your least-admired coworker. Practice.

Use the forms at the end of the book to prompt you to practice the variety of techniques in your daily life in a consistent basis over time.

Acceptance and Critical Thinking

The ACCEPT mnemonic above has an entirely different meaning when you attempt to actually increase your pain tolerance. Sometimes you are unable to successfully distract yourself and you tire of being mindful of the pain (because you have teased apart all the secondary from primary emotions, and even the remaining primary emotions are intolerably painful). At these times, what becomes of utmost importance is to increase your depression and anxiety tolerance itself. You need to increase your threshold of what you find acceptable. In fact, you need to accept the pain for what it is. You engage in acceptance as a method of reducing stress and depression (Hayes and Wilson 1994; Kabat-Zinn 1993). You say to yourself, I hurt, I feel like shit, and in this moment there is nothing I can do about it. I need to tolerate this pain. I need to accept that in this moment my pain and I are intertwined in ways I wish on no one.

Admitting Your Pain

What Dr. Linehan refers to as "radical acceptance" is validation that your pain hurts horribly, hurts continuously, and struggle is no longer an option (1993b). You can't move this emotional hurt, you can't distract it away, and just for this instant you choose not to improve the moment. You need to accept your pain for what it is, no more and no less. You hurt.

Radical acceptance does not mean that you run with your negative thoughts. It doesn't mean that you give up like your feelings tell you to do. It does not mean being pessimistic and giving in to the urge to destroy your life and thus end your depression. (Besides, you don't actually know this will work; maybe the end of the physical life doesn't mean an end to spiritual and emotional pain. You may just be limiting your options in the future.)

One of my favorite Greek stories is the myth of Sisyphus. He angers the Greek gods with his sin of avarice (insatiable greed) and is condemned to roll a heavy stone up a steep hill, which, at the top, rolls down again. And this condemnation is intensified with immortality. He can never die, so for all of eternity all he can do is roll the stone up the steep hill and watch it roll down. Sisyphus is condemned to the senseless repetition of inanity. However, Sisyphus handles it by cleaving to his task. He decides, if he is condemned to roll this stone up this steep hill forever, he might as well believe that the most important and meaningful thing in the universe is rolling that stone up the hill. The action itself, not its accomplishment, is what is important.

In essence, Sisyphus teaches us radical acceptance. We need to accept that which we cannot change. There is no need fighting it, since the struggle simply increases our suffering. To fight that which is inevitable increases suffering and brings agony; it does not inspire

191

hope or meaning. Radical acceptance is about tolerating your pain without making it worse (without adding suffering and agony to an already bad situation).

You choose to accept your pain as it is, without struggle, because you know the struggle itself creates even more pain. Your choice is based on a commitment to accept. You have turned over your pain to a Higher Power, a spiritual force who helps you suffer less through acceptance. You know that fighting your pain gets you nowhere. You know you cannot will your pain away, so you roll with it. You don't give in to it, you don't base your decisions for future actions on it—you simply experience it acceptingly because you know on a deep level that this acceptance makes the pain bearable. You allow rather than encourage; you accept rather than intensify; you experience rather than agonize over.

Thinking Critically

This act of choice is critical thinking. You have inventoried all the ways you could avoid your pain and all the ways you could tolerate your pain, and made the decision to accept it in this moment. You appreciate that all feelings change over time, that this pain also will pass, and you endure it willingly and without struggling with it. Acceptance isn't a behavior engaged in to intensify or practice the feeling. It's not a decision to engage in intentional actions of self-harm or to make matters worse by contributing to the pain. It is a choice of acceptance of that which already exists—nothing more and nothing else.

This is critical thinking in at least three ways. First, it is decisional. It is a choice among alternatives. It is not emotionally based, but a thought process that occurs about an emotion. Second, it's critical because it is made in the depths of agony. You engage your mind, your rational self, when it seems as if only your heart and soul speak. You raise your rational voice above the screams of emotionalism. Third, it is critical thinking because it precisely defines the true meaning of crisis management. You choose an alternative that results in the least harm both for this moment and for the future.

Acceptance is based in critical thinking, but fundamentally it is an emotional decision. You accept that which cannot be changed. But you accept your feelings of anxiety and depression with the deep belief, backed up with scientific evidence, that acceptance can decrease emotional pain over the long haul (Hayes 2002; Teasdale et al. 2000).

Distress tolerance is probably the least-favored strategy you will ever use to manage your emotions, but it does work to decrease the intensity and duration of your pain (Baer 2003; Davidson 2000). Fortunately, there are skills that you can use to decrease your need for distress tolerance in the future. In the next chapter we turn to strategic behavior that can decrease the probability of future depression and anxiety.

Chapter 9

Strategic Behavior Skills

Wisdom can be defined as an understanding of what is true, right, or lasting. It is the use of good judgment. I've had clients who, in the first session, warned me that they doubted the utility of psychotherapy for themselves. They said they understood that they had problems, but they doubted that I could help them because they were extremely intelligent. They would then give me a verbal resume of their accomplishments, both academically and in their businesses or careers. Some would tell me about their high IQ. If I am this intelligent, they reason, then how will you, Dr. Marra (who presumably are not quite as bright as I), possibly be able to help me?

I immediately tell such people that there is no doubt in my mind that they are more intelligent than I. I might even tell them briefly some of my own academic or life struggles (such as my total incompetence with math). In fact, I truly appreciate that many of the patients with whom I work *are* more intelligent, accomplished, and capable than I. And I then suggest to them that psychotherapy is not an intellectual process. While intelligence can tell us how to do things, wisdom tells us what needs to be done.

The Benefits of Wisdom

With intelligence you think logically, you conceptualize and abstract from reality. With intelligence you are thus able to accumulate knowledge. Knowing things (accumulating information and experience) certainly increases power and success in life. Psychotherapy, on the other hand, is about gaining wisdom. While knowledge can be fallible (your ideas or theories may sound good, but still be wrong), with wisdom you are able to strive for balance between knowing and doubting. Being intelligent is helpful in developing wisdom, but intelligence is not the same thing as wisdom.

Very bright and capable people, who by any standard are considered intelligent, can still have problems in living their lives in ways that optimize happiness and reduce emotional suffering. So psychotherapy, and this approach of DBT, isn't about developing skills only for those dimmer bulbs amongst us. You can easily be smart but not strategic or wise. DBT, in fact, presumes that people are basically logical, rational beings who struggle with developing coping mechanisms to reduce emotional pain.

Wisdom is about problem solving that goes beyond simply finding facts. With wisdom we take into account your appreciation of human nature, your doubts about knowledge as commonly accepted, your values that are less bound by time and culture, and your keen sense that timing and perseverance frequently have more value than skill. You may think this sounds pretty abstract and ambiguous—and you would be right. Developing strategic behavior skills while being mindful of using wisdom in leading your life can be ambiguous.

I will never forget what one of my undergraduate psychology professors, Ken Beauchamp, told me about the value of a liberal arts education. We were serving on a college committee and the debate turned to the students' demand for career preparation. After all, after an expensive four years of study at a private institution such as the University of the Pacific, students expect that they'll be prepared to get a job to pay off their student loans! Dr. Beauchamp politely and calmly explained that a liberal arts education does not prepare you for work, but rather for life. How? By developing tolerance for ambiguity. Not all things are known, and maybe much is even unknowable. Nevertheless, you strive to know. I did not realize it at the time, but this was my first introduction to dialectical thinking.

Strategizing with Wisdom

So, in this chapter you will develop strategies for using the coping techniques described in the previous chapters. Strategic behavior skills involve the use of behavior therapy principles to better analyze prompts (both internal and external) that keep unwanted behavior or feelings going or that make it difficult to sustain wanted behavior or feelings. So why not call this chapter "Behavior Therapy Skills" rather than "Strategic Behavior Skills"? In DBT, you attend to meaning and to meaning making. You are mindful that the only way you can truly sustain some of the difficult strategies proposed in this book over the course of your lifetime is by using your wisdom. Certainly if you had sufficient control over your environment such that you were somehow rewarded each time you engaged in your desired behavior, you would be able to sustain your plans to deal differently with life situations. Unfortunately, most of us don't have that kind of control over our environments. Most of us don't even have that much control over what happens in our immediate family or home, so why expect that we can control what happens at the workplace, in the community, or elsewhere?

Why are "wisdom" and "strategy" used in this chapter almost synonymously? A strategic approach to life is one that is defined by plans, methods, and techniques that optimize obtaining a goal. Strategic people are goal oriented. There is a specific result or outcome they are pursuing. While many people think immediately of selfish people who are only out for themselves or of greedy people who only care about wealth or power, strategic people can also be in pursuit of meaning in their lives. And isn't this one definition of wisdom? It is a wise person who is mindful of what will make their life worth living, in this moment and over the course of their life. It's a wise person who is mindful of what their long-term objectives are in life, what the obstacles are to obtaining more meaning in their life, and who adjust their techniques and strategy depending on the outcome of their previous stratagem.

Wisdom, DBT would argue, is about meaning and purpose in life. It goes beyond practical techniques that work but is very concerned with the practical. Human meaningfulness is thus grown through a combination of ambiguous commitment to values and practical attention to mundane, everyday details. The dialectics of this notion are interesting, and you can take a look at them in the following table.

Strategic Focus	<————>	Wisdom Focus
Attention to the moment	<————>	Attention to long-term objectives
Focus on the practical	<————>	Focus on values
Focus on self	<————>	Focus on others
Focus on techniques and procedures	<————>	Focus on ideas and ideals
Focus on knowledge and facts	<————>	Focus on doubts and feelings
Rational knowing	<————>	Intuitive knowing
From the head	<————>	From the heart
Confidence and pride	<————>	Humility and self-doubt
Behavioral focus	<————>	Emotional focus
Gets me what I want	<————>	Relinquishes what I want

Do these dialectic dimensions look somewhat confusing? They should. Strategic behavior is not a unitary concept. Being strategic demands that you attend to situational variables, variables that change from one circumstance to another. The continua or dialectical poles will thus shift (some being critical while others become irrelevant) depending on the situation you are strategizing. Some simple algorithm cannot define wisdom. What I am trying to describe is a general path to wisdom, not wisdom itself. This path involves attending to objectives and goals (rational processes), as well as affect and intuition (emotional processes). Strategic behavior, seen through the eyes of DBT, thus involves forming compromises among potentially conflicting aspirations and emotions. The goal is not to firmly plant you somewhere along the potential continua outlined above, but to have your interactions with the world ever ready to shift from one end to the other. Truth, that which is lasting or right, depends on judgment. And judgment depends on circumstances of the moment—an inherent dialectic. So this chapter is really about change and transformation, meaning creation within the context of hard-nosed realities of daily living. No simple task, indeed. But you have the courage to do this because it is important.

Urgency and Timing

The issue of urgency is a complex one, and one that most of us in emotional pain fall victim to. Why? Emotional pain, as we've already discussed, increases a sense of urgency. When you feel urgent, you want everything to happen now: "I can't stand my emotional pain any longer and want it to end now." So what do you do? You engage in impulsive behaviors. You want to do something, anything, to end what is happening or what you're experiencing. You begin to act, to impulsively try to do something that might work. Anger is a good example. If you're furious that someone failed to comply with a request you made, then the feeling of being ignored, taken advantage of, made unimportant by them, and having your wants unfulfilled all make you want to do something to make the situation right (in your eyes). You may yell and scream at them. You may call them names. You may say something inane, walk briskly away, and slam the door behind you. Does this increase the chances that they will comply with your requests in the future? No, of course not. It increases the chances that the other person will avoid you in the future, not make commitments to you of any kind, or engage in passive-aggressive behavior (i.e., say what you want to hear, but do something else). And that's not what you want.

Urgency, in general, is thus an enemy. In most cases, urgency derails you. It decreases the accuracy of your judgment because you no longer choose from available options. Instead, what you do is try as many things on your list of options as possible, frequently in rapid succession, and sometimes without waiting to see if the last thing you tried even worked. You are not using wisdom, you're not being judicial, and you are not keeping your important goals in mind. You're responding to your sense of urgency to remove the prompt for your strong emotion without attention to the effect this will have on your other purposes or wants.

A sense of urgency should thus always be seen as a red flag that perhaps you're about to be impulsive in your actions, forget your longer-term objectives, and engage in self-defeating behavior.

Urgency and What's Important

Obviously there is a time and place for urgency. You should urgently run from a burning building, urgently rescue your drowning child, and urgently apply your brakes when you're about to hit something with your car. But how urgent is it that you punish someone who infuriates you? How urgent is it that someone express affection or love for you right now or that you receive recognition or admiration for your abilities? Are these feelings of urgency really responding to short-term needs and wants? Most of your important and meaningful needs and wants are longer-term. No one should be surprised that you want recognition, love, affection, and respect from others. These are longer-term needs, and if you treat them with a sense of urgency, then you are more likely to make critical errors due to impulsivity.

Go back to your initial notes on "What Is Important to Me," beginning on page 86. In the first column of the following worksheet write a shorthand description of a thing or process you find meaningful. In the second column, rate if this need or want is an urgent one (one that needs to be met immediately), an intermediate one (one that needs periodic and ongoing satisfaction), or a long-term one (one that needs to be satisfied eventually and doesn't necessarily need to be displayed consistently). In the third column, rate the force or strength of the underlying feelings you have about it. The third column is different from the second in that you are rating how often you think about it or feel a need for it, or how often it influences you. With urgency we instead are considering the issue of time (how quickly you need it satisfied).

Important to me	Rate the urgency of having this want or need satisfied			Frequency (strength) of my feelings about it		
	Urgent	Medium	Long-term	Strong	Medium	Weak
Example: Being loved						
_____ _____						
_____ _____						
_____ _____						
_____ _____						
_____ _____						
_____ _____						
_____ _____						
_____ _____						
_____ _____						
_____ _____						
_____ _____						

If you find that many of your urgency ratings are in the "urgent" category, then you're probably confusing how important it is to you (your ranking in the third column) with how urgently it needs to be met. And that is precisely what happens when you become anxious, depressed, panic-stricken, guilt-ridden, or shamed. You confuse the strength of your desire or feeling with the issue of timing. You act as if quick action will bring quick relief.

Now take a look at your check marks in the third column. When your feelings are strong and you feel them frequently, this generally signals that the associated item is a long-term process. Being loved, for example, is something you work toward on a continuing basis. It need not be satisfied in each waking hour, and you certainly don't need it to be manifested now, in this precise moment. Instead, you need it periodically over the course of your lifetime. If you find that there isn't a correlation between those items you ranked as "strong" in the last column and "long-term" in the second column, then you may wish to reconsider how you approach your need-satisfying strategies.

Examine the first column, where you've written what is important to you. For those things you rated "strong," how often do you pursue them? Do you do something every day, or even multiple times per day, to achieve those things that you want? Strategic behavior is about having plans, but plans are rather useless unless you enact them. And typically there are both small (or short-term) and large (long-term) actions you can take to accomplish your objectives. While short-term plans may not bring you what you want immediately, they set the stage for getting what you want eventually. Short-term behaviors frequently set in motion reciprocal actions by others. For example, the more often you call your friends and plan recreational activities with them, the higher the likelihood that they eventually will begin calling you and including you in some of their recreational pursuits. This is one way that friendships are built.

In this next worksheet, list again what is important to you, and write both short-term and long-term behaviors, actions, and thoughts you can engage in that will increase the chances that you obtain what's important.

What is important to me	Short-term plans to accomplish	Long-term plans to accomplish
Example: Make more friends	1. Review the newspaper for upcoming events I can attend, particularly those that involve time to talk to others (show up early). 2. Make a point to engage in eye contact when running errands (the grocery store, gas station, parking lot, etc.) and say hello when possible. 3. Catch myself when I make excuses for not being friendly and outgoing. 4. Do more things. Stay out of my house or apartment.	1. Work on being less task focused and more friendly. 2. Work on talking more about me. 3. Ask more questions of others, showing interest. 4. Create recreational opportunities.

What is important to me	Short-term plans to accomplish	Long-term plans to accomplish
_____	_____	_____
_____	_____	_____
_____	_____	_____
_____	_____	_____
_____	_____	_____
	_____	_____
	_____	_____
	_____	_____
	_____	_____
	_____	_____
	_____	_____
	_____	_____
	_____	_____
	_____	_____
	_____	_____
	_____	_____
	_____	_____
	_____	_____
	_____	_____
	_____	_____
	_____	_____
	_____	_____
	_____	_____
	_____	_____
	_____	_____
	_____	_____
	_____	_____
	_____	_____

What is important to me	Short-term plans to accomplish	Long-term plans to accomplish
_____	_____	_____
_____	_____	_____
_____	_____	_____
_____	_____	_____
_____	_____	_____
	_____	_____
	_____	_____
	_____	_____
	_____	_____
	_____	_____
	_____	_____
	_____	_____
	_____	_____
	_____	_____
	_____	_____
	_____	_____
	_____	_____
	_____	_____
	_____	_____
	_____	_____
	_____	_____
	_____	_____
	_____	_____
	_____	_____
	_____	_____
	_____	_____
	_____	_____
	_____	_____
	_____	_____

Ask yourself the following questions about your short- and long-term plans. Spend some time and energy answering them, as their answers will help you strategize and plan your actions.

◊ What is going to prompt or remind you to actually do these things?

◊ What are the obstacles or barriers to accomplishing your plans?

◊ What has made it difficult for you to do these things in the past?

◊ What, if anything, do you stand to lose by engaging in these plans?

◊ How much of what you need to accomplish these plans is under your control?

◊ How much of what you need to accomplish these plans relies on others' efforts?

◊ If you're relying on others, what do you have to offer them that can make them more likely to want to assist you?

◊ Are you trying to do too much? Too little? People suffering from depression frequently try to do too much, and those suffering from anxiety try to do too little. Make your goals reasonable.

◊ Can you really sustain these things? Could any reasonable person be expected to do these things?

◊ Is there any way you can break these goals down into more manageable steps?

◊ Can you lower your short-term expectations in service of your long-term wants and needs?

◊ How much is your sense of urgency interfering with the accomplishment of your goals?

◊ How is your behavior being influenced by your moods?

Your answer to these questions can help you to revise your goals when you meet obstacles, maintain optimism within a realistic framework, and separate out strategy from mood-dependent behavior (the topic to which we turn next).

Does Your Behavior Reflect Mood or Strategy?

One of the most difficult barriers to overcome with emotional problems is mood-dependent behavior (Barrett et al. 2001; Tice, Bratslavsky, and Braumeister 2001). A behavior is mood-dependent when you engage in it because of the mood you're in. The behavior is thus acting more as an expression of the mood than as a way to meet a goal. An example is when you are feeling irritable and someone asks you for something and gets a surprisingly grumpy response. Adolescents, with their raging hormones, frequently respond to situations based more on their moods than on the situation to which they are responding. When you're angry and "kill the messenger," this is mood-dependent behavior. When feeling depressed, it can be difficult to overcome the mood-propelling tendency to reject, be judgmental, trivialize, or engage in generally pessimistic thinking. Your behavior under such circumstances reflects your mood, as you turn down opportunities, decrease activity, socially withdraw, push others away with your criticism or sarcasm, or engage in other self-defeating behaviors. Mood-dependent behavior is not strategic or wise. It does not help you to pursue your long-term objectives.

Getting Strategic

Strategic behavior requires that you become aware of your mood when you're responding to situations and ask yourself if the response you are contemplating is going to help you get what you really want (is based upon your goals, values, and objectives) or if it's mood-dependent (expresses your underlying feelings, but is counterproductive to your goals, values, and objectives).

In order to accomplish such strategic behavior, you have to break the situation down into its components.

1. What is the environmental (external) prompt? What is happening to which you're about to respond?

2. What is your (internal) mood?

3. What is your short-term goal or objective?

4. What is your long-term goal or objective?

5. What behavior (action) will accomplish your goal?

6. If you express your mood in this moment, will it interfere with your long-term or short-term objectives? Will it interfere with or enhance your goal obtainment?

This problem-solving process is pretty obvious, but under high emotionalism, most of us fail to use it. We respond to our emotions because they are immediate, powerful, and processed more quickly than our rational thoughts. Even those of us who are fearful of our emotions and try not to express them engage in mood-dependent behavior. While we may be reticent or downright obstinate about allowing ourselves to cry, express hurt, or (heaven forbid) let others see us as having needs, we will express these underlying feelings in other behavioral ways (withdrawal, criticism of others, sarcasm, temper tantrums, drug use, or passive-aggressiveness). As I said, such mood-dependent behavior is not strategic or wise. So we have to remind ourselves to use a problem-solving, strategic approach to life. Such reminders must be frequent and (over time) become habitual.

The mnemonic to use here to remind you about your goals and values is OBJECTIVES.

Outside. What's going on outside of you that prompts you to do this or that? What is happening in the environment?

Beliefs. What are your beliefs about what's going on outside of you? What are your thoughts, anticipations, and interpretations about the event to which you are about to react?

Judicial. How can you have a kind judge who will coach you toward an adaptive and correct course of action to take? Evaluate and judge your behavior in terms of your goals and aspirations.

Emotions. What are you feeling? Give voice and power to your feelings without being reactionary and mood dependent.

Consequences. What will happen if you express your emotion? What are the consequences of doing this or not doing this?

Time. Is it the right time to do this? Focus on the environment and your objectives, not on your feelings.

Introspection. Is this really that important to you? How important? What are the costs and the advantages? Are you willing to risk the consequences given your values?

Values. Does this have sustaining interest and value to you? Does it come from deep within you, or is it only situational?

Endings and Exposure. End this process. Make a decision, one way or the other. Face the consequences and gain the rewards.

Short-term and long-term objectives. Was this decision serving your short-term or your long-term goals? Be mindful of balance (sometimes focus on short-term goals, sometimes on long-term goals).

The "O" in OBJECTIVES stands for "outside." What's going on outside of you that prompts you to do this or that? What's happening in the environment? Outside is requesting some sort of action, or you are desiring something from outside of you to happen. It can be an event, process, or thing. What is precipitating you to do something?

The "B" is for "beliefs." What do you believe or think about what is going on outside of you? What are your thoughts, anticipations, and interpretations about the event to which you're about to react? These can be subtle "as if" interpretations or assumptions, as we discussed previously. If you are prone to act as if everybody must love you and you just got rejected, you'll believe that the situation is horrific (even if you never consciously say this to yourself, you surmise it must be so given your reaction to the event in "O").

The "J" is for "judicial." Wisdom involves a judicial stance toward the world. You evaluate and judge the adaptiveness and correctness of potential courses of action. You are the "judge" who decides if this set of beliefs or this way of interpreting the world is in your best interest. Since you're the judge, the judicial function should be self-serving and personal. You do not judge what others may think, what is politically correct, or mimic what you anticipate someone else may think is the correct interpretation of the beliefs in "B." Instead, your judicial function evaluates the beliefs for their functionality and goal directedness to your own aspirations. This is different than judgmentalism because the judicial function in "J" is designed to help you navigate the maps you yourself have formed. Judicial functioning is thus a kind court designed to help you get what you want, which is to find and increase the meaning you seek in your life. It is critical, in that it attempts to evaluate other potential interpretations or understandings of the world, but it is not invalidating. The judicial function works for you, not against you.

The first "E" in the mnemonic OBJECTIVES is for "emotions." What is it that you're feeling? The invitation here is to be mindful of what your emotions are and to give them voice and power over your problem-solving process. While mood-dependent behavior is not adaptive or wise, sensitivity to your emotional reactions is not mood dependent. What's the difference? In mood-dependent behavior you react unconsciously, without forethought or analysis. You just react to your moods because they are there. Here, what you're attempting to do is consider and give power to your emotions, since frequently they do communicate important information about how to react and how to understand the world. Mood-dependent behavior is reactionary, while mindful emotion recognition is considered. You are in touch with your emotions, without necessarily reacting to them. You feel, but don't yet behave.

The "C" stands for "consequences." What will happen if you express your emotion? What potential reactions of others or of the environment will occur if you express your emotions? What reactions or consequences will there be if you express your beliefs or thoughts? There are consequences to each action you engage in, some mild or lacking in meaning and others powerfully influential over both your long-term and your short-term goals and aspirations. Consequences can be interpersonal, intrapersonal (within oneself, such as self-esteem), financial, political, sociological, cultural, or environmental. What will happen if you react to your emotions or beliefs as you are prompted to do in this moment? The consequences do not relate to the validity of your emotion. Your feeling may be totally appropriate and expectable, but the consequence for expressing it might be quite negative.

The "T" is for "time." Evaluate the timeliness of your potential reaction. Is this the right time to express your emotion or belief? Timing can be the most powerful variable in evaluating the potential success or failure of your actions. Telling someone how you feel can provide comfort, reassurance, bonding, and increase meaningfulness at one point in time, and in another instance can bring criticism, anger, rejection, and punishment. For example, telling someone you love them on your first date could lead the person to believe you are superficial and devious (that you have an agenda that is not so cleverly hidden), but saying the same thing after the relationship has matured and both of you are entitled to and expecting emotional feedback will bring the exact reverse emotional response from the person. Attempting to enhance and sustain established relationships is an important goal, while expending great effort and strain attempting to gain the attention and admiration of someone who doesn't know you exist may be foolish. Is this the right time to express your thoughts and feelings? How do you know? How much of this decision is based on your beliefs and how much on your feelings? Have you consulted your judicial self? Should you wait for a more appropriate time? Or should you strike while the iron is hot?

By engaging in the above process you are entering the "I" of "introspection." Introspection is when you look into yourself, reminding yourself of your goals and objectives. What really is meaningful to you? Is this really that important to you? Does it speak to your goals and aspirations in life, or is it a temporary and transitory bump in the road? *You* are important, but is *this* really that important? Be mindful, and your reactions can be improved because you do not simply respond haphazardly to what you are confronting.

"V" is for "values." Remind yourself of what is important and valuable. Will this have sustaining interest and meaning to you, or is it just a distraction that you're using to avoid more important and perhaps scary outcomes about which you're insecure? Are you forming this value on the spur of the moment, in reaction to what just happened (in "O"), or is this something you've really pondered and considered in the context of your overall map of the world you want to live in? Including your values in your decision making is wise; simply reacting to strong emotions because they are strong is counterproductive. It does not get you to where you probably want to go. Living your values is strategic and brings wisdom.

"E" is for "endings and exposure." You have thought about the consequences of doing this or that, considered how your thoughts and feelings influence the possible courses of action, and now it is time to act. It is time to end your thinking and feeling about this possible reaction versus that one and to do something. You do not engage in this exercise simply to be confident of your situation—you do it because you want to obtain your objectives and get what you want out of life. You do it in order to increase meaning and develop wisdom in your daily functioning. End this emotional and rational encounter with the universe, act, do something, and then a new and different challenge will present itself. If you do not act, engaging in behavior in response to your analysis, then you substantially decrease your power over your world as you see it. Exposure to that which you fear can make you stronger.

In "S," finally, be mindful of both "short-term and long-term objectives." If what you just did served your short-term interests but had long-term negative consequences, then you need to repair the damage. Alternatively, if you decided to forgo your short-term desires, you need to be mindful of that fact and be certain that sometimes you engage in behavior that helps you satisfy your short-term objectives as well. Life is a series of compromises, some of them satisfactory and some of them pretty dismal. Balance is what you are seeking, not perfection. I don't know anyone who is able to always meet both their long-term and their short-term objectives. Sometimes one is sacrificed to serve the other. This is the core of dialectical therapy, that sometimes you compromise in one direction and sometimes in the opposite direction. You form a synthesis of competing and contradictory needs over time so that all needs are sometimes served and no need is always served.

Use the form below to practice OBJECTIVES and avoid mood-dependent behaviors. In so doing, you will be engaging in more strategic behavior that is self-enhancing. You will feel better about yourself and improve your problem-solving skills.

Your Cue	Example	Your Situation
Outside. What is happening outside of me in the environment? What caused or prompted me to react?	I've been offered a promotion at work.	
Beliefs. What am I saying to myself about this event? What are my thoughts?	I'll probably fail. I'll make a fool of myself. Better to stay where I am because it's safer.	

Judicial. Be critical, evaluating the reality or veracity of my beliefs.	Who knows if I'll fail! Maybe I'll be the best damn manager they've ever seen! I've been preparing for this move.	
Emotions. What am I feeling about this?	I'm scared, anxious, and excited at the same time.	
Consequences. What will happen if I respond to my beliefs or feelings?	If I respond to my first thought, I'll avoid. If I respond to my fear, I'll avoid. If I respond to my excitement, I'll probably take the job.	
Time. Is this the right time to do it? Is it based on emotion or thought that I conclude this is or isn't the right time? Am I avoiding or being impulsive?	Knowing this company, I probably won't be asked a second time. I either do this now or forgo the probability of future career advancement with this company. Of course, I could always take a job elsewhere and repeat my chances of promotion.	
Introspection. Have I really worked this through sufficiently? What are the variables?	I've been struggling with my perception of my abilities for a long time. This is probably not anything impulsive.	
Values. Is this potential response consistent with my values? Is it meaningful and important?	I like my job. I think what I do is important. Therefore this is about my feelings of worthiness, and I do want to promote myself. My new work will be meaningful to me also.	
Endings and Exposure. I have to make a decision, take a risk, let myself succeed or fail.	I'm going to expose myself to this anxiety, take this job, and see what happens.	

Short-term and long-term. Did what I just do serve my short-term needs or my long-term needs? I need to compromise between the two.	I'm serving my long-term needs. I'm exposing myself to something frightening in the now (the new job), so I'm not satisfying my short-term needs. I need to do something now to make myself relax so I'm better prepared to tolerate the anxiety of the new job in the future.	_____ _____ _____ _____ _____ _____

Each time you face difficult problems, experience high arousal, or find yourself feeling a sense of urgency, you can engage in OBJECTIVES in order to access and intensify your use of wisdom.

Emotional Sensitivity and Distrust of Emotions

Some people are extremely ashamed that they emote so easily (Gross, John, and Richards 2000). They feel they are different or even weird because they cry so easily (such as during a commercial that shows something lovely), get excited so quickly (begin talking a bit more loudly and rapidly when discussing something they like), or experience dejection so rapidly (become despondent when their plans are disappointed). The result can be that they protect themselves as much as possible from experiencing emotionally provocative events (Barrett et al. 2001) and look to others to decide how much to feel. The dialectic here is between emotional receptivity and emotional blunting—expressing or repressing what you experience.

Since you feel what you feel (just as you see what you visually observe), to begin to distrust your emotions is extremely invalidating. Although it's important to be able to work toward positive change in your life, it's equally important to be able to accept your basic nature. Some of us are born naturally expressive and responsive to our environments, and others are born rather reserved and less influenced by environmental events.

The question to ask is whether your expressiveness is natural or contrived. Do you spontaneously and without effort operate this way, or are you expending effort to be different from your natural inclinations? If you strain to suppress your emotions, you may be draining vital emotional energy that you could put to use more effectively elsewhere. Alternatively, if you find that you must strain to express your emotions, is this because of fear that you'll be wrong, be punished, or be overwhelmed by your emotions? Or is it because you're naturally thing or activity oriented rather than people oriented (more focused on tasks than on process)? Is your expression or repression of emotion natural or is it forced? Is it a defense against something else, where you feel anxiety and pressure, or are you simply more entertained with interaction in activities that are not emotion inspiring?

There is no one "right" personality predisposition. There is no "one size fits all" in psychology. It will serve you best to accept your natural inclinations once you have ruled out that these patterns are defenses against something else or responses to trauma or secrets that bring shame and anticipatory avoidance.

Dialectical thinking suggests that we should examine the pros and cons of the emotional expressiveness continua.

Emotionally Expressive	<————————>	Emotionally Reserved
Open to Experience	<————————>	Observing of Experience
Affected by what is going on around you	<————————>	Unaffected by what is going on around you
People get to know you fast	<————————>	People find you hard to know
More emotional changes	<————————>	Fewer emotional changes
Easy to establish relationships	<————————>	Difficult to establish relationships

The potential pitfall is deciding to evaluate these alternatives as "good" or "bad." They are neither. There are advantages and disadvantages to both. The emotionally expressive person is more easily influenced by what is going on around them, and that makes their lives more potentially vibrant and changeable. But it also makes them more susceptible to emotional shifts and more psychologically dependent on the environment. The emotionally reserved person, on the other hand, is better protected from environmental shifts. They are also less vulnerable to manipulation by others and experience less emotional turmoil. However, it is more difficult for the reserved person to make friends, sustain relationships, and change their mood once the mood begins. So there are advantages and disadvantages to each personality style.

Strategic behavior asks you to use this information about yourself rather than try to change it. Rather than an emotionally expressive person attempting to hide their feelings or an emotionally reserved person trying to express feelings they're not confident they have, simply use your knowledge about your propensities. How can you use it? The TRUST mnemonic can show you how.

Trust that the feeling you are having is okay and acceptable.

Redirect your attention to your objectives and goals.

Use your understanding of your personality to make rational choices.

Sense your face, muscles, voice, and posture.

Tame the expression of your emotion to fit your objectives.

TRUST will work differently with each personality style. For the emotionally reserved person, you Trust that it is okay not to be effusive and exceptionally demonstrative. However, you have to Redirect your attention to your objectives. If your objective is to begin a friendship with someone you just met, then you have to be aware that you send out too few signals to others to let them know this. Since you are less easy to read (because of your relative undemonstrativeness), you have to make specific verbal disclosure of your reactions to others. "I really like what you just said" will work just fine. If you're not sure of what you are feeling, you Use your understanding of your personality and issues to make rational choices.

This means you are exceptionally familiar with your priorities (reread your inventory of them on page 86. Strategic behavior demands that your analysis is in accord with your objectives. Our emotions (that are immediate and powerful) can influence over the short-term what we perceive our objectives to be. Go back to your original writing on what is important to you (that probably represents more long-term objectives), and compare it to what you now identify as the objective. If extending trustworthy relationships in your life is among your highest desires, then beware of the opposite (that you might be overly critical of the motivations of others and dismiss them too quickly). Sense your face, muscles, voice, and posture in order to get a clearer picture of what you might be feeling. For the emotionally reserved person, you are less likely to access your feelings and use them, so sensing your body can remind you to access your emotions. Pay attention to your body and your thoughts, and they will suggest the feelings you may be having. Taming the expression of your feeling does not mean that you attempt to be like everyone else. It means that you are aware of your relative lack of emotional disclosure and make conscious efforts to jack it up just a bit in service of accurate communication to others. You are trying to accomplish your objectives, to express what you want and get what you want, not to be someone else or change your total self.

With the emotionally demonstrative person, you also start with Trust your feelings, validating that what you're feeling is acceptable and important. However, because you use your understanding of your personality (that you're easily provoked and influenced by what's going on in the environment), you Redirect your attention from your feelings to your goals and objectives. If what you want is to establish more meaningful relationships in your life, then you must remind yourself (Use your understanding of yourself) how much of an open book you are and choose your words carefully so that you don't come off as so intense that you scare people (like your emotionally reserved friend) away. You, too, have to Sense your face, muscles, posture, and voice to communicate what you want to have communicated. You Tame the expression of your emotion to your objective. It's not that your feelings are wrong—it's that you measure your expression of that feeling so that you can reach your goal.

Some people have difficulty with this reasoning. You might say, "Why should I have to tame my emotion if it is valid and acceptable? Why can't others just accept my valid feelings? Isn't it their problem if they can't accept how I feel?" No! Again, the confusion is between behavior and emotion. You accept your feeling for what it is, and you validate it as okay. However, what you choose to do with that feeling is another matter. If you use strategic behavior and your wisdom, then you know that your expression of your emotions is an act of communication. As the communicator to another person, it is your responsibility to get the message across that you want received. It's not their responsibility to read between the lines and somehow know what you mean.

Taming the emotion is thus about communication, about accurate reception of messages, and about sending out cues about your objectives and perceptions. It is not about trying to feel differently than you feel.

Let's try an example to see how TRUST works with both emotionally expressive and emotionally reserved personalities. The example situation for both personality types is that you're frustrated that your spouse is constantly criticizing you over the last two days.

Emotionally Expressive Type	Emotionally Unexpressive Type
Trust my feelings. It is okay that I'm frustrated. I just need to make sure I don't bowl him over with my expression of it.	**Trust** my feelings. It is okay that I'm frustrated. I just need to make sure I get my message across.
Redirect to my objectives. I'm really frustrated, but what I really want in this situation is to make him understand that I need support. I want him to know that he is eager to criticize and has been skinny on compliments.	**Redirect** to my objectives. I'm frustrated, but he probably doesn't know it. Redirect my attention to him. What do I need to say to him to let him know how I feel?
Use my personality. I'm expressive. I tell him a lot. Probably because I say so much, my message can get lost. I need to slow down, look him directly in the eyes, and let him know that this is important to me and not another one of my stream-of-consciousness verbalizations.	**Use** my personality. I'm quiet. I don't tell him much. Maybe he doesn't have any idea that his criticisms are bothering me so much. I need to just tell him, in plain English, what I'm feeling and thinking.
Sense my face, body, posture, voice. I'm tense, but not that tense. This is not the end of the world. I know he loves me, so maybe I should temper what I tell him. But when I tell him, it will be important that I let him know that this is a real issue and not something that I just thought of on the spur of the moment.	**Sense** my face body, posture, voice. I'm tense. I'm usually not affected by him, because I know that he loves me. But these critical remarks have gotten out of hand. I need to let him know how I feel. I need to be strategic and let him know what I want from him.
Tame my feeling. Since this is not the end of the world, I won't beat him silly with arguments proving that what he's doing is wrong. I'll get close to his face, look him in the eyes, and just tell him what I'm feeling. Nothing dramatic.	**Tame** my feeling. I'm typically so meek and uncommunicative that sometimes it's difficult to get my point across. I'll practice what I'm going to say to him. I'll use feeling words, telling him that I've been feeling nervous about talking to him about this, but that it has been bothering me so I decided to do it anyway. I'll tell him that it hurts when he criticizes me so much and gives so few compliments.

With both types of emotional expressiveness the goal is to have the other person understand what you're feeling. You use your knowledge of your personality to temper or tame your expression so that you are understood accurately. This is strategic behavior, and it uses your wisdom. It helps you get what you want because it's objective oriented, rather than simply expressing each emotion as it might naturally come out.

When a situation occurs where you are concerned about your emotional expression (no matter if your basic predisposition is be under- or overexpressive), use the TRUST mnemonic to help in your problem-solving process. In the following worksheet you can write about a situation involving emotional expression that concerns you. For Trust, identify and validate your feeling. For Redirect, state your objective (what you want to have happen). For Use, writing your anticipation about how your natural under- or overexpressiveness will affect your strategy. For Sense, take stock of your bodily reaction. Tame is for writing how your understanding of your personality type will cause you to tame your expression of your emotion in order to get what you want.

Trust my feelings.	_____ _____ _____ _____
Redirect to my objectives.	_____ _____ _____ _____
Use my personality.	_____ _____ _____ _____
Sense my face, body, posture, voice.	_____ _____ _____ _____
Tame my feeling.	_____ _____ _____ _____

Behavior Focus

Being strategic, having your objective or purpose in mind, is difficult to do when you are extremely anxious and depressed. Your attention and focus is on the pain itself, and you may fail to attend to other variables affecting or promoting your pain. This is natural and normal, but not helpful. Wisdom requires that you attend to all aspects of your situation, that you pay attention to what might be causing your pain so that you can eliminate those causes and thus reduce your emotional suffering. Frequently you identify only global or generic causes such as loneliness, potential humiliation in the face of your peers, loss of something that was powerfully important to you, or loss of meaning in your life. Strategic behavior requires you to be more specific, to drill down further and search more completely. The BEHAVIOR mnemonic can help you to do just that.

<u>B</u>ehavior

<u>E</u>nvironment

<u>H</u>ealing versus Hurting

<u>A</u>ntecedents

<u>V</u>alues

<u>I</u>nterval

<u>O</u>utcome

<u>R</u>einforcement

While DBT attributes most psychological difficulties to the emotional realm (you don't trust your feelings, you avoid your feelings), it is also true that emotional maladies are behaviorally reinforced or sustained by your environment. If you find that issues appear to surface out of the blue and repetitively, then there is something that you or the environment is doing that keeps these "new" and "different" crises developing.

I'm not trying to blame the victim here. I'm not suggesting you're at fault because your behavior may tend to sustain your pain. I'm suggesting that a more specific behavioral analysis of your situation may help you feel better.

Use the BEHAVIOR mnemonic to do your own behavioral analysis. You can do it, even if preliminarily, on your own. If you don't come up with something significant and explanatory, then maybe you need a coach (a trusted friend, sponsor, mentor, or therapist) to help you tease out the details.

The BEHAVIOR analysis can help you keep yourself focused on what's important, can keep your responses effective, and can help to decrease the mixed anxiety and depression that has decreased your quality of life. I mentioned earlier that strategic behavior can be ambiguous because it's so situational. Your strategy must take into account the specifics of what is going on now, what you anticipate to be the conditions in the future, and what your objectives are. The BEHAVIOR mnemonic is thus designed to provide a global analytical framework you can use with any situation you find especially confusing, anxiety provoking, or powerful over the course of your life. We will review some examples so you can get a feel for how to use the mnemonic in actual problem solving. Later, there is a blank worksheet for you to write down your own responses. Choose a situation that is important to you, in which you find yourself unable to make a decision and you care about the long-term consequences of your actions. There is also a blank version at the back of the book for you to photocopy before completing, so that you can use the strategy on an ongoing basis to improve your behavioral effectiveness.

Behavior. Could you be doing something that is causing this to happen? What do you do immediately before the undesired event occurs? What do you do immediately after the prior event occurs? How do you influence other people's behavior? While you may consider yourself powerless and lacking in influence, the truth is that we are all mutually influential on each other. You do influence the behavior of others, even if many times it feels like you don't. This is about frustration in not accomplishing your goals, not about proof that you don't have a role in what is going on around you. What is your specific behavior, perhaps as observed by an alien who wants to know how these darn humans interact with one another? You have to look at the situation and your own part in it with some distance and objectivity.	Example: I express depression, then my mother and my spouse reassure me and tell me that everything will be okay. People in my environment provide the soothing that I refuse to give to myself. I'm still depressed, but I've been reassured that my worst fears are not true. I feel just a little bit better, and this encourages me to express my depression again. I begin to practice the feeling, and it grows.
Environment. Is there something in your immediate environment that is prompting this to occur? What does the environment "want" or prompt others and you to do? What are the "demand characteristics" of this environment? What does it expect of you?	Example: I'm petrified that I'll fail at work. I'm scared to enter the employment market because then, as my mother always told me, I'll be discovered to be the inadequate, lazy bum she told me I'd amount to. Result: I do not try. I anticipate failure. I'm convinced that I'm no good, and I don't want evidence that it's true.
Healing versus Hurting. We all want to not hurt. But maybe you're doing something to try to heal yourself that is actually hurting you. Are you avoiding? Escaping? Seeing what you want to see rather than what is really happening? Are you reasoning based on your emotions (what you want and need) rather than your rational self? Are you fooling yourself into thinking and feeling this?	Example: I quit taking my antidepressant after three weeks because I didn't notice any improvement. In fact, I noticed my sexual interest and performance was decreased. No improvement, some worsening of symptoms; it is reasonable to stop my medications. My doctor warns me that the medication does not kick in for up to six weeks, but why put up with this?
Antecedents. We all tend to focus on the powerful feelings we have now. The intensity of your emotions skews your perspective. Antecedents remind you to look to what came before. What took place prior to the event that caused you pain?	Example: I avoid sexual contact with my wife. I "forget" that this avoidance all began after I was unable to sustain an erection to complete intercourse. I was humiliated, felt less than a man, and never wanted to experience those feelings again. It has now been months (maybe years) since the performance problem, but I keep the avoidance up because (unconsciously) the humiliation is worse than sexual deprivation.

Values. Even in a behavioral analysis, you need to take in to account what motivates you or is important to you. Your values, your needs, and your sense of deprivation provide powerful motivation to engage in certain behaviors. What is it that you're getting out of this situation? You're staying in it, in spite of your pain, so (on balance) there must be something in it for you. Otherwise you would have left that which causes pain. What is motivating you within this painful situation?	Example: I put up with a physically abusive husband. He beats me. I have bruises that I try to hide from others. I feel ashamed that I stay with him, but I'm afraid that my family will judge me about my poor choice of boyfriends. They warned me, and their opinion of me is more important to me than my own opinion of myself. Keeping the secret reduces anticipated greater emotional pain, which is worse than the physical pain inflicted by my husband.
Interval. We tend to pay attention only to things that occur regularly and steadily. However, we know from extensive research that things that occur infrequently but occasionally are even more powerful sustainers of behavior. (How often does a person have to punch you in the nose before you rationally decide that you're in danger?) What powerful but infrequent events may be sustaining these crisis situations?	Example: Once, when I visited a large shopping mall, I had a panic attack. Last time I tried to visit that same mall, I began to have the same heart palpitations, dizziness, and perspiration that I had before. I never go the mall now, even though it has been years since I last tried.
Outcome. The proof is always in the pudding. What effect do these events have on you? The outcome, and it may not be emotional on the face of it, may be keeping these undesired events going. What is the payoff? What do you get out of it? What bad thing is avoided by keeping this going?	Example: I want to get married and have a family. However, every time I go on a date, the person turns out to be a dud. But I can see that by concluding they are duds before I really get to know them, I'm spared the anxiety of intimacy (even if I'm not always aware of the anxiety). I don't know the anxiety is there because it's all anticipatory. I tend to interpret my slight feelings of anxiety as a signal that the other person is a dud. I usually just refuse another date with them, so I never really know if it is them or me.
Reinforcement. What is the payoff? Like our examination of values (what you know to be important to you), reinforcement asks you to examine what it is that increases the probability of your behavior. What sustains your participation in this process? What keeps this cycle going?	Example: I go see my therapist, who is warm and supportive. In fact, he is the only person who is warm and supportive in my life. I find that the more problems I have, the more support he provides. While intending to help me, he is giving me what I need and not encouraging me to get these needs met in my routine day-to-day life.

While this is simplistic behavioral analysis, and "real" behavioral analysis is much more specific and sophisticated, a full behavioral analysis is beyond the scope of this book. Now let's look at another example of the BEHAVIOR technique.

Behavior. What are you doing that is causing this to happen? How do you influence other people's behavior? What role do you have and what do you do in this situation? Look at the situation and your own part in it with some distance and objectivity.	Example: I'm tense and depressed all the time. I feel that no matter what I do, nothing changes. Life is no fun anymore. My behavior is negative. I see the glass as half empty all the time. I complain and criticize others. Now they don't want to be around me, and I don't want to be around them.
Environment. Is there something in your immediate environment that is prompting this to occur? What does the environment "want" or prompt others and you in it to do?	My environment is depressing and rejecting. I guess I've pushed people's buttons so often that now they feel they have to defend against me even before I open my mouth.
Healing versus Hurting. Are you doing something to try to heal yourself that is actually hurting you? Are you avoiding? Escaping?	I'm trying to protect myself by keeping people at a distance. I'm safe from attack that way. But now I'm lonely and depressed, so my attempt to heal myself really is hurting me.
Antecedents. Look to what came before. What took place prior to the event that caused you pain?	Kids teased me in school because I was so shy. I came to expect that they would attack me. I came to believe that it's better to be on the attack rather than on the defense. So now I'm quick to verbally strike out before they have a chance to be critical of me.
Values. What is it that you're getting out of this painful situation? What is motivating you?	My anticipatory attack strategy expresses my value of being safe and of not getting the short end of the stick. I value safety, so I keep myself prepared with an army of critical comments.
Interval. Things that occur infrequently but occasionally are powerful sustainers of behavior. What powerful but infrequent events may be sustaining these crisis situations?	I must feel so vulnerable that I can't take being teased, even though it does not happen any more like it did in elementary and high school.
Outcome. What effect do these events have on you? What is the payoff? What do you get out of it? What bad thing is avoided by keeping this going?	The outcome is that I'm lonely, depressed, and always expecting to be attacked by others, even people I don't know. Though I'm protected from possible harm from other people, I also feel very alone.
Reinforcement. Examine what it is that increases the probability of your behavior. What keeps this cycle going?	What keeps this cycle going is my perception that it keeps me safe. People don't have the chance to get close enough to be critical of me. But I end up lonely and depressed, so it's not serving my real value or objective.

If you find that use of the BEHAVIOR mnemonic below does not result in any substantial ideas for behavior change, then you may need professional assistance. However, even if you are under the care of a mental-health professional, try to identify behavioral dynamics that may play a role in your emotional difficulties. Completing the following worksheet will help. Choose a situation that seems to repeat itself over time and causes both anxiety and depression in you. Give it as much consideration as you can. The point is to be self-observant, not to become a behavior therapist yourself. Do as much as you can, even if some of the responses are left blank. You can always return to them later. This is a process to be completed over time.

Behavior. What are you doing? How do you influence other people's behavior? What role do you have in this situation? What do you do? Look at the situation and your own part in it with some distance and objectivity.	_____ _____ _____ _____
Environment. Is there something in your immediate environment that is prompting this to occur? What does the environment "want" or prompt others and you in it to do?	_____ _____ _____ _____
Healing versus Hurting. Are you doing something to try to heal yourself that is actually hurting you? Are you avoiding? Escaping?	_____ _____ _____ _____
Antecedents. Look to what came before. What took place or came before? What took place prior to the event?	_____ _____ _____ _____
Values. What is it that you're getting out of this situation? What is motivating you within this painful situation?	_____ _____ _____ _____
Interval. Things that occur infrequently but occasionally are powerful sustainers of behavior. What powerful but infrequent events may be sustaining these crisis situations?	_____ _____ _____ _____

Outcome. What effect do these events have on you? What is the payoff? What do you get out of it? What bad thing is avoided by keeping this going?	
Reinforcement. Examine what it is that increases the probability of your behavior. What keeps this cycle going?	

Emotionalism

I outlined at the beginning of this book that DBT is designed to treat emotional difficulties having a certain topography: high emotional arousal, high emotional sensitivity, slow reduction in emotional tension, distrust of one's emotions, emotional escape, emotional avoidance, and a sense of urgency to solve problems immediately. It is fitting to return to this bare-bones outline at the conclusion of this book to examine how I have proposed to deal with each of these difficulties and how to decrease the chances that they continue to operate in your life.

With emotion regulation skills we break our experiences down into their smaller components (how expressed bodily, in your thoughts, in your behavior, and in the environment); you learn to be mindful of your current emotions (both pleasant and unpleasant) in order to decrease escape and avoidance conditioning from previous experience and to be more open to current experience; and you learn to tease apart primary from secondary emotional reactions. By increasing positive experiences and at times taking an opposite action, you're able to terminate cyclical patterns of painful anxiety and depression that, over time, have become self-sustaining. New feelings and moods can emerge.

With distress tolerance skills you learn to decrease pain by being mindful to it, and you learn to self-soothe or distract from your pain when you can't change the situation prompting the pain. You also learn to improve the moment, and you learn critical-thinking skills (acceptance) that can increase your pain tolerance.

Used together, mindfulness, emotion regulation, and distress tolerance skills (when applied rigorously over time) should decrease high emotional arousal and allow a faster return to a calm state once you are stressed. By exposing yourself to your emotions in new ways (mindfully), you should learn to trust your emotions and, over time, your emotional sensitivity can begin to work for you rather than against you. Finally, with the use of strategic behavior skills you can become more effective in gauging the appropriateness of your decisions based upon your own objectives and aspirations in life.

This set of strategies do work. They work exceptionally well with a variety of emotional problems and when applied to people having a variety of personality types. They're especially good for people who have the double whammy of both depression and anxiety. I have used these procedures in both acute hospital facilities and outpatient settings. The psychological research literature also validates that these procedures are effective (Koons et al. 2001; Linehan 1993a; Linehan et al. 1994).

Occasionally, however, a client tells me it's not working. The most frequent reason DBT does not work is due to emotionalism and a lack of practice. You may remember from our previous discussion that emotionalism is when you are urgently caught up in your emotions. You are running so fast from your anxiety or frantically trying to escape or avoid depression that you have no leftover brainpower to focus on anything else. With emotionalism, you cannot really complete any of the therapeutic strategies of DBT because you can't simultaneously be experiencing urgency to escape and be mindful. You can't be plunged into the heart of your feelings and reasonably expect to engage rational thought processes about your emotions. You can't do both at the same time. Emotionalism means you have put your brain on the back burner, and all of your resources are focused on your emotional self.

Certainly wisdom demands that we attend to all forms of knowing available to us: rational knowing, emotional knowing, and intuitive knowing. With emotionalism, we are using only one kind of knowing. Just like the rigid intellectual who refuses to accept that emotions are of any importance whatsoever, so too the person experiencing emotionalism is crippled by their inability to use all of the intellectual resources available to them.

If, as you attempt to practice any of the therapeutic techniques in this book, you find that they are not influencing you one bit, then the cause is either that you are simply going through the motions and not participating in the activity or that you are experiencing emotionalism.

CARES

It can be quite difficult to get out of emotionalism. When your feelings are exceptionally intense, doing something else (anything else) can be challenging. Therefore, CARES is designed to set the stage for greater calmness and thus lower the likelihood that emotionalism will occur in the first place. CARES is about preparation for calmness, a recognition that each moment influences each future moment. You need to engage in CARES each day, knowing that this is vital and strategic preparation for feeling good in the future.

Calm, coached practice

Arousal monitoring, **A**bstinence

Relaxation and **R**est

Emotions and **E**nvironment

Sleep

Practice

With "calm, coached practice" I invite you to choose someone to do something soothing with (go for a walk, jog, meditate, pray, or sunbathe). It can be "coached" in a number of different senses. You are coached or encouraged to engage in an activity when it is planned with someone else. You have a date and a plan, and you are less likely to back out of it if you know someone else is counting on you to do that activity. It can also be coached in the traditional sense. You invite someone to help you monitor your engagement in the activity.

Simply tell a friend that there is too much stress in your life and you want them to come over on Thursday evenings and make sure you do your yoga, music mindfulness, progressive muscle relaxation, imagery, and the like.

While most people acknowledge that stress is a problem in their lives and most people have some exposure to stress-management techniques, most people I know don't apply or practice the strategies they already know (let alone the variety of new strategies they could learn). So you're not alone if you feel challenged by maintaining a practice. Most people don't do routinely what they know is good for them. Many people, probably most people, allow themselves to be controlled by the environment (respond to this or that event) rather than being strategic in managing stress. So, you're not the only one, but the fact that you are doing what most people do won't alleviate your stress or make you feel good.

Be strategic in planning something that is calming every day. Take control of the environment by making some part of the day your stress-reliever break. Take five minutes before you leave for work each morning and do deep breathing. Take one minute in your car, before you start the engine, to engage in positive imagery before your trip home. Take five minutes just prior to brushing your teeth at bedtime to meditate. Whatever you do, make it routine and calm. There is no place for urgency with calmness. It has to be a long-term strategy that is implemented daily. It works, but only if it is applied routinely and rigorously.

Monitor

"Arousal monitoring" means paying attention to your body, your thoughts, and your feelings on a continuing basis. Once you are in a state of panic, your body screams at you, and you can no longer ignore it. Don't wait for the arousal to become so intense that you can no longer avoid it. Monitor it in an ongoing way. Since it's so much easier to decrease mild to moderate stress and extremely difficult to decrease intense stress, by monitoring your arousal or stress level consistently you will be in a better position to engage in emotionally corrective exercises that will work. Arousal and abstinence go hand in hand. Many people attempt to control their arousal by use of nonprescription or illicit drugs. Abstain from such practices. Use behavioral stress-management techniques whenever possible. Be compliant with the medications your physician prescribes. If you do not like the effects the medications the physician has given you, speak with them openly about it. Collaborate with your physician. Yes, it is your body, and your physician is your consultant and advocate. They want you to be better, and if you provide them with the information they need, you can cooperate to make changes to your medications so that they work better.

Relax

Relaxation should be something that occurs each day, every day. You should stretch, get in the hot tub, listen to great music, walk the dog mindfully, enjoy your shower mindfully, plan recreational activities, and do nothing that is goal oriented for at least a few minutes each day, multiple times each day.

Know Your Environment

"Emotions and environment" reminds you that it is the external world, your relationship with it and expectations about it, that influence your emotions. Refuse activities occasionally that are stressful. Give yourself permission to say no to something that you know will increase stress. Leave environments, even if only for a few minutes, that cause you anxiety or depression. Take a time-out on your own. Be aware of your feelings in the moment, and then shift your attention to what in the here and now is prompting or causing these feelings to be activated. Don't see yourself as a prisoner of your environment.

Sleep

Sleep is something that many people see as the most easily manipulated "discretionary" activity in their daily lives. You may stay up and watch the evening news, missing that extra half hour of sleep. You'll finish the movie you rented and miss that hour of sleep you normally get. While there is no immediate consequence that most of you are aware of when you reduce your sleep time, the consequence is indeed immediate and powerful. When you get too little sleep your mood is influenced. Perhaps you do not become the devil personified, but your potential for irritability, anger, and tension is increased. You become more reactive to your environment. There is a greater probability of emotionalism in your life. Get the sleep you need.

Modern sleep researchers have generally given up on their recommendations for how much sleep is needed. The eight to nine hours per day recommendation was a "one size fits all" approach that sounded good, but was wrong. Now we know that each person has their own internal clock that demands a certain amount of sleep. For some, four hours is plenty. For others, nine hours is barely enough. Become mindful of what your body wants. Don't just follow your previous habits. If you find that by getting that extra half hour of sleep you feel rested, your dreams are calmer, and the world doesn't provoke you as readily, then give yourself that extra sleep.

Too much sleep can be just as bad as too little. People suffering from depression often use sleep as way of escaping from their feelings. The consequences are the same for the depressed person who gets too much sleep as for the anxious person who gets too little. You need to adjust your hours of sleep to your body's signals. Your body and mind can let you know what the right amount of sleep is for you, if only you'll listen over a period of time and heed its communications.

Think of CARES the way it sounds: you are taking care of yourself, treating yourself with care. The more you engage in CARES, the lower your emotionalism will be and the more you will be able to profit from the other powerful strategies of DBT.

Below, identify ways you plan to use CARES to reduce your emotionalism.

	Examples	Write Your Plans
Calm, coached practice	I'll invite Jane to go with me to yoga on Wednesdays. I'll ask Tom at work to remind me to take my lunch hour rather than working through it.	_____ _____ _____ _____
Arousal monitoring, **Abstinence**	I'll stop smoking pot when I come home from work each day. During my lunch hour I'll take stock of my bodily sensations of tension and take stretch breaks during the afternoon.	_____ _____ _____ _____
Relaxation and **Rest**	No more work on the weekends, except cleaning my house. Each weekend I'll have a plan to do something that I find to be restful (rather than just hoping that it will happen automatically).	_____ _____ _____ _____
Emotions and **Environment**	I'm going to stop gossiping about all the politics that go on at work. It just makes me angry, and that increases my anxiety and contributes to my depression.	_____ _____ _____ _____
Sleep	I'm going to make it to bed by 10:00 P.M. every weeknight and 11:00 P.M. each weekend night. I'm going to sleep in one hour each weekend morning.	_____ _____ _____ _____

Mixed anxiety and depression can feel like a curse. You feel you have done nothing to deserve the emotional pain that you're required to deal with. The emotional struggle is often heightened by sleeplessness, nightmares, indigestion, and ever-present fear. It's hard to be confident that any strategy, no matter how powerful, can reduce your sense of futility. I invite you to work through the exercises in this book. Look for small changes over time. No single exercise by itself will rid you of your mixed anxiety and depression. Even doing all the exercises once will not help much. You need to do them repeatedly. Just like when your doctor prescribes an antibiotic for an infection, you must take all of the tablets, or your visit to the doctor, her diagnosis, and her prescription have been in vain.

See the techniques and strategies of this book like an antibiotic. You have to complete the full prescription. You have to practice daily. After each implementation, after each episode of practice, rate your tension and depression on a scale from 1 to 10. Don't look to go from a 10 to a 1 after one practice. Look for small, incremental changes over time. The changes may not be dramatic, but they will stick.

Some behaviors are so entrenched and automatic that you are not able to identify what may be maintaining your mixed anxiety and depression on your own. The assistance of a psychologist or psychiatrist cannot be replaced with a book if you need coaching and support to implement the strategies suggested by DBT. If you don't see the changes you want after sincerely working with the exercises for a period of months, seeking help from a therapist will enable you to make the progress you want.

On the following pages are a summary of the mnemonics of DBT and a chart that will allow you to record your practice of the DBT technology. Photocopy the charts before you write on them so you can make multiple clean copies to record your daily practice of the techniques. Remember, if you don't deploy the techniques, they can't help you. If you simply read this book, understand it, and then lead your life the way you always have, you cannot expect to feel better.

Conclusion

Mixed anxiety and depression is an especially painful set of disorders because it can test your very humanity (your understanding and acceptance of your emotions, your identity, and your relationships with others and the world in which you live). You can begin to question everything in your world, and few things are spared being affected, including your appetite, your sleep, your sex drive, your self-esteem, your concentration, and even the meaning you attribute to things in your life that previously were unquestionably important to you. The World Health Organization (Thornicroft and Maingay 2002) now understands that emotional disorders are among the most debilitating of all medical disorders (causing more suffering than all other specific medical disorders and leading to comparable disability days). There is thus little doubt that comorbid anxiety and depression can be a catastrophic experience. The modern techniques, procedures, and exercises in this book can eliminate your emotional suffering, but only if you use them systematically and frequently.

John was a patient of mine who used these procedures. His lower productivity at work caused him to be fired. His lack of affection, interaction, and interest in sex led his wife to leave him. John's wife could no longer tolerate his pessimism and withdrawal from life. She took the children with her. John felt, perhaps quite accurately, that his entire life had fallen apart. No means of economic support, no wife, no children, and no social life. Indeed, he had many reasons to be anxious and depressed. It took this much loss to force John into treatment. When he came in for treatment he had lost over twenty pounds in the preceding four months, bathed infrequently, and spent every day in his new little apartment, smoking cigarette after cigarette, and drinking more than he ever had in his life. He was in an emotional stupor, behaviorally paralyzed but feeling an intense sense of urgency to win his life back.

John and I began the laborious process of identifying and increasing meaning in his life, practicing meaning making on a daily basis, disengaging his emotional experiences of the past from his sense of identity, increasing emotion regulation strategies, increasing mindfulness to his daily experiences, applying distress tolerance procedures, and forcing him (sometimes against his will) to analyze his behavior so he could be more strategic and goal oriented in everything he did. After a month of practicing the principles of this book, his mood-dependent behavior began decreasing. His anxiety initially increased, since he was doing the very things he feared the most (experiencing his feelings rather than avoiding them). He increased joy in his life. He began planning social dates with his wife, who was hesitant and distrustful. Over time, he was able to show his wife that he could be fun to be with again, take interest in the children, and come out of his self-absorption. His renewed interest in the world and in having meaningful relationships with others (including his own family) resulted in a reuniting of his family. Although the new job he obtained was not totally satisfying to him, he had a plan for career advancement and used his free time to deepen his relationship with his wife and children. As his depression reduced, so did his fear of new experiences. His fear of his own emotions decreased, and he was thus better able to express himself in ways consistent with his emotional sensitivity. After three months, John had his life back. In addition to the application of the principles of this book, John had to engage in trial-and-error behavior, take risks, and refer to the worksheets of this book on a daily basis. It wasn't easy work, but it was the most important work he had ever done in his life.

There is no magic bullet in mental-health care that can easily and effortlessly reduce emotional suffering. In fact, the reverse is true. Reducing emotional suffering is difficult and requires sustained effort and strain. It's hard work. But it's hard work that pays off. Use the techniques and strategies presented in this book systematically. Think of this book as your emotion manual to decrease your mixed anxiety and depression. Don't just read it once through, scribble a few notes, and wait for emotional transformation. Unfortunately, it does not work that way. Practice. Practice daily. Photocopy the worksheets in the back of this book, and use them as daily prompts to engage in both emotional and behavioral strategies different from the ones to which you have become accustomed. Different behavior and a different approach to your suffering can progressively result in the changes you seek and deserve.

Symptoms and How to Treat Them

Symptom	Techniques to Resolve	See Pages
I lack energy, hope, direction.	Identify what is important to you. Do SPECIFIC PATHS daily (practice this technique, don't just read it).	p. 81–82
I'm confused and unable to achieve my goals.	Identify the dialectics in your life and attempt to form better compromises between your competing needs and wants. Engage in OBJECTIVES.	p. 16–32 p. 203–204
I have self-doubt and self-hatred.	Identify the self versus self dialectical conflicts in your life.	p. 39
I have frustrated or failed interpersonal relationships.	Identify the interpersonal dialectical conflicts in your life.	p. 40–42
I doubt that DBT is the right approach to my problems.	After reading the book and beginning to complete the workbook assignments, retake the self-test. If you continue to answer a significant number of items in the yes direction, then this approach is for you. You may need a psychologist to help you do the work of this approach.	p. 11–13
My emotions are contradictory and inconsistent. It's hard to tell what I really feel.	Reread the "Contradictory Emotions" section of the book, and move from blame to problem solving. Redo the "Compromise Formations" workbook sections. Practice EMOTIONS.	p. 43–48 p. 47–51 p. 164

I'm self-absorbed, always in my head and thinking about myself and my problems.	Redo the self-focus versus other focus dialectical domain. What compromises can you make in the other focus direction?	p. 20–22
I'm codependent. My needs rarely get met.	Redo the self-focus versus other focus dialectical domain. What compromises can you make in the self-focus direction?	p. 20–22
I'm a pushover. People take advantage of me.	Redo the trust versus suspicion dialectical domain. What compromises can you make in the suspicion direction? Less transparent? More self-efficacious?	p. 22–23
I'm paranoid. Everyone is a potential threat to me.	Redo the trust versus suspicion dialectical domain. What compromises can you make in the trust direction?	p. 22–23
I have few friends.	Redo the transparency versus privacy section of the workbook. What ways can you become more transparent and less private? Less independent? More help seeking?	p. 23–26
I'm set in my ways. My habits in living are so strong, I'll never be happy.	Redo the understanding versus approval dialectical domains. Find out how you're approving of, rather than simply understanding, your personality issues.	p. 29–30
My feelings of depression and anxiety have been with me so long, I can't imagine life without them.	Redo the "Emotion Regulation versus Emotion Tolerance" section of the book. Practice EMOTIONS.	p. 32–35 p. 164
I hate my feelings. I just want them to go away.	Reread chapter 5.	p. 73–97
I'm a despicable person.	Reread chapter 6. Do the exercises on gathering evidence.	p. 98–118 p. 70–72
I can think of an argument against most of what you say in your book. I have no hope that this approach will work for me.	It is easy to devalue supreme concerns. See the list on pages 83–84. Think dialectically.	p. 83–84
The world is bland because of my anxiety and depression. Nothing excites me. I just can't get motivated.	Do ONE MIND every day. Use the variety of inputs from the world. Use EMOTIONS.	p. 105–106 p. 164
I'm so anxious, self-absorbed, inadequate, and full of doubt that I don't have the confidence to do the DBT exercises.	Use mindfulness and the ONE MIND mnemonic. Each time you do this, ask yourself the questions from the second stage of mindfulness practice.	p. 105–106 p. 112–113

My bad feelings stick with me, no matter how much I try to increase positive daily experiences.	Practice the third stage of mindfulness. Practice breaking down situations from the "Emotion Regulation Skills" worksheet. Be mindful of your pain. Break down your primary from secondary emotional reactions. Do the "What to Do" exercises. Afterward ask yourself the questions on page 135. Act opposite.	p. 113–116 p. 127–128 p. 177 p. 131–138 p. 157–158 p. 135 p. 158–164
There is no fun in my life.	Increase positive emotional experiences. Apply the guidelines. Be mindful of them. Do the "What to Do" exercises.	p. 149–150 p. 150 p. 155 p. 156
I feel anxious and depressed.	Use EMOTIONS to change your feelings. Use ONE MIND to be mindful of your distress. Self-soothe. Use ACCEPTS. Use IMPROVE.	p. 164 p. 105–106 p. 175–183 p. 183–186 p. 186–191
My life is always in crisis.	Examine your sense of urgency and timing.	p. 195–202
My plans never work out. I don't get what I want.	Work on both long-term and short-term objectives daily. Examine your answers to the questions on page 202.	p. 199–201
I get so emotional that I just can't problem solve. I know I'm smart enough, but my emotions get in my way.	Use OBJECTIVES to break down each situation.	p. 203–208
People tell me I'm too emotional.	Think dialectically. Engage in TRUST. Engage in CARES.	p. 209 p. 209–212 p. 219–222
Because of my anxiety and depression I've taught myself to cut off my feelings.	Think dialectically. Engage in TRUST. Engage in CARES.	p. 209 p. 209–212 p. 219–222
While these strategies make some sense, I find myself too anxious to use them. My emotions take over.	Practice ONE MIND. Engage in CARES to reduce emotionalism in your daily life.	p. 105–106 p. 219–222

Mnemonic Review

Creating or Increasing Meaning in Our Lives

SPECIFIC PATHS (p. 81–82)

Supreme concern

Practice

Energy

Concentration

I ("I," me, not others)

Faith

Important

Courage

Patience

Attention

Tasks

Humility

Sensitive to self

Mindfulness Skills

ONE MIND (p. 105–106)

One thing

Now

Environment

Moment

Increase Senses

Nonjudgmental

Describe

Emotion Regulation Skills

EMOTIONS (p. 164)

Expose yourself to emotions

Mindful of current emotions

Outline plan to deal only with primary emotion

Take opposite action

Increase positive experiences

Outside precipitants?

Notice what's going on

Secondary emotions dealt with later

Distress Tolerance Skills

ACCEPTS (p. 183–186)

Activities

Contributing

Comparisons

Opposite Emotions

Pushing away

Thoughts

Sensations

IMPROVE (p. 186–191)

Imagery

Meaning

Prayer

Relaxation

One thing at a time

Vacation

Encouragement

Strategic Behavior Skills

OBJECTIVES (p. 203–208)

Outside

Beliefs

Judicial

Emotions

Consequences

Time

Introspection

Values

Endings and Exposure

Short-term and long-term objectives

TRUST (p. 209–212)

Trust your emotion

Redirect to objectives and goals

Use your personality (understand)

Sense your body

Tame the emotional expression

BEHAVIOR (p. 213–218)

Behavior

Environment

Healing versus Hurting

Antecedents

Values

Intervals

Outcome

Reinforcement

CARES (p. 219–222)

Calm, Coached practice

Arousal monitoring, Abstinence

Relaxation and Rest

Emotions and Environment

Sleep

DBT Log

Photocopy these blank forms before using.

Skill Sets	What I did to practice the coping skills.
SPECIFIC PATHS	
ONE MIND	
EMOTIONS	
ACCEPTS	
IMPROVE	
OBJECTIVES	
TRUST	
BEHAVIOR	
CARES	

Dialectics

Most situations you confront have competing and potentially contradictory goals and wants that you wish satisfied. Below, take stock of the situation you are confronting and identify those dialectics so that you can make informed choices about what to give up, what to sacrifice, and what to pursue in service of your goals. The examples below are just memory prompts. Your dialectics may be unrelated to these examples.

Activity	<——>	Passivity
Trust	<——>	Suspicion
Independence	<——>	Dependence
Changing	<——>	Observing
Skill Enhancement	<——>	Self-Acceptance
Focus on Feelings	<——>	Focus on Goals and Behavior
Focus on Blame and Guilt	<——>	Focus on Problem Solving

Self Focus	<——>	Other Focus
Transparency	<——>	Privacy
Self-Efficacy	<——>	Help Seeking
Understanding	<——>	Approval
Emotion Regulation	<——>	Emotion Tolerance
Focus on Judgments	<——>	Focus on Experience
Keeping Things the Same	<——>	Making Changes

Opposing or competing needs or wants in this situation

<——>

<——>

<——>

One set of needs or wants in this situation

What I'm willing to sacrifice or give up in order to reach my short-term goals:

What I'm willing to sacrifice or give up in order to reach my long-term goals

What I'll be gaining by sacrificing the above:

Meaning Making: SPECIFIC PATHS

On the form below, makes notes to yourself about how you are using SPECIFIC PATHS this week.

Supreme concern. Identify importance, reason, why.

Practice. How can I repeat this in my daily life?

Energy. How can I put emphasis on this? How can I be disciplined?

Concentration. How can I focus on this, making it more than passive?

I. "I", me, not others. What is it that I want to happen in me?

Faith. How can I have faith that this will work, that it makes a difference?

Important. How can I increase the attention and direction of this?

Courage. What can I do when I begin to question or be negative?

Patience. How can I remind myself that this takes time, effort, and energy?

Attention. Be mindful of it when I'm doing it, not automatic or by habit.

Tasks. What are the specific things I need to do? Behavior, not just thoughts

Humility. It's not all about me. I'm imperfect and supposed to be that way.

Sensitive to self. What am I experiencing? How does this feel?

Supreme concern	
Practice	
Energy	
Concentration	
I. ("I," me, not others)	
Faith	
Important	
Courage	

Patience	
Attention	
Tasks	
Humility	
Sensitive to self	

Mindfulness Skills

Mindfulness is paying attention in a focused way without trying to change that which we observe. Increase your powers of observation (both of the environment and of yourself) by practicing this powerful strategy of meditation on a routine basis. Make a check in the box that day when you practice mindfulness in each of the sensory areas.

One thing

Now

Environment. What is happening out there?

Moment. Immediate

Increase senses. Touch, taste, vision, hearing

Nonjudgmental. Not good or bad, right or wrong

Describe. Words, descriptive not prescriptive or proscriptive

Date	Sound	Smell	Tactile	Visual	Body	Thought	Feeling	Taste

Emotion Regulation: Mindfulness to Current Emotions

Many times you may wish to avoid your current emotions. Such avoidance can actually at times increase the intensity and pain of your anxiety and depression. Take the time (and the courage) to be mindful of what you are feeling before you try to change it.

Identify the emotion (label it)	How expressed bodily	Thoughts about the emotion	Environmental precipitants	Behavior	Afterward
Example: Shame that I misled my supervisor	Back muscles tighten, heart rate increases, shortness of breath	I'm a coward who can't face up to my responsibilities. I'll always be a coward.	Supervisor asked me how far along I was in getting in the report.	Told her it was almost done when I hadn't even begun it.	Feel even more anxious and pressured. Take work home to complete so I won't get caught. Feel resentful that I'm working at home and not paying attention to the children.

Distress Tolerance: Acceptance

Most of the time you want to eliminate anxiety and depression feelings. Paradoxically, sometimes the best strategy is to accept the emotional pain, and in so doing, have it fade in intensity. Write your responses below.

Acknowledge the emotion	Identify the judgment	Dispute the judgmental	Be mindful of the emotion	Reassure (soothe) yourself	Tolerate the emotion
Example: I'm feeling ashamed that I feel vulnerable.	I don't feel it is acceptable to be vulnerable. I should always be strong and capable.	Vulnerability is a part of life. While I don't like it, it is not an experience that I must feel shame about.	I feel this shame. It's about inadequacy and not being good enough. I'm paying attention to this feeling of shame.	I can take this shame. It won't destroy me, I just don't like it. I can put up with it forever, if I have to—but I don't have to put up with it forever. I will put up with it for a few moments.	I experience this shame feel its full intensity. I tolerate it for just this moment.

Emotion Regulation: Discriminate Primary from Secondary Emotions

The intensity of your emotion increases when you pile secondary emotions on top of primary emotions. Below, write your thoughts about which of your feelings are primary reactions to the current event about which you are feeling strongly, and how many of your feelings are about past situations (secondary emotions).

Identify the emotion	Differentiate primary from secondary emotions	My plan to deal with the primary emotion	My plan to deal with the secondary emotion
Example: I'm upset that my friend is ignoring me. I'm feeling lonely, unworthy, and angry that I'm always the person who has to initiate in relationships.	My primary feeling is being lonely that my friend is not calling me or initiating social plans with me. My secondary emotions are the feelings of anger and unworthiness because I feel that others have done this to me in the past.	I'm not going to take my anger out on my friend. It is not his fault that others have been passive in my past social relationships. I'm going to react only to the feeling of being lonely by picking up the phone and calling my friend.	My resentment and anger that I'm always setting up social encounters is something I'll be better prepared to handle when I'm not actively feeling lonely. I'll take a look at these resentful and angry feelings when I'm not feeling so alone.

Emotion Regulation: Challenge Your Assumptions

Your thoughts can cause unnecessary anxiety and depression when they're based on assumptions that may not be true. Below, identify the assumptions you're making that increase your mixed anxiety and depression, and challenge them.

Identify the emotion	Anticipation	Question your anticipation	Practice different anticipation, and notice emotion changes
Example: Fear that I'll be seen as stupid	If I don't pass the bar exam the first time, everyone will know and think that I'm not smart enough to be an attorney.	People won't know when I plan to take the test unless I tell them. Anyway, no one cares as much about whether I pass as I do so I just need to prepare as best I can and reduce my anxiety.	What I think and feel is more important than what others think and feel. Trying to please others just takes my mind off the real task of study and preparation. Having a certain amount of test anxiety is normal, I just need to manage the anxiety. I'm now paying more attention to the task at hand, and less to anticipatory feelings. And that feels better.

Emotion Regulation: You Are Not What You Feel

Frequently, people with mixed anxiety and depression have their feelings overly color and influence their sense of identity. Help to separate out your feelings from your identity by practicing the exercise below when you begin to doubt your self-esteem.

Identify the emotion	Personality or identity statements I'm making	Question these statements	Practice desired identity statements	Identify feelings I'll have with practice
Example: Self-loathing	I'm a habitual liar. I can't seem to tell the truth to save my life. I want to believe my lies so badly.	I do lie frequently. I so badly want other people's approval and acceptance. However, this is not a personality thing. It's a behavior—the behavior of telling lies. I can change my behavior. I was not born with a "lie gene" that makes me this way. I have control over this behavior.	I want to see myself as a person who is connected and compassionate to other people and who encourages these interpersonal connections by being honest and trust-worthy. I want to like myself and my behavior. I want to trust in myself.	As I tell the truth more often, I'll feel good about myself. There is nothing wrong with wanting others to like me, but I have to like myself first. When I feel the impulse to lie, I'm going to keep my mouth shut and say over and over to myself, "I am a trustworthy person. I'm honest with myself. I like me."

Emotion Regulation: Increase Positive Experiences Mindfully

Depression and anxiety prompt you to do less for yourself. Help regulate your emotions by engaging in daily positive experiences (and be mindful of those experiences). Both anxiety and depression cause you to pay too much attention to negative experiences (always seeing the glass as half empty), so decrease your mindfulness to negative emotions and experiences. Take opposite action in order to increase positive experiences and decrease negative experiences. Record your daily practice of these principles below.

Positive Experiences I Had Today	How I Practiced Being Mindful of That Positive Experience

Negative Experiences I Had Today	How I Practiced Not Being Mindful of That Negative Experience

How I Took Opposite Action Today	How I Practiced Being Mindful of How That Made Me Feel

Emotion Regulation: EMOTIONS

Intense anxiety and depression, especially when experienced together, often prompt us to use old, unhelpful strategies to feel better. EMOTIONS is a global strategy that can help you to better problem solve in your current situation. Use this technique whenever you feel stuck (when situations and feelings keep reoccurring even though they are unwanted).

Expose yourself to emotions

Mindful of current emotions

Outline plan to deal only with primary emotion

Take opposite action

Increase positive experiences

Outside precipitants?

Notice what's going on

Secondary emotions dealt with later

Expose self to emotions	Example: I'm terrified. I'll let myself feel this terror.	
Mindful of current emotion	My heart is racing, I feel like I'm going to die. I'm afraid others will see this terror.	
Outline plan to deal only with primary emotion	Fear is the primary emotion. I'll use deep breathing and mindfulness to deal with the fear and leave the shame that others may notice to deal with later.	
Take opposite action	I'm going to smile and have a nice swing to my gait. I'm going to act as if I'm happy and carefree, even though I'm feeling terror.	
Increase positive experiences	In fact, I'm going to turn on my favorite music CD and listen through my earphones. In my head I'm going to sing along to the pleasant music.	
Outside precipitants?	My supervisor is about to come in to give me my annual performance evaluation. I know this terror is caused by things that I fear. I'm not making it up. It is normal.	
Notice what's going on	As I take opposite action I find that my anxiety is going down a little. I can handle this.	
Secondary emotions dealt with later	So what if my supervisor knows that I'm afraid. She can't fire me for that! I have rights just like everyone else. It's not a crime to feel anxiety.	

Distress Tolerance: Self-Soothing

Sometimes there's nothing you can do to decrease the intensity of your anxiety and depression. Self-soothing is a way to talk yourself through such situations so that you can tolerate the pain that is unavoidable. Write below the things you tell yourself that are reassuring, positive, or give meaning to the pain you're enduring. Writing this down can increase your belief in what you are saying to yourself, as well as temporarily distract you from paying so much attention to your feelings.

Thoughts. What can I think about that will make me feel reassured?	
Vision. What can I look at that will make me feel good things?	
Hearing. What is pleasing to the ear? What can I listen to that soothes me?	
Smell. What aromas make me feel good?	
Taste. What can I put in my mouth that makes me feel great and prompts fond memories?	
Touch. What can I touch that will invoke feelings that are so different from my pain?	

Distress Tolerance: ACCEPTS

The ACCEPTS mnemonic (Linehan 1993b) is about use of distraction skills that may help dispel much of your depression and anxiety. Write below what you have done in each category to decrease the intensity of your feelings.

Activities. What can I do now to distract myself?	
Contributing. What can I do for others?	
Comparisons. How am I better off than some? Worse off than some?	
Opposite Emotions. What can I do to feel the opposite of what I'm feeling right now?	
Pushing away. Don't let the emotion in. Protect myself from it.	
Thoughts. Think about something else. Engage my mind.	
Sensations. Expose my senses to something else.	

Distress Tolerance: IMPROVE

Using the IMPROVE mnemonic (Linehan 1993b), you can improve the moment by at least temporarily (even for just one moment) having a more pleasant experience than the anxiety and depression that you suffer.

Imagery. What can I "see" in my mind that will be reassuring, pleasant, and invoke great memories?	
Meaning. Review what I wrote on pages 86–87. Which of these things can I do, remember, or remind myself of when I'm depressed or anxious.	
Prayer. How can I develop my spiritual or meditative power in this moment of depression and anxiety?	
Relaxation. What relaxation technique can I more faithfully practice?	
One thing at a time. What gets in the way of me really focusing? How can I stay on track better?	
Vacation. What small vacation from the ordinary can I take today, or at least in the next couple of days?	
Encouragement. What can I say to myself that will inspire hope and make me more positive?	

Strategic Behavior Skills: OBJECTIVES

With mixed anxiety and depression, the sense of urgency you have to resolve issues immediately increases, leading to mood-dependent behavior and impulsivity. You sacrifice long-term goals for short-term gains. This is not strategic. It does not help you get what you really want out of life. When you feel a sense of urgency, focus on long-term as well as short-term wants. Practice OBJECTIVES daily as a method to increase your effectiveness in life.

Outside. What is happening outside of me in the environment? What caused or prompted me to react?	
Beliefs. What am I saying to myself about this event? What are my thoughts?	
Judicial. Be critical or evaluate the reality or veracity of my beliefs.	
Emotions. What am I feeling about this?	
Consequences. What will happen if I respond to my beliefs or feelings?	
Time. Is this the right time to do it? Is it based on emotion or on thought that I conclude this is or isn't the right time? Am I avoiding or being impulsive?	

Introspection. Have I really worked this through sufficiently? What are the variables?	
Values. Is this potential response consistent with my values? Is it meaningful and important?	
Endings and **Exposure.** I have to make a decision, take a risk, let myself succeed or fail.	
Short-term and long-term objectives. Did what I just do serve my short-term needs or my long-term needs? I need to compromise between the two.	

Strategic Behavior Skills: TRUST

Especially with mixed anxiety and depression, you become overly concerned with how you think you appear to others. You're afraid that others will see your emotions. Actually, emotions should communicate to others. They should help us to get our wants and needs, perspectives, and demands, across to others. If you view yourself as "overly emotional" or "unreactive," the result may be the same: you don't communicate effectively to others. TRUST your emotions below whenever you're concerned how others perceive you.

Trust my feelings. Identify them. The feeling is not wrong.	
Redirect to my objectives. What is it I want to accomplish?	
Use my personality. Am I very expressive emotionally or not? How will this affect the listener?	
Sense my face, body, posture, voice. Be mindful.	
Tame my feeling. Express myself according to my objectives, mindful of my style of relating.	

Strategic BEHAVIOR

This technique demands that you analyze what is going on both inside of you and in your environment. Break situations that cause you pain down into smaller components. BEHAVIOR asks questions that may make your analysis more complete and allow you to understand how better to change the situations that cause you anxiety and depression.

Behavior. What are you doing? How do you influence other people's behavior? What role do you have in this situation? What do you do? Look at the situation, and your own part in it, with some distance and objectivity.	
Environment. Is there something out there in your immediate environment that is prompting this to occur? What does the environment "want" or prompt others and you in it to do? What are the "demand characteristics" of this environment?	
Healing versus Hurt. Are you doing something to try to heal yourself that is actually hurting you? Are you avoiding? Escaping?	
Antecedents. Look to what came before. What took place prior to the event that caused you pain? Maybe it's not you specifically causing this, but something that comes immediately prior to your behavior (you may be reacting to something you're not aware of yet).	
Values. What is it that you're getting out of this situation? What is motivating you within this painful situation?	

Interval. Things that occur infrequently but occasionally are powerful sustainers of behavior. What powerful but infrequent events may be sustaining these crisis situations?	
Outcome. What effect do these events have on you? What is the payoff? What do you get out of it? What bad thing is avoided by keeping this going?	
Reinforcement. Examine what it is that increases the probability of your behavior. What keeps this cycle going?	

Strategic Behavior: CARES

The CARES mnemonic also demands that you be prepared for inevitable stresses and strains while you are overcoming your anxiety and depression. You must prepare for stressors by having balance in your life between work and play and by participating in activities that reduce your baseline stress level. This will help you to be calm to begin with, so when trouble situations arise you are better prepared to handle them. Engage in CARES daily, and prepare with the exercise below.

CARES	Plans for Monday	Plans for Tuesday	Plans for Wednesday	Plans for Thursday	Plans for Friday	Plans for Saturday	Plans for Sunday
Calm, Coached practice							
Arousal monitoring, and Abstinence							
Relaxation and Rest							
Emotions and Environment							
Sleep							

DBT PRACTICE SHEET

The mnemonics of this DBT approach are designed to help you remember the psychological coping strategies presented in this book. You must use them in your daily life in order for them to have any benefit to you. Below, simply place a check mark in the box of the specific mnemonic within the time frame you have used it. This should prompt you to use the full variety of coping skills regularly. Photocopy the blank form before using it.

	Mon A.M.	Mon P.M.	Tues A.M.	Tues P.M.	Wed A.M.	Wed P.M.	Thurs A.M.	Thurs P.M.	Fri A.M.	Fri P.M.	Sat A.M.	Sat P.M.	Sun A.M.	Sun P.M.
SPECIFIC PATHS														
ONE MIND														
CARES														
EMOTIONS														
ACCEPTS														
IMPROVE														
OBJECTIVES														
TRUST														
BEHAVIOR														

Dates: Monday, _____ (month) _____ (date) to Sunday, _____ (month) _____ (date)

References

American Psychiatric Association. 1994. *Diagnostic and Statistical Manual of Mental Disorders: Fourth Edition: DSM-IV*. Washington, D.C.

Anxiety Disorders Association of America. 2003. Web site (www.adaa.org).

Arean, P. A., and B. L. Cook. 2002. Psychotherapy and combined psychotherapy/pharmacotherapy for late life depression. *Biological Psychiatry* 52(3):293-303

Baer, R. A. 2003. Mindfulness training as a clinical intervention: A conceptual and empirical review. *Clinical Psychology: Science and Practice* 10:125-143.

Baily, C. 2002. Is it really our chemicals that need balancing? *Journal of American College of Health* 51(1):42-47.

Barrett, L. F., J. Gross, T. C. Christensen, and M. Benvenuto. 2001. Knowing what you're feeling and knowing what to do about it: Mapping the relation between emotion differentiation and emotion regulation. *Cognition & Emotion* 15(6):713-724.

Basco, M. R. 2000. Cognitive-behavior therapy for bipolar I disorder. *Journal of Cognitive Psychotherapy* 14(3):287-304.

Brody, A. L., S. Saxena, M. A. Mandelkern, L. A. Fairbanks, M. L. Ho, and L. R. Baxter, Jr. 2001. Brain metabolic changes associated with symptom factor improvement in major depressive disorder. *Biological Psychiatry* 50(3):171-178.

Brown, T. A., M. M. Antony, and D. H. Barlow. 1995. Diagnostic comorbidity in panic disorder: Effect on treatment outcome and course of comorbid diagnosis following treatment. *Journal of Consulting and Clinical Psychology* 63:408-418.

Casacalenda, N., J. C. Perry, and K. Looper. 2002. Remission in major depressive disorder: A comparison of pharmacotherapy, psychotherapy, and control conditions. *American Journal of Psychiatry* 159(8):1354-1360.

Colenda, C. C., M. A. Mickus, S. C. Marcus, T. L. Tanielian, and H. A. Pincus. 2002. Comparison of adult and geriatric psychiatric practice patterns: Findings from the American Psychiatric Association's practice research network. *American Journal of Geriatric Psychiatry* 10(5):609-617.

Coyne, J. C., and I. H. Gotlib. 1983. The role of cognition in depression: A critical appraisal. *Psychological Bulletin* 94:472-505.

Davidson, R. J. 2000. Affective style, psychopathology, and resilience: Brain mechanisms and plasticity. *American Psychologist* 55:1196-1214.

de Jonghe, F., S. Kool, G. van Aalst, J. Dekker, and J. Peen. 2001. Combining psychotherapy and antidepressants in the treatment of depression. *Journal of Affective Disorders* 64(2-3):217-229.

Dimidjian, S., and M. M. Linehan. 2003. Defining an agenda for future research on the clinical application of mindfulness practice. *Clinical Psychology: Science and Practice* 10(2):166-171.

Eisenberg, N. 2000. Emotion, regulation, and moral development. *Annual Review of Psychology* 51:665-697.

Fava, G. A. 2002. Long-term treatment with antidepressant drugs: The spectacular achievements of propaganda. *Psychotherapy & Psychosomatics* 71(3):127-132.

Fedoroff, I. C., and S. Tayor. 2001. Psychological and pharmacological treatments of social phobia: A meta-analysis. *Journal of Clinical Psychopharmacology* 21(3):311-324.

Fromm, E. 1956. *The Art of Loving.* New York: Harper & Row.

Gorman, J. M. 2003. Treatment of generalized anxiety disorder. *Journal of Clinical Psychiatry* 64:24-29.

Granit, L. Neurobiology of attachment and sdult psychotherapy. *The California Psychologist* 35(1):16.

Gross, J. J. 2001. Emotion regulation in adulthood: Timing is everything. *Current Directions in Psychological Science* 10(6):214-219.

Gross, J. J., O. P. John, and J. M. Richards. 2000. The dissociation of emotion expression from emotion experience: A personality perspective. *Personality & Social Psychology Bulletin* 26(6):712-726.

Hayes, S. C. 2002. Acceptance, mindfulness, and science. *Clinical Psychology: Science and Practice* 9:101-106.

Hayes, S. C., and K. G. Wilson. 1994. Acceptance and commitment therapy: Altering the verbal support for experiential avoidance. *Behavior Analyst* 17(2):289-303.

Heldt. E., G. G. Manfro, L. Kipper, C. Blaya, S. Maltz, L. Isolan, V. N. Hirakata, and M. W. Otto. 2003. Treating medication-resistant panic disorder: Predictors and outcome of cognitive-behavior therapy in a Brazilian public hospital. *Psychotherapy & Psychosomatics* 72(1):43-48.

Huxley, N.A., S. V. Parikh, and R. J. Baldessarini. 2000. Effectiveness of psychosocial treatments in bipolar disorder: State of the evidence. *Harvard Review of Psychiatry* 8(3):126-140.

Jacobson, E. 1948. *You Must Relax: A Practical Method of Reducing the Strains of Modern Living.* Oxford, England: Mcgraw Hill.

Kabat-Zinn, J. 1993. Mindfulness meditation: Health benefits of an ancient Buddhist practice. In *Mind/Body Medicine*, edited by D. Goleman and J. Gurin. Yonkers, NY: Consumer Report Books.

Kabat-Zinn, J. 2003. Mindfulness-based interventions in context: Past, present, and future. *Clinical Psychology: Science and Practice* 10:144-156.

Klein, D. F. 2000. Flawed meta-analyses comparing psychotherapy with pharmacotherapy. *American Journal of Psychiatry* 157(8):1204-1211.

Kolar, D., and S. Bojanin. 2001. Obsessive-compulsive disorder in children and adolescents—integrative approach. *Psychiatry Today* 33(1-2):81-99.

Lazarus, R. S. 1991. Progress on a cognitive-motivational-relational theory of emotion. *American Psychologist* 46(8):819-834.

Linehan, M. M. 1993a. *Cognitive-Behavioral Treatment of Borderline Personality Disorder.* New York: Guilford Press.

———. 1993b. *Skills Training Manual for Treating Borderline Personality Disorder.* New York: Guilford Press.

Maser, J. D., and C. R. Cloninger, eds. 1990. *Comorbidity of Mood and Anxiety Disorders.* Washington, D.C.: American Psychiatric Press.

McLaren, N. 2002. The myth of the biopsychosocial model. *Australian & New Zealand Journal of Psychiatry* 36(5):701.

McNally, R. J. 1994. *Panic Disorder: A Critical Analysis.* New York: Guilford Press.

Meichenbaum, D. 1996. *Mixed Anxiety and Depression: A Cognitive-Behavioral Approach.* New York: Newbridge Communications, Inc.

National Institutes for Health. 1991. Web site (www.nih.gov).

National Institute for Mental Health. 2003. Web site (www.nimh.nih.gov).

Overholser, J. C. 2000. Cognitive-behavioral treatment of panic disorder. *Psychotherapy: Theory, Research, Practice, Training* 37(3):247-256.

Rivas-Vazquez, R. A., S. L. Johnson, G. J. Rey, M. A. Blais, and A. Rivas-Vazquez. 2002. Current treatments for bipolar disorder: A review and update for psychologists. *Professional Psychology: Research & Practice* 33(2):212-223.

Rothbaum, B. O., and M. C. Astin. 2000. Integration of pharmacotherapy and psychotherapy for bipolar disorder. *Journal of Clinical Psychiatry* 61(Suppl9):68-75.

Rusting, C. L., and T. DeHart. 2000. Retrieving positive memories to regulate negative mood: Consequences for mood-congruent memory. *Journal of Personality & Social Psychology* 78(4):737-752.

Selignan, M. 1995a. Mental health: Does therapy work? *Consumer Reports* November, 734-739.

———. 1995b. The effectiveness of psychotherapy: The Consumer Reports study. *American Psychologist* 50(12):965-974.

Strunk, D. R., and R. J. DeRubeis. 2001. Cognitive therapy for depression: A review of its efficacy. *Journal of Cognitive Psychotherapy* 15(4):289-297.

Teasdale, J. D., J. M. Williams, J. M. Soulsby, Z. V. Segal, V. A. Ridgeway, and M. A. Lau. 2000. Prevention of relapse/recurrence in major depression by mindfulness-based cognitive therapy. *Journal of Consulting and Clinical Psychology* 68:615-623.

Thornicroft, G., and S. Maingay. 2002. The global response to mental illness: An enormous health burden is increasingly being recognized. *British Medical Journal* 325(7365): 608-609.

Tice, D. M., E. Bratslavsky, and R. F. Baumeister. 2001. Emotional distress regulation takes precedence over impulse control: If you feel bad, do it! *Journal of Personality and Social Psychology* 80(1):53-67.

Zinberg, R. E., D. Barlow, M. Liebowitz, L. Street, et al. 1994. The DSM-IV field trial for mixed anxiety-depression. *American Journal of Psychiatry* 151:1153-1162.

Some Other
New Harbinger Titles

Angry All the Time, Item 3929 $13.95

Handbook of Clinical Psychopharmacology for Therapists, 4th edition, Item 3996 $55.95

Writing For Emotional Balance, Item 3821 $14.95

Surviving Your Borderline Parent, Item 3287 $14.95

When Anger Hurts, 2nd edition, Item 3449 $16.95

Calming Your Anxious Mind, Item 3384 $12.95

Ending the Depression Cycle, Item 3333 $17.95

Your Surviving Spirit, Item 3570 $18.95

Coping with Anxiety, Item 3201 $10.95

The Agoraphobia Workbook, Item 3236 $19.95

Loving the Self-Absorbed, Item 3546 $14.95

Transforming Anger, Item 352X $10.95

Don't Let Your Emotions Run Your Life, Item 3090 $17.95

Why Can't I Ever Be Good Enough, Item 3147 $13.95

Your Depression Map, Item 3007 $19.95

Successful Problem Solving, Item 3023 $17.95

Working with the Self-Absorbed, Item 2922 $14.95

The Procrastination Workbook, Item 2957 $17.95

Coping with Uncertainty, Item 2965 $11.95

The BDD Workbook, Item 2930 $18.95

You, Your Relationship, and Your ADD, Item 299X $17.95

The Stop Walking on Eggshells Workbook, Item 2760 $18.95

Conquer Your Critical Inner Voice, Item 2876 $15.95

The PTSD Workbook, Item 2825 $17.95

Hypnotize Yourself Out of Pain Now!, Item 2809 $14.95

The Depression Workbook, 2nd edition, Item 268X $19.95

Beating the Senior Blues, Item 2728 $17.95

Shared Confinement, Item 2663 $15.95

Getting Your Life Back Together When You Have Schizophrenia, Item 2736 $14.95

Do-It-Yourself Eye Movement Technique for Emotional Healing, Item 2566 $13.95

Call **toll free, 1-800-748-6273,** or log on to our online bookstore at **www.newharbinger.com** to order. Have your Visa or Mastercard number ready. Or send a check for the titles you want to New Harbinger Publications, Inc., 5674 Shattuck Ave., Oakland, CA 94609. Include $4.50 for the first book and 75¢ for each additional book, to cover shipping and handling. (California residents please include appropriate sales tax.) Allow two to five weeks for delivery.

Prices subject to change without notice.